# Chinese Imperial Cooking and Eating Secrets

## Translated by Zhang Tingquan

**Panda Books**

Panda Books
First Edition 1998
Copyright © 1998 by CHINESE LITERATURE PRESS
ISBN 7-5071-0376-5/I.334
ISBN 0-8351-3194-7

Published by CHINESE LITERATURE PRESS
Beijing 100037, China
Distributed by China International Book Trading Corporation
35 Chegongzhuang Xilu, Beijing 100044, China
P.O. Box 399, Beijing, China
Printed in the People's Republic of China

# CONTENTS

# Introduction

China's traditional customs for eating and drinking have always emphasized food and its nutrition. For example, around the time of the Zhou Dynasty (1122-247 B.C.), palace food doctors, or medical nutritionists as they are known today, headed the imperial medical staff. Between the Han and Tang Dynasties (206 B.C.-A.D. 907), doctors supervised the imperial food. And almost all traditional Chinese medical books include such descriptions as "medical care and food from the same source" or "food and drugs from the same source."

Traditional Chinese medicine (TCM) pharmacology originated from people's search for food. Through their long years of practice and experimentation, the ancestors of the tribes in ancient China learned that many animals and plants were not only delicious, they also built health and prolonged life. When pathological changes arose in the human body, eating the appropriate plants or animals in a prescribed way could help cure illness and improve the physique. Because localities, seasons, physiques, ages, sexes, and illnesses differed, people began paying special attention to food and drinks.

During the Chinese feudal society, the Confucian system, which is the foundation of the Chinese spirit, prompted special attention to be paid to palace food and drinks. As a result, imperial food and drinks improved dynasty after dynasty. Chinese imperial food and drinks, a collection of the world's delicacies prepared by the best cooks, helped raise the dietetic culture of the common people to a new height. Actually, many palace delicacies originated from the common people; the imperial cooks just made them more healthy, delicious, and aesthetically pleasing.

Dr. Sun Yat-sen (1866-1925), the great Chinese democratic revolutionary, once said: "A painting pleasing to the eye and a piece of music pleasing to the ear are both works of art, and why not a dish pleasing to the mouth?! Cooking is also an art." (*Plans for National Reconstruction*)

Food and drinks demonstrate the characteristics of a culture, therefore, the Chinese imperial food provides a key to China's dietetic culture. At present, the concept of a dietetic culture is still vague. Some regard it as just eating and drinking or how to eat, drink and cook. Others believe dietetic culture has spawned six branches of science: cooking, food preparation, dietotherapy, dietetic folklore, dietetic literature and art, and dietetic resources.

Imperial diets were closely tied to knowledge about building health through foods, dietetic aesthetics and dinnerware. Unfortunately, few historical records on these subjects exist prior to the Ming Dynasty (1368-1644).

This book focuses on imperial food and drink in the Ming and Qing Dynasties. Because imperial food and dishes originated from the common people, this book devotes a great deal of space to traditional cuisines, tea drinking in the palace, and related references for readers who wish to do additional research. The two chapters, "Imperial Food in the Ming Dynasty" and "Imperial Food in the Qing Dynasty," plus the appendix of 54 imperial dishes are meant to arouse readers' interest in cooking

Chinese dishes.

Because this book was compiled quickly, I would like to receive your comments concerning what is missing or incorrect. Some chapters are based on data from many sources and for that reason are not credited.

I would like to thank Xu Qixian of the research section of the Palace Museum, Lin Jing of the Forbidden City Publishing House, and Zhang Hongkuan, the chief physician at the Fangda Drugs Group, for their help and support in the course of this compilation.

August, 1997

# The History of Chinese Imperial Food

Chinese imperial food dates back to slave society. Ever since there were emperors and palaces, there has been imperial food, which was served mainly to the emperors, their wives and concubines, and the royal families. Emperors used their power to collect the best delicacies and called upon the best cooks to make delicious food for them. Imperial food represented a dynasty's best cuisine.

Although imperial food was made exclusively for the royal family, generals, ministers, and nobility, it was the peasants, herders, and fishermen who provided the raw materials, craftsmen who made the kitchen utensils, the cooking staff who provided the service, civil officials who named the dishes, and protocol officials who drafted the dietary and culinary rules. Imperial food comprised the dietetic culture of the Chinese palaces and it is part of China's valuable cultural heritage.

Imperial foods often were improved dishes invented by the common people. The inventors were not princes, dukes, or ministers, but cooks and commoners. The original model for a dish might have been similar to a dish you once prepared for yourself.

Food preparation is impossible without cooks, so emperors in ancient times cherished excellent cooks. *The Historical Records* by Sima Qian, a famous historian of the Han Dynasty (206 B.C.-220), reports that Yi Yin, the first famous prime minister in known Chinese history, helped Tang (the first ruler of the Shang Dynasty, enthroned 1766-1760 B.C.) destroy Jie (the last ruler of the Xia Dynasty, enthroned 1818-1766 B.C.).

Yi Yin had been a famous cook before he became prime minister. Yi Yin, whose original name was Ah Heng, was a slave of the Youxinshi family. He wanted to convince Tang of his good ideas, but lacked a way, so he brought his kitchen utensils with him and won Tang's trust by demonstrating his cooking skills. Tang described him as cooking delicious dishes and having the ability to govern the country, so he appointed Yi Yin as his prime minister.

Later cooks also participated in politics. Peng Zu, who is called the founder of Chinese cooking, was chef to Emperor Yao around the beginning of the 21st century B.C. Yi Ya of the Qi State in the Spring and Autumn Period (770-476 B.C.) won the trust of Prince Huan of Qi by being good at cooking and identifying flavors. Shao Kang, the seventh emperor of the Xia Dynasty, had been an official in charge of the kitchen service for Youyushi before the Xia Dynasty was founded.

Zhuan Zhu of the Wu State was an assassin in the late years of the Spring and Autumn Period. In order to help Prince Guang ascend to the throne, he learned the unique skill of "roasting fish" from a famous chef. Through his cooking skills, he was able to meet Prince Liao of the Wu State and assassinated him.

In the late Shang Dynasty (16th-11th century B.C.), the government became corrupt and held lavish banquets and feasts in the palace. The following was written of the reign of Emperor Zhou (the last emperor of the Shang Dynasty, enthroned 1154-1122 B.C.): "With a pool of wine and a forest of hanging meats, men and women chased each other naked, drinking all night." (*Records of Kings and Princes*) This lavish and licentious lifestyle led to the fall of the Shang Dynasty.

Chinese imperial food originated around the Zhou Dynasty (11th century-476 B.C.). Although China's dietetic culture developed and grew prior to the Zhou Dynasty, it truly flourished during the Zhou, Qin, and Han dynasties (1122 B.C.-A.D. 220).

The Spring and Autumn Period witnessed an unprecedented development in the history of Chinese thinking. Theories from the different schools of thought touched upon the universe, society and life. Pragmatic thinkers studied how food and drink related to the everyday life of the people. As medical science developed, the idea of dietotherapy arose and attention was given to dietetic hygiene.

Chinese eating and drinking habits differ greatly from those in the West. Westerners eat more meat while Chinese eat more vegetables, especially the traditional cereals. (Cereals are said to have been discovered by Shen Nong, the chief of the ancestors of remote antiquity.) China began growing the five cereals as food crops during the Zhou Dynasty.

The Zhou Dynasty was the most prosperous period of the slave society, and during this time politics, economics and culture advanced greatly. It was the strongest of the three slave dynasties: Xia, Shang and Zhou.

The imperial cuisine of the Zhou Dynasty was a great improvement over the cuisines of the Xia and Shang dynasties. Beginning with the construction of the Xia Dynasty palace and the establishment of the imperial court, an organization was set up to prepare and serve food to the emperor and empress. Officials were appointed, royalty began seeking pleasures, and an imperial kitchen system was conceived.

The Shang Dynasty imperial cuisine was even better than the cuisine of the Xia Dynasty. The foods for the emperors, princes, and dukes were stratified, and a system of stratified foods for the nobility was developed, however, a system for managing imperial food was still lacking.

During the Zhou Dynasty, such a complete system was developed. It included procurement, diets and preparation as well as staffing, supervising the imperial food, and developing grades for the emperor, princes and dukes. Everything was done in a fixed order according to the "eating rites."

The Zhou Dynasty imperial food was of a higher standard than the imperial food of the Xia and Shang dynasties, and famous dishes, feasts and banquets appeared one after another. During the Zhou Dynasty, Chinese imperial cuisine took shape. Staple and non-staple foods were plentiful and many imperial and famous dishes were developed.

The fairly advanced economy in the Western Zhou Dynasty resulted in abundant cereals, vegetables and meats. The cereals available included rice, corn, millet and beans. The *Book of Songs* states there were in excess of 130 plants, which included more than 30 kinds of common vegetables. Fruits and nuts included peach, plum, apricot, date, wild jujube (Chinese date), chestnut, hazelnut, pear, sweet crabapple, persimmon, melons, cherry, orange, tangerine and shaddock (a fruit similar to a grapefruit).

Around 100 different animals were available. These included the ox, sheep, dog, pig, horse, deer, bear, wolf and elephant. There were several dozen varieties of fowl, such as the chicken, pheasant, sparrow, and wild goose;

and nearly 20 kinds of cold-blooded creatures including the carp, triangular bream, turtle, snake and shark. The imperial cuisine used these abundant meats, fish, fowl, cereals, fresh fruits and vegetables, and nuts as well as vegetables pickled in vinegar and soy sauce.

The imperial drinks were known as the *six clears, five qis*, and *three jius*. The six clears were water; thick liquids, such as vinegar and sour wine; sweet wine, a wine made from cooked rice; mellow wine, a wine thinned by adding cold water; *yi wine*, a wine made from yeast and rice porridge; and *ye wine*, a wine made from thin porridge.

The five *qis* were five wines with residue made from rice, sorghum, and millet. They were *fan qi*, a sweet wine with thick, floating matter; *li qi*, a very mild, sweet wine made by soaking half liquid and half grain overnight; *ang qi*, a turbid, slightly clear, sweet wine; *ti qi*, a red wine with more clarity than *ang qi*; and *shen qi*, a wine with bottom sediment and clear liquid above.

The three *jius* were wines that had been filtered to remove the residue, and which differed from the five *qis*. The *qis* were used for sacrificial rites, while the *jius* were used for drink. The three *jius* referred to the categories of wine. *Shi jiu*, also known as occasion wine, was made immediately whenever there was a special occasion. *Xi jiu* was an aged wine that took longer to make. It usually was made in winter and matured in the spring; its liquid was clear and mellow. *Qing jiu* was aged even longer and its liquid was even clearer than *xi jiu*. It was made in winter and became mature in the summer.

The four drinks were *clear*, which referred to the clear wine that remained after the *li qi* of the five *qis* was filtered; *mellow*, which was a wine made from rice porridge after yeast was added; *thick*, which was a sour, vinegary wine; and *yi*, which was a wine made from thin porridge. (Some history books say *yi* was made from millet porridge.)

Under the rules described in the *Rites of the Zhou Dynasty*, "when the emperor took a meal, there were 12 deep bowls with legs and 12 plates. Music was played to urge him to eat." This was the custom during the Shang Dynasty. The Western Zhou Dynasty continued the custom in its early years but later made adjustments. The rites indicate the food served at the emperor's three daily meals were beef, mutton, pork, fish, cured meat, intestine, stomach, small pieces of cooked meat, fish, and fresh cured meat.

A diet system later was instituted for the emperor, princes, dukes, and ministers. According to the *Book of Rites*, "There were 26 bowls for the emperor, 16 for the princes and dukes, 13 for the marquis, 8 for the senior officials, and 6 for the junior officials." There were five grades of meals, one each for the emperor, princes and dukes, marquis, senior officials, and junior officials. Meals were arranged according to this rule.

Banquets and feasts given by the emperor and his officials also had rules. According to the *Rites of the Zhou Dynasty*, "When the emperor gives a banquet, there must be six cereals and six animals for food, the *six clears* for drink, 120 delicacies, eight dainties, and 120 urns of sauce."

The six cereals included rice, millet, broomcorn, sorghum, wheat, and wild rice stem. The six animals were the horse, cow, sheep, pig, dog, and chicken. The *six clears* were water, thick liquid, *li* wine, *chun* wine, *yi* wine, and *ye* wine. The 120 delicacies referred to all the delicacies the emperor ate.

Regarding the meals for senior officials, the records of the *Ceremonial Rites* say: "Senior officials have 20 delicacies more than junior officials, including pheasant, rabbit and quail." According to the annotations for the *Book of Rites* by Zheng Xuan, "The meals for senior officials included broomcorn, millet, rice, sorghum, white millet and yellow sorghum." The non-staple foods included cow, sheep, pig, roast beef, beef pieces cooked in soy sauce, minced beef, roast mutton, mutton pieces cooked in soy sauce, roast pig, minced fish, pheasant, rabbit and quail.

Junior officials' meals included the same staple foods as the senior officers' meals. Their non-staple foods included cow, roast beef, beef cooked in soy sauce, minced beef, roast sheep, mutton pieces cooked in soy sauce, roast pig, pork pieces cooked in soy sauce and minced fish.

A complete organization was responsible for the imperial food served in the Zhou Dynasty palace; it included a large staff and a clear division of labor. The functions and responsibilities of the different departments and staff follow:

Chief cook: The chief cook was in charge of the food, drinks, dishes, and delicacies for the emperor, empress and crown prince. The emperor's food included the six cereals, six animals, six clears, 130 delicacies, eight treasures, and 120 urns of sauce. The chief cook held an official rank.

Internal cooks: The internal cooks cooked the dishes for the emperor, empress, and crown prince. They chose the foods and tasted them. Internal cooks carried a title of nobility and were ordinary officials.

External cooks: The external cooks cooked dishes for the sacrificial rites. External cooks carried a title of nobility and were ordinary officials.

Assistants: The assistants were responsible for food

11

preparation, serving, maintaining the cooking fires, and carrying water for the kitchen.

Nutritionists: The nutritionists studied the nutrients in the emperor's food and drink.

Wine officers: The wine officers were responsible for the drinks for the emperor, empress, and crown prince.

Altogether, there were 22 departments with more than 2,300 staff. Thus it can be seen that the organization surrounding the imperial foods in the Zhou Dynasty was huge, the establishment was complete, and the division of labor detailed and clear. This guaranteed a standard of performance and quality for imperial meals, state banquets, and sacrificial feasts.

As the ruling class extended imperial food to include sacrificial rites as well as banquets given when the emperor met with princes and dukes, imperial food became linked with politics. Lao Zi, a famous thinker during the Spring and Autumn Period, said: "Governing a big country is like cooking a small fish." He meant that when governing a large country, one should not make too many changes, and policies should remain stable.

Even 50 years ago, the old Chinese government still called the job of the chief executive "making adjustments to the tripods". Tripod in ancient Chinese refers to all sizes of cooking utensils. "Making adjustments to the tripods" means adjusting the flavors of the dishes being cooked in the pots and pans to please the palates of the diners.

The relationship between food and politics was especially important during the Zhou, Qin, and Han Dynasties (circa 1122 B.C.-A.D. 220). Banquets and feasts were the norm whenever the emperor met with princes or dukes or whenever the latter met with each other.

Chinese dietetic culture flourished after the Han Dynasties (206 B.C.-A.D. 220) and became a conscious matter. Numerous writings on dietetic culture appeared, including the *Book of Foods*, by Cui Hao and some parts of the *Essentials for Common People* (on food), by Jia Sixie in the Northern Wei Dynasty (386-535). These writings, which record the popular thoughts on diets during this period and tell how to cook many dishes, mark the beginning of cooking as a specialty.

During the Han and Wei Dynasties (206 B.C.-A.D. 265), imperial food and drink followed the system initiated in the Zhou Dynasty. By this time China's strengthened economy and its cultural exchanges with other countries had provided new sources of raw materials, better cooking utensils and cooking skills, wider adoption of ironware, and higher standards for imperial dishes.

The *Seven Advices* was a book written by Mei Cheng, a politician in the State of Wu, to give advice to the crown prince of the State of Chu in the Western Han Dynasty (206 B.C.-A.D. 8). Although the book exaggerates the deliciousness of the food, it still gives a glimpse of imperial food at that time:

Tender calf meat, fresh bamboo shoots and vegetables, thick soup of flattened dog meat, good cooked rice covered with fresh rock mushrooms, rice cooked with mushrooms and made into balls that melt the moment they enter the mouth. It was just as if Yi Yin were in charge of the cooking and Yi Ya had cooked the dishes of tender bear's paw mixed with seasonings, roast tenderloin slices, raw fish slices, flavored autumn eggplant, vegetables so fresh they still had dew upon them, and wine with an orchid flavor.

13

Rinse the mouth after eating. Mountain pheasant, domesticated leopard fetus, less rice, more porridge, as if the hot soup were splashed upon snow, making it easy to digest.

The Han Dynasty imperial kitchens grew vegetables in hothouses, so their availability was not limited by the season. In the final years of the Eastern Han Dynasty food sweetened with honey began to appear in the palace.

It is said that during the period of the Three Kingdoms (A.D. 220-280), Cao Zhi, Prince of Chenliu and son of Cao Cao, made a thick soup of camel's hooves that cost 1,000 ounces of gold. Cao Zhi called it "Seven-Treasure Soup." Cao Cao usurped the power by taking the emperor hostage and acting in his name during the final years of the Eastern Han Dynasty, so their eating habits were representative of the palace customs. They paid great attention to the variety, taste, and flavor of food, and to the quality of the dinnerware. By that time, it had become fashionable to drink tea in the palace instead of wine.

Stir-frying was the chief cooking method during the Southern and Northern Dynasties (A.D. 420-589), and stir-fried dishes became popular as everyday meals among the common people. Buddhism was spreading in China by this time, and vegetarian dishes began appearing because the Buddhist monks ate vegetarian food. In response to the demand for vegetarian dishes, the cooks of Emperor Wu of the Liang Dynasty (502-557) introduced the use of gluten.

After the Han Dynasty, thick soup became a less important non-staple food, and roasted, broiled, and baked meats were eaten only when people drank wine; they were not eaten with cooked rice. Some famous delicacies appeared during this period, and they were given special names that reflected Chinese history and culture. In previous dynasties, the names of dishes reflected how the dishes were cooked. (The naming of dishes is discussed in greater detail in the later chapter, "How Chinese Dishes Were Named.")

The technique of using fermentation to make staple foods, such as steamed buns, stuffed buns, and steamed cakes, which are still popular foods today, was already being used in the final years of the Han Dynasty. Other staple foods were baked cakes and noodles.

The system of people taking separate meals, which was popular before the Han Dynasty, changed gradually into joint meals with several people or a family sitting together around a table, as is done today. The gradual change began with the use of wooden armchairs. This transition took more than 1,700 years.

The imperial food of the Sui, Tang, and Song Dynasties (581-1279) followed the system and rules of preceding dynasties, but the varieties of food and meal procedures changed tremendously. During Yang Di's reign in the Sui Dynasty (enthroned 605-618), seafood appeared much more frequently on imperial menus.

The imperial dishes of the Sui and Tang Tynasties (581-907) had far greater variety than did the dishes of previous dynasties, and more attention was paid to their flavor, taste, color, presentation and naming. Famous imperial dishes that have been passed down to today include fried ringing bells, quick-fried prawns, crab rolls, crystal dragon and phoenix cakes, and steamed Mandarin fish without soy sauce.

The characteristics, habits, and customs surrounding food in the Southern and Northern Dynasties and in the

Sui and Tang Dynasties belong to the same period. There were also similarities in the imperial food prepared and served in the Song and Yuan Dynasties (960-1368). And, there is almost no difference between the food of the Ming and Qing Dynasties (1368-1911) and the food served today.

Several hundred writings about using food and dietotherapy for better health have appeared throughout Chinese history. A few examples, listed by dynasty, follow:

The *Book of Food*, by Cui Hao and the *Transactions of Famous Physicians*, by Tao Hongjing during the Southern and Northern Dynasties.

The *Book of Food*, by Xie Feng and the *Collection of Writings and Copyings in the North Hall*, (the section on wine and foods), by Yu Shinan, an outstanding calligrapher (558-638) in the Sui Dynasty.

The *Prescriptions Worth a Thousand Gold for Emergencies*, (the article on dietetic treatment), by Sun Simiao; the *General Descriptions of Diets*, by Lou Juzhong; and the *Experiences of Chefs*, by Yang Ye in the Tang Dynasty.

The *Records of Chefs*, by Zheng Wangzhi; the *Remarks on Delicious Dishes*, author unknown; the *Records of Mutual Influences of Things*, the *Simple Remarks on the Hows and Whys*, (the part on animals, fowl and fish), by Su Shi; and the *Five Looks of Officials at Meal Time*, by Huang Tingjian in the Song Dynasty.

The *Collection of Dietetic Systems in the Yunlintang*, by Ni Zan (a famous painter, 1301-1374) and the *Principles of Correct Diet*, by Hu Sihui in the Yuan Dynasty.

The *Health Building of the People in the Song Dynasty*, by Song Xu; the *Gentlemen's Remarks on Diets*, by Chen Jiru (an outstanding painter); and the *History of the Ming*

*Palace — Preferences for Diets*, by Liu Ruoyu in the Ming Dynasty (1368-1644).

The *Grand Secrets of Diets*, by Zhu Yizun; the *Chance Leisure for Enjoyments*, (the part on diets), by Li Yu; and the *Menus of the Sui Garden*, by Yuan Mei in the Qing Dynasty (1644-1911).

Most of these books were written by scholars, literati, medical specialists, calligraphers, painters, or historians. This implies that diets, cooking, and dietotherapy to maintain good health constituted an important part of ancient Chinese culture.

To some extent each nation is closed, and this sense of being closed makes the uniqueness of a nation possible. Being closed often means adopting an attitude of hesitation or refusal toward things foreign, but a willingness to adopt the strong points of others, especially their foods. Many historians hold that after the Ming Dynasty, China gradually closed its door to the outside, yet many foods from the South and West entered China. They were brought to China not by Westerners and their warships, but by Chinese on their own initiative.

Some people brought foods into China even at a risk to their own lives. The sweet potato entered China in the middle of the Ming Dynasty. Texts say that Lin Huaizhi, a famous physician in Wuchuan, practiced medicine in Vietnam, where he cured many people. The king of Vietnam gave him sweet potatoes to eat. Because he wanted to bring one back to China, he asked for an uncooked sweet potato. The king gave him one, but Lin only ate two bites and kept the rest. At that time Vietnam prohibited anyone from taking sweet potatoes out of the country. When Lin left, a frontier guard discovered the sweet potato, but because Lin had cured his illness, the officer let him keep the sweet potato as a tribute.

Corn, which originated in America, came to China during the Ming Dynasty, but it was not commonly grown and was regarded as a rare and treasured delicacy. Kaoling or sorghum, which originated in Africa, also entered China during this period.

Soybeans originated in China, but other beans came from abroad. Mung beans (green beans) came from India during the Northern Song Dynasty.

Potatoes, which are eaten both as a staple food and as a vegetable, came from the West. They are believed to have been brought to China by pirates during the Ming Dynasty and were grown in the coastal provinces of Fujian and Zhejiang.

After the Han Dynasty, vegetable oils gradually replaced animal fats as the main heat conducting medium and flavoring agent in cooking. Daily-use vegetable oils came to include sesame, rapeseed, peanut, soybean, and sunflower. Sesame came to China during the Western Han Dynasty and soybeans were native to China, but the other oil-bearing crops did not enter China until after the Southern and Northern Dynasties.

Sugar, China's most important sweetener, first appeared during the Tang Dynasty (617-907). During the Warring States Period (475-221 B.C.), people in the State of Chu had learned to extract the sweet flavoring from sugar cane juice. Emperor Taizong of the Tang Dynasty sent an envoy to the Western Region to learn how to make sugar. After the envoy returned home, he used sugar cane from Yangzhou to make sugar. Its color and flavor were superior to that produced in the Western Region, so granulated sugar came to play a key role in Chinese cooking.

Because sugar is water-soluble, it became an important

flavoring used to make food sweet and delicious. It is used in soup and in cooking all kinds of dishes. Malt sugar and honey, which were used as sweeteners and flavorings before the Han Dynasty, now are used mostly to make thick soup.

Hot peppers are eaten widely in China. People in Hunan, Hubei and Sichuan are addicted to eating them and call them "meat for the poor" or salt, meaning they go well with rice like meat or salt. Hot peppers stimulate the appetite and dispel internal cold. They originated in South America, and were brought into China from Southeast Asia about the 15th century during the final years of the Ming Dynasty or the early years of the Qing Dynasty.

One of the first vegetables brought into China was spinach. At first it was called the Persian vegetable because it came to China from Persia (present-day Iran) when Emperor Taizong of the Tang Dynasty was in power. Because it has red roots, it was also called the red-root vegetable. As spinach is tender, it cannot be cooked very long. It grows in all seasons in areas south of the Yangtze River, so it is considered an ordinary vegetable.

A popular, nutritious vegetable grown in North China that originated elsewhere is the carrot, which came from Europe. It is used in cooking or eaten raw. People along the northern bank of the Yangtze River in Jiangsu Province developed the habit of eating it raw at noontime.

Eggplant originated in India and was brought into China along with Buddhism during the Southern and Northern Dynasties. It grows as tall as two meters (almost 80 inches), in southern China, but in northern China it is considered an annual herb.

Some other vegetables are native to China, but they were not well known in ancient times. They became recognized only after the Han Dynasty. Among these is *song*, known today as Chinese cabbage, which became known as an autumn vegetable in the Southern and Northern Dynasties. *Song* was an important winter vegetable for all of northern China.

Water shield became important after Zhang Han, a high-ranking official of the Western Jin Dynasty (265-316), became homesick for the vegetables and other native delicacies. Bamboo shoots, mushrooms, wax gourds (winter melons), and vegetable beans also became common after the Song Dynasty. These vegetables, plus chives, radishes, onions, cucumbers, three-coloured amaranths, and turnips were the principal vegetables during this period. Cabbage, tomato, and cauliflower were only introduced into China several decades ago.

Shark's fin and edible bird's nest, which are indispensable ingredients at modern, opulent banquets, were treasured by people in the Qing Dynasty. These two foods were brought into China from Southeast Asia in the early years of the Ming Dynasty when the eunuch, Zheng He, returned from there. During the middle period of the Qing Dynasty, edible bird's nest and shark's fin headed the menus at extravagant banquets. Sea cucumbers and prawns are native to China, but only became imperial dishes much later.

As cities and towns began to develop and thrive, cooking became a commercial activity and many restaurants were opened. Some cooks freed themselves from their slave status of serving the royal family and nobility by becoming independent laborers who sold their cooking skills. Many famous cooks and chefs emerged, among them Song Wusao in the Southern Song Dynasty and Wang Eryu in the Qing Dynasty.

Scholars also became interested and involved in cooking during this period by recording the cooks' knowledge, creativity, processes, and recipes for later generations. Using their education and aesthetic ability, they urged the cooks to make dishes more appealing to the senses of sight, smell, taste and touch. They were gourmets who knew diets and cooking very well, and they helped the cooks create a dietetic culture. They were connoisseurs and critics, propellers of progress, and recorders of the cooking experience.

Because of cultural exchanges between China and other countries, foods not native to China, such as corn, sweet potatoes, peanuts, and hot peppers, gradually entered the daily lives of the Chinese people. Many regions developed cuisines with unique flavors as a result of these exchanges.

To some extent peoples' food and drink are influenced by regional divisions, but the primary influences are peoples' income, education, culture, and religious beliefs. For these reasons, China developed several dietetic cultures. These include the imperial, aristocratic, literati, market, and temple cuisines. Especially during the Ming and Qing Dynasties, imperial food and drink were closely tied to preserving health, which led to the development of unique imperial food.

# Imperial Food in the Ming Dynasty

Zhu Yuanzhang, the founding emperor of the Ming Dynasty, established his capital in Nanjing (Chinese for southern capital). He ate mostly food cooked with the flavors of South China during his ruling years. His fourth son, Zhu Di, declared himself the emperor in 1403 and gave his reign the title of Yongle.

In September 1420, the 18th year of his reign, Zhu Di moved the capital to Beijing (Chinese for northern capital), so the palace cooks moved with him. Most of the raw materials they used in Beijing were grown locally, so the imperial food in Beijing had both southern and northern flavors.

Because tributes were sent to the palace from all parts of the country, delicacies of all kinds were available in the Forbidden City. Beijing had been the capital of the preceding Yuan Dynasty. The food in the Yuan palace had been influenced by the Mongolian flavorings. The food in the Ming palace, however, was mainly that of the southern Han people, so it totally changed the Mongolian style of food served in the palace.

The Mongolian food served in the Yuan palace was mainly meat from animals and fowl, especially mutton, but little seafood was served. The Yuan imperial food consisted of meats and vegetables with mixed flavors from the Muslims, Hans, and other ethnic groups. This was because Beijing, having been the capital city of the Yuan Dynasty, was an important communication center and was inhabited mainly by Han people. Therefore, the food of the Mongolian rulers had been influenced by the Hans and other ethnic groups.

The imperial food of the Ming and Qing Dynasties had one common attribute: Diet was used to protect health. Kublai (1215-1294), the first emperor of the Yuan Dynasty, paid great attention to protecting his health through diet.

During the Reign of Tianli in the Yuan Dynasty (1328-1330), Hu Sihui, the imperial physician at the imperial hospital in charge of the emperor's food, wrote a book entitled *Principles of Correct Diet*, which he gave to the emperor. The book dealt with questions about nutrition and hygiene. It also told how to make soup, thick soup, syrup, paste, oils, tea, sesame cakes, stuffed buns, steamed buns, porridge, and noodles, and described their nutritious effects. The book had a great influence on the food and drinks served in the Yuan palace. It encouraged health protection and parental education, listed taboo foods during pregnancy, and banned alcoholic drinks. It described foods for use in all seasons, prevented the wrong use of flavors, and stressed dietotherapy and regimen.

Shortly after Zhu Yuanzhang (1328-1398) ascended to the throne, he summoned Jia Ming, a 100-year-old man from Haining to ask him the secret of his long life. Jia Ming gave *The Instructions on Foods and Drinks* to the emperor.

Hu Sihui's *Proper and Essential Ways of Drinking and Eating* also received great attention from the Ming emperors. Zhu Qiyu, Emperor Daizong of the Ming Dynasty, even wrote a preface for the book before it was reprinted.

As in previous dynasties, food and drinks in the Ming Palace were supplied in season. Fresh fruits, vegetables and meats were supplied in their times. In the Ming Palace, more vegetables and fruits were eaten than meat and fish. Among the meat and fish eaten were chicken, pheasant, goose, duck, carp, golden carp, Mandarin fish, bream, rabbit, and deer.

The menu in the Ming Palace changed daily and dishes were not repeated. Light refreshments also changed daily. This variation in the daily diets continued until the end of the Qing Dynasty.

In the middle of the Ming Dynasty there were great varieties of food and drinks, their quality was improved, and new cooking methods were used. During festivals, sacrificial rites, and celebrations, the court ministers and officials were given food. On the Dragon Boat Festival, court officials were presented outside the Meridian Gate with a pyramid-shaped dumpling of glutinous rice wrapped in bamboo or reed leaves. When there was a ceremony, those called by the emperor were given a cake wrapped in red silk. When Imperial College students paid tribute to Confucius, they received food from the emperor, but the variety of the food given to them was not great.

In autumn, residents of the Ming Palace liked to eat fat ground squirrels, which were an annual tribute from Shanxi. The eating of ground squirrels was a Mongolian custom handed down from the Yuan Dynasty. But as a whole, the customs of the Han ethnic group most influenced the food and drinks served in the palace.

*The Chronicle of Ceremonies and Rites*, by Sun Chengze, listed the appropriate food and drinks by lunar month:

One: Chives, romaine lettuce, chicken, and duck

Two: Celery, liver mosses, *artemisia vulgaris*, and goose

Three: Tea, bamboo shoots, and carp

Four: Cherry, apricot, green plum, cucumber, and pheasant

Five: Peach, plum, Chinese pear-leaved crabapple, eggplant, barley, wheat flour, and chicken

Six: Lotus seedpod, sweet melon, watermelon, and wax gourd (winter melon)

Seven: Date, grape, fresh water chestnut, amaranth, and pear

Eight: Lotus roots, young taro plant, wild rice stem, tender ginger, semi-glutinous rice, millet, broomcorn, and Mandarin fish

Nine: Orange, chestnut, small red beans, granulated sugar, and bream

Ten: Mandarin orange, tangerine, Chinese yam, rabbit and honey

Eleven: Sugar cane, buckwheat flour, red bean, deer, and rabbit

Twelve: Spinach, leaf mustard, golden carp, and whitefish.

Vegetables and fruits accounted for a large percentage of the foods. Of the meats, there were many kinds of poultry, fish, and animals.

In the Ming Palace, most foods had southern flavors, with the foods of the Han ethnic group being dominant. The Ming Palace was characterized by opulent banquets, sumptuous feasts, and voracious eaters. According to Liu Ruoyu:

The food and drinks for the royal family were bought by their own grants, and poor officials were hired to do the cooking. Those who were highly skilled could earn several taels (one tael is approximately 30 grams) of silver every month, but received no odd bonuses.

Clean baskets had to be used to cleanse the rice before cooking.

Sesame seed oil, sweet sauce made of fermented flour, fermented soybeans, soybean sauce, vinegar, and other sundries were bought from outside at any price.

All foods taken by the Royal Family and court officials were roasted or fried.

When members of the Royal Family fell ill and had to take drugs, they took them carelessly and refused to avoid rich foods.

In short, the members of the Royal Family most favored those court officials who were good cooks.

As the eunuchs' sexual physiology was altered and destroyed, they paid special attention to eating foods that invigorated their kidneys and stimulated their male virility.

The court officials are fond of eating the sexual organs of the ox and donkey. When they say *arm-in-arm*, it means the penis. If they say *the white kidney of the sheep*, it means the testis. The ovaries of the white horse is a very rare and precious thing that is difficult to get. It is called the *ovaries of the dragon*.

If an old male duck is cooked so as to melt in the mouth, it has the same positive effect as ginseng. For this reason, eunuches like to eat the kidneys of male ducks.

The Ming Palace paid more attention to dinnerware than had previous dynasties. Besides the porcelain ware fired in the Chai, Ru, Guan, Ge and Rao kilns, there were porcelain treasures from the Xuande, Chenghua, Jiajing, and Wanli reigns. In addition to horn and jade ware, there were cloisonne ware, countless exquisitely shaped, pure gold ware, silverware, and gold and silver ware inlaid with precious stones. Yan Song (1480-1567), a prime minister of the Ming Dynasty, had many high-grade sets of dinnerware among his articles of tribute.

The Ming Palace had no special menus for imperial dishes. Based on available historical data, following are how some representative dishes were cooked in the Ming Palace:

**Roast Mutton**: Cut the mutton into large pieces. Mix soybean sauce to an even consistency and add kernels of *Fructus amoni*, Chinese prickly ash, and the whites of scallions. Cook sesame oil in a wok for a little while. Add the ingredients, a little water, seal the pan with paper, and cook it over a low fire, or roast it again after it is cooked. (*Song's Way to Build Health*)

**Roast Sliced Mutton**: Slice the raw mutton and grill it on an iron mesh over a charcoal fire. Dip the mutton pieces in salted water and soy sauce occasionally until they are well cooked on both sides and ready to eat. (*Collection of Making Adjustments to Tripods*)

**Quick Stir-Fried Sheep Tripe**: Wash the sheep stomach until it is clean and then cut it into small strips. Heat water to boiling in a soup pot and heat oil in a wok. Put the tripe into the boiling pot, scald it, remove it with a wire strainer, wring it dry in a piece of coarse cloth, and stir-fry it in the wok. Add cut onion, sliced garlic, Chinese prickly ash, aniseed, soy sauce, rice wine, and vinegar. Stir-fry it quickly until it becomes crisp and delicious. If it is fried slowly, it will become moist and difficult to eat. (*Eight Commentaries on How to Live*)

**Stir-Fried Sheep Tripe**: Cut the cleaned sheep stomach into small pieces. Place them in a heated wok with chicken fat, soy sauce, wine, ginger, and onion and stir them quickly. Or, cut the stomach into long strips, boil them quickly in boiling water, and wring them in a piece of cloth. Stir the pieces in heated oil until they become slightly yellow. Add wine, soy sauce, and onion, and stir them again. (*Collection of Making Adjustments to Tripods*)

**Steamed Mutton**: Clean the fat mutton and cut it into large pieces. Rub the pieces with Chinese prickly ash salt and shake off the excess salt. Crush some walnuts and put them in with the meat. Wrap the meat and walnuts inside mulberry tree leaves using softened rice stalks to tie them tightly. Put the bundles with some walnuts on top in a wooden steamer. Cover it tightly and steam until the meat melts in the mouth. (*Grand Secrets of Diets*)

**Steamed Cow's Milk**: Mix three cups of cow's milk, eggs, one walnut (crushed into powder), and a little crystal sugar (crushed into powder) and steam the mixture. It is good for the health. (Add a spoonful of ginger juice for old people who are short of breath or for those with phlegm.) (*Collection of Making Adjustments to Tripods*)

**Cold Sliced Sheep Tail**: Steam the sheep tail until the meat melts in the mouth. Cool the meat and cut it into slices. Dip the slices in sugar. (*Collection of Cooking Tripods*)

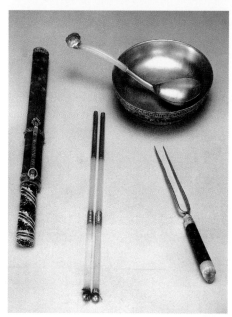

清宫进膳餐具
Eating Implements

清宫火锅
Qing-Dynasty Hot Pot

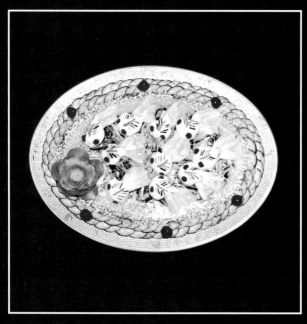

金鱼鸭掌
Goldfish-Shaped
Duck's Webs

罗汉大虾
Buddha Prawns

干贝冬瓜球
Dried Scallop
and Wax-Gourd Balls

沙舟踏翠
Sail the Desert Boat
on Green

龙凤丝
Shredded Dragon
and Phoenix

金蟾望月
Golden Frogs
Look at the Moon

肘子菜心
Pork Leg
with Rape Hearts

桃仁鸭方
Duck Squares
with Walnuts

鱼藏剑
Fish with Hidden Swords

肉末烧饼
Sesame Cakes Stuffed with Fried Minced Pork

**Sausage**: Clean the casings of the large intestines. Fill them with minced meat. Tie them on both ends and cook them in water. (*Song's Way to Build Health*)

**Meat Balls**: Mince two portions of lean pork and one portion of fatty meat. Add a little onion, green pepper, apricot jam, and dried steamed cake crumbs (or bread crumbs) and mix it all together. Use your hands to form the mixture into balls, then coat the meatballs with fine flour. Quick-boil the meatballs in boiling water; remove them as soon as they float. Eat them with hot pepper juice. (*Collection of the Dietetic Systems in the Yunlin Hall*)

**Stewed Pork**: Wash the pork clean. Rub the meat with wine and salt and place it in a pot. Add a little onion, Chinese prickly ash, honey, and bamboo shoots to the pot. Add a small cup of water and a small cup of wine. Cover the pot and seal it with wet paper. When the paper dries, dampen it with water. Burn a large bunch of straw under the pot without poking it. When it dies out, burn another bunch. After the fire dies out a second time, wait for a while. Open the cover when it becomes cool to the touch and stir the meat. Cover the pot again and seal it with wet paper. Burn another bunch of straw. Wait until the pot cover again becomes cool; the pork is ready. (*Collection of the Dietetic Systems in the Yunlin Hall*)

**Pickled trotters** (feet): How to pickle a pig's head and trotters. Cook the pig's head and trotters until they are very soft, then remove the bones. Spread the meat on a cloth and press it flat overnight with a large stone. It is very delicious when pickled in grains. (*Eight Commentaries on How to Live*)

**Steamed Pork**: Use good pork and boil it for a short time, then remove the meat and cut it into square pieces. Rinse the meat in clean water. Scrape the skin clean, then crush the skin into pieces with a knife. Put aniseed, Chinese prickly ash, caoguo (*Fructus tsaoko*), and Chinese cinnamon in a small bag and place it in a soup pot. Put the meat squares on top of the bag. Mix goose and chicken stock together and pour it over the meat. Cover the meat with onions, pickled vegetables and garlic. Put the lid on the pot, and steam it. Remove the onions, garlic, and small bag of flavorings before you eat the meat. (*Eight Commentaries on How to Live*)

**Boiled Meat**: Use a sharp knife and scrape the skin three or four times. Rinse the meat and boil it in a pot. Stir it continuously (do not cover the pot) until you smell a meat aroma. Put out the fire when you smell the meat and cover the pot with a lid for a while. Eat it in slices; it is delicious. (Another version: Place a basin of cold water by the pot. Add some cold water to the pot when it begins to boil. Repeat this process three times. The meat will taste even more delicious.) (*Records on Waking up in the Garden*)

**Intestine in Intestine**: Choose small, fat pig intestines and clean them. Place one intestine inside another and cook them in broth. Cut them diagonally into one-inch pieces. Mix the pieces with fresh bamboo shoots and mushroom stock, and cook them well. The flavor is excellent. It is also good when made with rice wine and oil. (*Grand Secrets of Diets*)

**Stir-Fried Shredded Pork**: Remove the sinews, skin and bones. Shred the pork, then soak it in soy sauce and wine for a moment. Boil rapeseed oil until the white smoke changes to gray smoke. Put the pork in the pan and stir-fry it constantly. Add corn starch, a drop of vinegar, a pinch of sugar, and onion stalk, chives or cabbage. Use just half a catty of meat (1 catty is equal to about 1.3

pounds) and use a slow fire without adding water. Another method: After soaking the meat in the oil, cook it with soy sauce, water, and wine slightly over a slow fire until the pan becomes hot and red. It smells even more delicious if some chives are added.

**Stir-Fried Sliced Pork**: Cut the half-lean, half-fat pork into thin slices, mix them with soy sauce, and stir-fry them in an oiled wok. Add soy sauce, water, onion, gourd, bamboo shoots, and chives as soon as the pan hisses. The fire must be large and strong when you stir the meat. (*The Menus of the Sui Garden*)

**Deep-Fried Sparrows**: Pluck the feathers from the sparrows. With the sparrow's breast in one hand and a knife in the other, make a small opening by the tail and squeeze out the internal organs. Cut the sparrows from their tails along their spines. Remove the breastbones. Break the spines and leg joints, cut off the beaks and claws, and remove the eyes. Rinse and dry them, then marinate them in Shaoxing rice wine, salt, ginger, and onion stock for a short while. Roll the sparrows in glutinous rice flour and deep-fry them slightly in hot peanut oil. Drain the oil until the sparrows are cool. Deep-fry them again in oil until they become crisp and golden yellow. Mix minced garlic with sugar, vinegar, and starch and put it in the hot pan, then add some sesame oil. Pour it over the sparrows and place them on a plate. (*Chinese Menu*)

**Steamed Chicken**: Choose a tender chicken and clean it in water, then rub it all over with salt, soy sauce, Chinese prickly ash, and aniseed powder. Keep it preserved for half a day. Steam it until a joss stick burns out. Tear the chicken into pieces, remove the bones, and add a proper amount of flavorings. Steam it again until another joss stick burns out. The taste is very delicious. Goose, duck, pork, and mutton can all be steamed the same way. (*Grand Secrets of Diets*)

**Egg Rolls**: Fry whipped egg in a thin layer in a wok, then fill it with minced meat and flavorings and roll it up. Cook it in lard with sugar and sweet soy sauce. Slice it into pieces. (*Grand Secrets of Diets*)

**Deep-Fried Whitebait** (young fish): Use dried whitebait. Steam it with wine, Chinese prickly ash, and onion. It is good stir-fried in oil and better with chives added. It is good quickly fried in oil and wine, and better with edible gourd (squash) or fresh bamboo shoots added. It is good rolled in wheat flour and fried in oil; it is better in soup. (*Song's Way to Build Health*)

**Abalone**: Wash it clean and cook it over a slow rice-husk fire for a while. Change the water and immerse it. Cut it into pieces. (*Collection of the Dietetic Systems in the Yunlin Hall*)

Abalone is very good thinly sliced and stir-fried. Abalone was cut into slices and put into chicken soup with bean curd in the home of Imperial Inspector Yang. It was called abalone bean curd. Pour some rice wine and oil over it. Magistrate Zhuang stewed a whole chicken with abalone and it was also very delicious. (*The Menus in the Sui Garden*)

**Steamed Hilsa Herring**: Remove the intestines, but not the scales. Wipe away the blood and water with a cloth and put the herring in a soup pot. Crush Chinese prickly ash and kernels of Amomum xanthioides (Fructus amomi) and mix them well with soy sauce, water, wine, and onions. Steam the herring and remove the scales before eating. (*Eight Commentaries on How to Live*)

**Sea Cucumber**: Sea cucumber has no taste but it contains a lot of sand and it has a bad smell. Its natural consistency is thick and heavy. It should never be cooked in broth over a slow fire. Choose small sea cucumbers with thorns. Remove the mud and sand in water. Boil the sea cucumbers three times in meat soup, then stew them in chicken and pork stock with soy sauce until they become very soft. Add mushrooms and fungus that have a similar black color. If you host a dinner, stew the cucumbers the day before. (*The Menus in the Sui Garden*)

**Stir-Fried Chicken Legs with Mushrooms**: The monk in the Wuhu Buddhist Temple cleaned the chicken legs and mushrooms in water. He then added oil and wine to a wok and stir-fried the chicken legs and mushrooms until they were well done. Serve them on a plate; it is a very good dish for your guests. (*The Menues in the Sui Garden*)

# Imperial Food
# in the Qing Dynasty

## Xu Qixian

The imperial food served within the walls of the Forbidden City by the Qing Dynasty had an important effect
on Chinese dietetic culture. Using the traditional diet of
the Manchu ethnic group as its foundation, the best of the
Chinese dietetic culture, mainly foods of the Han ethnic
group, were assimilated to develop the dietetic culture of
the Qing Palace. Even today this cuisine is important to
people at home and abroad.

The "Imperial Kitchen," a special organization within
the Qing Palace, was responsible for the emperor's meals.
It was located south of the Yangxin Hall (Hall of Mental
Tranquillity), where the emperor lived and handled political affairs. The Imperial Kitchen was managed by the
General Office of Internal Affairs, an office directed by
several ministers personally appointed by the emperor.

The Imperial Kitchen had a director, deputy and assis-
tant directors, manager, executive manager, and clerks to
handle the emperor's daily meals, employing more than
200 officials, cooks and eunuchs. The empress had both an
internal and an external kitchen, and the Empress Dowager had a special external kitchen. The crown prince and
his son got special kitchens after they were married.

For good luck, the Royal Family used the terms *yong shan* (use the meal), *chuan shan* (pass the meal), or *jin shan* (advance the meal) instead of *chi fan* (eat the meal) when they ate. They did this because the Chinese character *shan* (meaning meal) has the same pronunciation as another character for *shan* (meaning kindness) and they wanted to imply a close friendship with the people. The word "fan" has the same sound as another Chinese character that means "rebellion," so it was considered unlucky. Moreover, the Royal Family wanted to stress their difference from the common people, their supreme authority, and their extravagant lifestyle.

Within the Forbidden City the emperor's meals were divided into two categories: The regular meals he took every day and his large banquets and occasional feasts.

In its early years, the Qing Dynasty had a tea kitchen (for tea with milk), a clear tea kitchen (for plain tea), and meal kitchens. The tea kitchen and clear tea kitchen were special places for making milk tea and clear tea. The meal kitchens were distributed throughout the palace and usually made the dishes as well as the porridges and cooked wheat food.

There was a special bakery for making pastries, cakes, and other baked foods. There was an internal and an external bakery. The internal bakery made staple foods for the emperor and his family; the external bakery prepared all rice and wheat foods for the banquets, feasts, and sacrificial rites. Both bakeries were under the palace Secretariat of the Office of Administration.

During the rule of Emperor Qianlong (1736-1795), the imperial tea and meal kitchens were divided into the Internal Kitchen and the External Kitchen.

The Internal Kitchen had departments for meat dishes,

vegetables, roasting, baking, and rice cooking. The meat department cooked all delicacies from land and sea: domesticated animals, poultry, wild fowl, and dishes like roast pig, roast duck, and roast chicken. The bakery made cakes and pastries; and the rice cooking department prepared cooked rice and porridges.

In addition, the Imperial Kitchen had a meat supply department, inner house, vegetable house, and dried-meat house to guarantee its daily supply of raw materials. Each kitchen (including the tea kitchens) had its own dinnerware storehouse where all variety of gold, silver, jade, tin, bronze, copper, and porcelain ware were kept for use at any time.

The External Kitchen prepared the palace banquets, feasts, and sacrificial rites.

The Yuanmingyuan Imperial Garden, the Summer Palace, and the Imperial Palace for Short Stays in Jihol also had imperial kitchens.

The Qing Palace imperial meals formed an important part of the royal family's daily life. The rites for the meals, the number of people, and the use, cost, variety, and quality of sumptuous courses at each meal were the greatest of all the dynasties in China.

## Imperial Cooks

When the first Qing Dynasty emperor ascended to the throne in 1644, the Qing Palace cooks were Manchus and the cooks from the Ming Palace who had remained. Therefore, the imperial meals and other palace meals were similar to those in the preceding capital city of Shenyang. The cooks from the Ming Palace were afraid to make Han style dishes for fear of offending the habits of the Manchu rulers and their national sentiments. So, for a very long time the imperial meals in the Qing Palace were, in fact, cooked by Manchus.

Nevertheless, the dietetic establishment, organization, and many dietetic matters in the Qing Palace followed the systems of the Ming Palace.

Early in the first emperor Shunzhi's reign, an organization called the Guanglu Temple was in charge of state banquets. The officials at all levels of this organization were eunuchs and imperial bodyguards. Most of the cooks from the Ming Palace were from Shandong and were skilled in cooking Shandong cuisine. Given their long service in the palace, the skills they displayed naturally influenced the Manchu cooks. These skills helped the imperial kitchens improve the quality and variety of the dishes served during the Qing Dynasty.

The Qing Palace banquets and dinners given in the Guanglu Temple were classified as either Manchu dinners or Han dinners. All Manchu dinners had cooked wheat foods, the staple food in traditional Manchu style.

Han dinners had dishes of goose, chicken, duck, fish, and pork as the major ingredients. Han dinners also included many Manchu dishes, with the major ingredients coming from Northeast China. Moreover, under the influence and restrictions of the Manchus' sacrificial activities, the dishes also reflected the features of sacrificial offerings, but most of the dishes were from the Shandong cuisine.

The Qing Palace imperial meals reflected the Manchus' strong ethnic feelings. After the Manchus came to power, their rulers took many measures to strengthen their rule and prevent assimilation by the Hans, including which foods were served in the Qing Palace. The imperial meals were mainly Manchu dishes, yet they were influenced by the flavors of the Han cuisine. At banquets held in the House of State Banquets, dishes from the Manchu and Han cuisines were well blended.

During Qianlong's reign, the composition of the imperial cooks in the Qing Palace and the flavors of the imperial meals changed somewhat. During his reign there was a stable political situation, a developed economy, and a thriving food market. Restaurants mushroomed in the ancient cities of Suzhou, Hangzhou, and Yangzhou along the Yangtze River and their cooks skillfully prepared excellent dishes.

Emperor Qianlong visited the southern cities six times during his reign and tasted their delicacies. He personally selected a number of uniquely skilled cooks to work in the Qing Palace. At that time the palace cooks had lifetime, inherited positions. When old cooks died, their children succeeded them. Most of the cooks were Manchus, but because the cooks followed this system of succession, the Shandong cuisine, Suzhou cuisine, and Hangzhou cuisine were all well preserved. Therefore, Qing Palace imperial meals had the distinct flavors of Northeast China, Central China, and East China.

More than 400 cooks worked in the Qing Palace during the reigns of Qianlong and Jiaqing (1736-1820). This could be called the period of full bloom. As national power declined during Daoguang's reign (1821-1850), he simplified his diet and reduced his cooking staff to 200.

However, the number of cooks increased greatly when Empress Dowager Cixi took power, and her meals had unparalleled extravagance. For details, please read "Western Kitchen, Cixi's Private Kitchen."

There were only a few highly skilled cooks in the Qing

Palace. Most staff were assistants or laborers who tended the fire, washed dishes, cleaned, and did other odd jobs. Others were waiters.

The palace cooks' remunerations differed by person. The best enjoyed the salary of a seventh grade official, or the equivalent of a magistrate's salary. Common cooks received three, four, five, or six taels of silver daily, which was not a low income at that time. Besides their salaries, the best cooks also received bonuses from the emperor and members of the Royal Family, so they were quite well-off.

The cooks' families lived around the town of Haidian, a western suburb of Beijing. During the final years of the Qing Dynasty and in the early years of the Republic, the cooks from the Imperial Kitchens began to wander about Beijing, Tianjin, and Northeast China. Some opened restaurants and brought the imperial food to the common people.

# Meals for Emperors

The Qing Dynasty emperors did not take their meals in just one place. Often they ate where they lived, worked, or played. Banquets, feasts, and dinners were given in Taihe Hall (the Hall of Supreme Harmony), Baohe Hall (the Hall of Preserving Harmony), Qianqing Palace (the Palace of Heavenly Purity), and the Ziguang (Purple Light) Pavilion in the Western Garden (the South and Central Lakes, where the headquarters of the Chinese government is located today).

The emperors took their daily meals in Yangxin Hall (the Hall of Mental Cultivation), Chonghua Palace (the Hall of Double Glory), or the Imperial Library. These details are clearly recorded in the archived imperial diets of the Qing Palace General Office of Internal Affairs. The following was recorded about Emperor Qianlong. "At about 7 a.m. on the 30th day of the ninth month in the 12th year of Qianlong's Reign, His Majesty (Emperor Qianlong) took his breakfast in the Hongde Hall (the Hall of Grand Virtue)." And, "at about 2 p.m. on the first day of the 10th month, His Majesty took his late meal in the eastern heated room of the Chonghua Hall." On the same day, "His Majesty asked for a dinner of 15 courses with wine, wild game, and fowl to be served on red porcelain plates in Yangxin Hall." He selected three different places for his meals in just two days.

The Qing Dynasty emperors ate two formal meals a day: breakfast after 6 a.m. and the second meal after 12 or 2 p.m. Besides the two formal meals, there was a cocktail and snacks, usually after 4 p.m., the exact time and menu as ordered by the emperor.

At meal time the emperor ordered his bodyguard to summon the meal. The senior or junior officials in the imperial kitchen immediately ordered the eunuchs to set the table in the hall where the emperor wanted the meal served. The eunuchs then brought the dishes prepared according to the menu the emperor had ordered and placed them on the table according to the strict rules.

The emperors were always afraid of being murdered and did not trust even their closest attendants or body-guards, much less the officials and eunuchs in charge of the imperial meals. Therefore, when the dishes were put on the table, the emperors did not immediately eat. First they took a small silver plate and inserted it several times into each dish. It was believed that if poison were present, the silver plate would change color.

Even when the silver test was negative, the emperors

still had fears so they asked the waiting eunuch to taste all the dishes. If there were poison, the eunuch would get poisoned, not they. It was thus evident that the emperors, once they were enthroned, regarded everyone as their enemy and isolated themselves totally.

On those days when officials wanted to present memorials or be called in, they each submitted a plate at the emperor's meal time. Princes, dukes and members of the Royal Family used red plates. Civil officials above the rank of Deputy Chief of the Court of Censors and military officers above the rank of Provincial Military Governor used green plates. Civil officials from outside the capital above the rank of Chief Prosecutor of the Provincial High Court and military officers above the rank of Area Commander used common plates.

The Memorials Office officials gave the plates to the emperor to decide whether the memorials would be presented and who would be called in. Because the plates were submitted at the emperor's meal time, the plates for calling in the officials were called "meal plates".

Profound philosophical thought and a thorough base of knowledge went into the emperors' diets during the Qing Dynasty. According to the ancient Chinese classic, *The National Language — The Language of the Zheng State*, dishes should not be of a single ingredient or several monotonous ingredients, but should be diverse. The diversification should not be a simple mixture, but a reasonable blending. The precise term for this reasonable blending was "harmony," which meant scientific coordination.

The ancient Chinese philosophy reflected in the emperor's diets was "harmony is precious." "Harmony" meant the foods should include the five cereals and five flavors. Only by eating the five cereals plus foods with the five

41

flavors of sweet, bitter, sour, salty, and spicy could all nutrients be obtained to stimulate the appetite and maintain good health. The diverse food and reasonable blending of ingredients were intended to achieve "harmony." The imperial meals for the emperors in the Qing Palace represented the philosophy that "harmony is precious."

The emperors' diets in the Qing Palace were roughly divided into two periods, with the dividing line being Qianlong's reign. First, there were changes to the raw materials: During the early Qing Dynasty, most raw materials came from Northeast China. These included live and processed ducks from different parts of the country, duck eggs, edible bird's nest, fish, deer and its products, river and roe deer, bear, wild fowl, wild game, and ham. Fruits and vegetables included small root vegetables, bamboo shoots, lily, Chinese yam, and mountain pears. More red meats were eaten than cereals, vegetables, and fruits.

After Qianlong's reign, more cereals appeared in the diet. Glutinous millet, rice, and purple rice came from Jade Spring Mountain and the Lush Green Garden near Beijing, and the Tang Spring in Zunhua. Good-quality rice, wheat, flour, dried noodles, and cereals came from other parts of the country.

To make sure the royalty had an abundant supply of fresh and dried fruits, all the local governments sent their specialties and fresh fruits to the palace. These included peanuts, dates, dried persimmons, and lotus seeds from Shandong; dried persimmons, lily, and preserved peaches from Henan; sweet-scented osmanthus blossoms and Hami melons from Shaanxi and Gansu; oranges, litchis, tangerines, and round cardamom from Guangdong and Guangxi; tangerines, oranges, crystal sugar, areca (palms, especially betel palm) and longan from Zhejiang and Fujian; fresh fruits from Hunan, Hubei, Sichuan and Guizhou; and plums, pears, hazelnuts, hawthorn berries, and grapes from Northeast China. Vegetables were bought at the market, but pickled and salted vegetables were tributes from different parts of the country.

The imperial diets included multiple nutrients, multiple flavors, and a vast number of dishes. One meal included both hot and cold dishes, meat and vegetable dishes, sweet and salty pastries, soup, thick soup and milk, pickles, rice, wheat foods, desserts, and fruits.

The diversity of foods in the Qing Palace was clearly evident in the emperors' daily menus. Following are examples of menus prepared for Emperor Qianlong:

Example one: On the 1st day of the 10th month in the 12th year of Qianlong's reign, His Majesty (Emperor Qianlong) took his late meal in the eastern warm room of the Zhonghua Hall at a Japanese-lacquer dinner table. He was served bird's nest, shredded chicken, shredded mushrooms, shredded smoked meats, shredded cabbage and cashew nuts, and a pink bowl of eight delicacies — bird's nest, duck, sliced smoked meats, pork leg, cabbage, chicken wings, pig stomach, and mushrooms. The two courses were cooked by Zhang Dongguan.

Courses of chicken with Chinese cabbage, stewed pig's offal, hotchpotch (a thick stew of meat, vegetables, and potatoes), a soup, tender duck, shredded pheasant, and pickled vegetables were served in bronze enamel bowls.

Afterward, chive sprouts stir-fried with shredded dried venison were offered in the Imperial Temple along with roast venison *hors d'oeuvres*, lightly fried chicken slivers, cold mutton, and courses of pork and mutton for sacrificial offering, both on silver plates. Other dishes included rice cakes, small cakes, and small buns served on yellow plates; folded milk skins served in a silver bowl; sacrificial cakes on a silver plate, bean flour mixed with butter served in a silver bowl; honey in a small purple dragon dish; lala (porridge) with bean paste served in a gold bowl; pickles served in a sunflower enamel box; cold dishes with southern flavors; spinach; mutton soup with a poached egg and vermicelli; turnip soup; pheasant soup; and radish with osmanthus flowers served in enameled copper dishes decorated with a birthday peach surrounded by five bats to symbolize prosperity and longevity. Spoons, chopsticks, and napkins were prepared. A bowl of round-grained glutinous rice, as usual, was served in an enamel bowl with a gold cover.

Example two: On July 28th in the 35th year of Qianlong's reign, at about 6:15 a.m. His Majesty asked for breakfast and took it in the Yangxin Hall (Hall of Character Cultivation) at about 7 a.m. A lacquer table was laid and Chief Director Wang Cheng brought him eight courses.

Bird's nest with shredded duck meat, stewed chicken with mushrooms and sweet beans, sweet duck, smoked duck and mushrooms without soy sauce, hotchpotch of duck meat — half cooked with soy sauce and the other half cooked without soy sauce, pork stewed with wine, spiced mutton, bird's nest with smoked chicken, *hors d'oeuvres* of roast duck, peaches stuffed with duck meat, deep-fried cakes, steamed chicken, stewed roe deer meat, steamed rolls shaped in bamboo knots, small buns, pickles served in a silver sunflower box, four courses of cold dishes served on silver plates, a course of longevity noodles, (brought in by Wang Cheng), and cooked round-grained non-glutinous rice.

During the Qing Dynasty, food and drink were used to improve the emperor's physique and preserve his health. This was an ancient Chinese tradition clearly stated in the ancient Chinese medical classic, *Huang Di Nei Jing*, under "Plain Questions": "The five cereals are staple foods, fruits are auxiliary foods, meats are beneficial, and vegetables are available in abundance." This means that cereals, fruits, meats, and vegetables guarantee good health.

The imperial kitchen adjusted the emperors' diets with the change of the seasons. The emperors ate more light foods in spring and summer and more fatty, nutritious foods in autumn and winter. Light food increases body fluids while fatty, nutritious food increases vital energy. This conforms to the metabolic rule of the human body. We will use another example of Qianlong's diets to illustrate this point. Emperor Qianlong ate more light food in spring and summer. For example, on June 8 in the 54th year of his reign, Qianlong "took his breakfast in the Yihong Hall (Hall of Partial Rainbow) at a lacquer table on which were served a hot pot of game with bird's nest, roast duck and roast meat; a hot pot of thick duck soup with Chinese yam; courses of wild herb salad, cold bean jelly, duck stewed with wine and cauliflower, stir-fried spinach with small dried shrimp, cooked lotus root, steamed lotus root with glutinous rice, bean curd stewed with mushrooms, sliced chicken and duck cooked with soy sauce, bamboo knotted rolls and steamed small buns, steamed buns stuffed with minced pumpkin and mutton, braised chicken with cowpea (black-eyed peas); pickles served in an enamel sunflower box; four cold dishes on flange plates; a bowl of cooked round-grained non-glutinous rice; and a bowl of boiled cowpeas."

Emperor Qianlong ate more fatty food with a higher calorie content in autumn and winter. For example, at 1:30 p.m. on December 13 in the 54th year of Qianlong's Reign, the emperor "took his late meal in the eastern warm room of the Yangxin Hall at a lacquer table. His meal included a hot pot of chicken with bird's nest and pine nuts; a hot pot of chicken, smoked meats, and Chinese cabbage; a hot pot of shredded lamb stomach and shredded mutton; courses of steamed chicken with fresh mushrooms, pork fried in salt with fresh mushrooms, cold steamed chicken and mutton, cold steamed duck and deer's tail, pork in thick gravy, bamboo knotted dumplings and small buns, red spoon-shaped cakes, spiral buns with filling, steamed dumplings with minced chicken, salted pork, pickles served in a silver sunflower box; four small cold dishes put on silver plates; chicken soup with cooked rice; a thick wild duck soup with Chinese yam; and some bird's nest soup with spinal cord."

An analysis of the menus from the two different seasons shows that hot pot, a traditional Manchu dish, roast duck, and roast chicken were served at every meal. The other dishes changed from season to season.

The Qing Dynasty emperors also ate foods that had medicinal effects. Many records in the meal archives of the Qing Palace included the use of wines, juices, extracts, preserved fruits, and sugar. Examples are: Songling Taiping aphrodisiac wine, longevity wine, medicinal wine for old people, Zhuangyuan wine to stimulate the spleen and kidneys, realgar (red orpiment) wine, rose extract, watermelon juice, papaya extract, pineapple extract, longan extract, peppermint tea extract, cakes with osmanthus flowers, eight-treasure cakes, ginger cakes, lily cakes, haw jam, chrysanthemum jam, date jam, glutinous rehmannia (a medicinal herb) preserved in syrup, preserved gingko, preserved fingered citron, preserved rose, peppermint, almond sweets, and walnut sweets.

These foods were used to stimulate the stomach, kidneys, and appetite; reduce internal heat; reduce phlegm; nourish the body; and prolong life.

The emperors' imperial meals not only represented the Qing Dynasty's dietetic culture, they were also an important component of the Chinese dietetic culture. The meals taken by the Qing emperors were varied in content and form, followed strict rules and rites, and were based on profound cultural thoughts. They comprised Manchu dishes, Han dishes, and dishes cooked in both southern and northern styles. The foods reflected the colorful, dietetic culture and multiple nationalities of the Qing Dynasty. What the Chinese eat today is mostly a continuation of the dietetic culture of the Qing Dynasty.

Our study of the imperial meals, regular meals, snacks, imperial wines, and medicinal meals of the Qing Dynasty is an important effort to identify, continue, and develop this cuisine as well as an important task in understanding and further developing today's dietetic culture.

As part of our study of the imperial meals of the Qing Dynasty, I would like to tell you about some of the foods the emperors ate in order to help you better understand the imperial meals and the dietetic culture.

Hot pots included:

Steamed duck, bird's nest, and fresh mushrooms without soy sauce; duck, bird's nest and lotus seeds; bird's nest and wild game; stewed pork leg and grouse; stir-fried shredded pork, chicken, and kelp; stir-fried chicken slices and stewed bean curd; stir-fried chicken slices, stewed spinach, and bean curd; stir-fried chicken and quick stir-fried pork, pickled vegetable and stewed pork leg; quick stir-fried pork and stir-fried Chinese cabbage; shredded pork and bamboo shoots; duck stewed in soy sauce and duck stewed without soy sauce with Chinese cabbage; sheep's intestines and stomach with vinegar and pepper; Chinese yam and smoked duck with onion and Chinese prickly ash; stewed chicken and braised meat balls of three delicacies; and omelet with scallion, shredded sheep's stomach, roast dog's meat, and duck kidney sautied with vinegar.

*Hors d'oeuvres*:

Steamed chicken and deer's tail; roast duck, barbecued pork, lotus root, duck, and pork leg; stewed venison and deer's tail; steamed chicken and stewed roe deer; steamed chicken and deep-fried mutton slivers; roast pig; and duck with fruits.

Soups:

Shredded chicken and bird's nest, bird's nest and shredded duck, sliced bean curd, bird's nest and eight delicacies, sheep's intestine and stomach, duck and broad bean, and mixed duck.

Staple food:

Cooked non-glutinous rice, small buns, steamed white sponge cake, lotus leaf cake, spoon-shaped red cake, steamed wheat cake, steamed broomcorn cake, steamed wheat cake with Chinese dates, cowpeas recooked in boiling water, steamed buns filled with minced duck meat, steamed buns stuffed with minced duck and mushrooms, steamed dumplings with the dough open at the top filled with minced duck and mushrooms, steamed dumplings with the dough open at the top filled with minced chicken and mushrooms, steamed buns filled with chives, deep-fried triangular dumplings filled with minced pork, and steamed buns filled with minced mutton and pumpkin.

# Characteristics of Imperial Meals in the Qing Palace

Imperial meals in the Qing Palace were dominated by the Manchu cuisine, but they also included the Shandong and the Suzhou-Hangzhou cuisines. These three cuisines were influenced by and blended with one another. A course might be made of raw materials from Northeast China, but its cooking method and taste might have Shandong or Suzhou-Hangzhou cuisine characteristics. Likewise, a dish of the Shandong or Suzhou-Hangzhou cuisine was often prepared by a cook of the Manchu nationality.

Through longtime cooperation and exchange, the cooks of the Manchu and Han nationalities catered to the Qing rulers' tastes and desires for the banquets and feasts. Under the restrictions of the Qing Palace regulations, systems, and rites, they learned from each other and helped each other create new imperial meals that varied from the cuisines of the three different localities and also varied from the imperial meals of the preceding dynasties.

The eating habits and traditional cooking methods of the Manchus dominated in the preparation of the Qing Palace imperial meals. The imperial meals were limited to dishes from the imperial kitchen and the bakery under the Office of Palatial Affairs. The imperial kitchen and bakery only served the emperors and the royal family.

The imperial kitchen and bakery prepared mainly Manchu foods early in the dynasty, but mixtures of Manchu and Han foods in the latter period. There was a strict difference between the Manchu and Han dishes served at the banquets and feasts. The standards for the Manchu courses were higher than for the Han courses.

Of all banquets held in the Qing Palace, the most famous and magnificent were the old men's birthday banquets (especially the grand birthday banquets given by Emperor Kangxi in 1713 to celebrate his 60th birthday and by Emperor Qianlong in 1790 to celebrate his 80th birthday). Both banquets served mainly hot pots of wild game and Manchu buns, which are representative dishes of the Manchus.

The Manchu sacrificial rites were fixed by the Qing Palace as national rites. Rules were fixed for the sacrifices, the sacrificial meat, sacrificial wine, and the offerings. The offering of food had to follow the ancestral system.

Every year the Qing Palace had large quantities of sacrificial offerings. As a rule, these offerings were shared by the emperors, the Royal Family, palace officials, eunuchs, and guards. The eating customs for the sacrificial offerings profoundly influenced the imperial meals and were a component of the imperial food. This was because the meats, fruits, wines, cakes, buns, vegetables, dried dishes, and sweet foods were often the foods served at the emperors' meals.

The raw materials from Northeast China that were used for the imperial meals far surpassed those from other provinces in the number of tributes, quantity, and expense. It was cold in Northeast China, nearly the same as in Beijing, and the transportation was easier. More importantly, the people in Northeast China catered to the eating habits of the Qing Dynasty rulers.

After the raw materials came to Beijing, the annual family dinners the emperors gave on the eve of the lunar

New Year's Day were prepared in the Manchu tradition. Moreover, the delicacies and wild game, native specialties, and river and sea food from Northeast China were more nutritious and could be made into various exotic dishes. In the early years of the Qing Dynasty, the raw materials from Northeast China were the ones used in imperial meals. The eating habits and cooking of the Manchu nationality dominated the imperial meals of the Qing Palace.

The valuable raw materials used in the imperial meals were gathered from all parts of the country. They were a collection of rare foods, and the dishes prepared from them were rare and in the highest quality.

Originally, most of the cooks and cooking staff in the Qing Palace were Manchus, but this began changing around the middle of the dynasty. Because of the social and economic developments in the more than 260 years of the Qing Dynasty, changes also occurred in the expenses allocated for palace banquets, feasts, and dinners; the taste preferences of the royal family; and the composition of the ingredients for the imperial meals.

Before Kangxi's Reign (1662-1722), the Manchu rulers maintained their traditional eating habits, so the raw materials generally came from around Beijing, Mongolia, and Northeast China. A few ingredients also came from other parts of the country. After Qianlong's reign, a clear change took place in the source of the raw materials, so that more came from Northwest China, including Xinjiang, and China's southern provinces.

The tributes from the south helped increase the variety in the imperial meals, and Emperor Qianlong preferred southern-style food. Emperor Daoguang and Emperor Xianfeng (1821-1861) ate less food cooked in the southern style. Emperor Daoguang occasionally took a meal of the

Qianlong reign, but his regular food was cooked in the northern style.

The imperial food during the Tongzhi Reign (1862-1875) was even richer and more colorful than in the Qianlong Reign. Its raw materials came mainly from areas north of the Yellow River and from Northeast China. Except for bird's nest from Fujian, an indispensable tribute to the palace, the specialties originally produced in the south, like ham, mushrooms, bamboo shoots, and vegetables, could also be made or cultivated in northern areas. Because Emperor Guangxu liked seafood, the coastal areas greatly increased their tributes of shark's fin, abalone, sea cucumber, prawns, jellyfish, and kelp. In short, the raw materials for the imperial food varied with the emperors' preferences.

Some products rarely found among the common people were kept in regular supply in the Qing Palace. According to a record, "different varieties of grapes from Xinjiang are found in white, red, and purple colors, the longest looking like horse nipples. A small variety is named Gonglingsun, another small variety is called Suosuo. They were transplanted to the imperial garden during Kangxi's reign.

"Prior to the 20th year of Kangxi's reign, the ancestral emperor happened upon an ear in the rice field in the Lush Green Garden quite different from the common ears. This rice was slightly red. The ear was gathered to be grown in a fertile field the next year. For more than 40 years afterwards, the rice was used for imperial meals, and it could not be obtained elsewhere outside the palace...

"In the autumn hunting season of the 16th year of Qianlong's reign, Taijibiligunda from Mongolia outside the Great Wall presented an albino roe deer to the emperor. It was as pure white as snow and its eyes were as red as cinnabar. It was presented on the 60th birthday of the Empress Dowager. Emperor Gaozong (Qianlong) called it good luck and tied a poem to it. In the next autumn hunting season, the roe deer gave birth in an enclosure built by the mountainside to a young roe deer with pure white hair. This was the only one ever seen...

"Kandahan was found in Heilongjiang. Bigger than deer, it lives in mountains but takes to water."

During the more than two centuries of the Qing Dynasty, all rare fruits, fowl, animals, fish, and birds that could be found in the world were either captured personally by His Majesty or by the army, or were sent as tributes to the emperor. These delicacies were then cooked in the imperial kitchen.

The dishes had simple names, and more importance was attached to their taste than to their variety. Most imitation Qing Palace imperial dishes served today are named for the dragon or phoenix, or else their names sound beautiful, òstentatious, mysterious, or fantastic. This is contrary to the imperial meals in the Qing Palace where the dragon was likened to the emperor and the phoenix to the empress; therefore, dishes could not be named after them. It was unlike the style of the Qing Palace to give showy or mysterious names to dishes, or to give more importance to appearance than to quality and taste.

In our research of related historical data and the Qing Palace dietetic archives, we found none of the imperial dishes from Emperor Kangxi down to Emperor Puyi named after the dragon or phoenix. All the names were simple and told what raw materials were used, how the dishes were cooked, or what containers were used to hold them. The only difference between dishes served in the restaurants at that time and the imperial dishes was that the dishes in the imperial kitchen were more carefully and tastefully prepared.

Greater attention was paid to imperial meals during Qianlong's reign, but giving dishes simple names, monitoring the duration and degree of cooking, and flavoring dishes consistently were constant characteristics of the Qing Palace imperial meals.

The palace had strict standards for cooking and fixed rules for using raw materials. The Qing Palace imperial dishes were handed down from generation to generation. Although the menus were prepared by the chief cook in the imperial kitchen, the emperors checked all dishes and ate more of what they liked and less of what they disliked. The chief cook had to change the unpopular dishes when he prepared the new menu. The common dishes in the menus were what the emperors most liked. These dishes had to be standardized so the flavors and taste did not change regardless of how many times the same dishes were cooked. There were strict rules for the composition of the ingredients and the cooks could not change them at will.

Attention was paid to primary extracts and primary taste. For example, in preparing a duck course, only duck fat, duck stock, or duck soup could be used, chicken soup or other oils could not be used. In preparing a chicken dish, only chicken fat, chicken stock, or chicken soup could be used. Mutton and pork were prepared the same way.

There were also strict rules for flavorings and auxiliary materials. Only duck was used to make duck soup, only chicken to make chicken soup, and only mutton to make mutton soup. Only water from the Jade Spring Hill was used to cook soup and dishes: "The water from Jade

Spring Hill is the lightest and clearest. It has always been used for meals and tea, and is brought to the palace every day by people under the Office of Internal Affairs." (*Collected Records of the Hall of Ancient Cultivation*, Vol. 24). While imported flavorings such as pepper, ketchup, and cream were already popular in the markets, they were not used for imperial meals.

Fixed amounts of the major ingredients, auxiliary ingredients, and flavorings were used in the imperial dishes. The weights of dishes and the size, length, and height of the buns and other staple foods were all controlled by strict rules. Increases or decreases were forbidden.

Because the emperors' tastes differed from person to person, the dishes on their menus also varied. The major ingredients used for Kangxi's meals were meats of beasts produced in Northeast China, mutton, chicken and pork.

Emperor Qianlong's menus were richer and more varied. Apart from the delicacies of land and sea produced in Northeast China, he liked bird's nest, duck, Suzhou cuisine, vegetarian dishes, tea, and fruits, but he disliked river and sea foods. From among the preserved records of his daily meals, it is clear that almost no dishes were made of shark's fin, sea cucumber, prawn, abalone, or fish.

Emperor Guangxu liked seafood. Empress Dowager Cixi liked duck, smoked and roasted dishes, and dishes made with sugar and vinegar and with fruit flavoring. She also liked mushrooms and fresh vegetables. Emperor Puyi, the last emperor of the Qing Dynasty, liked vegetarian food and Western food, and he did not drink wine.

# Western Kitchen, Cixi's Private Kitchen

## Wang Laiyin

Toward the end of the Qing Dynasty, Empress Dowager Cixi arrogated all powers onto herself. This period, called the Guangxu-Xuantong Reign, was China's darkest and most corrupt political period.

Cixi was known for her overbearing, extravagant, dissolute, and self-indulgent attitude. She was a ruler who brought calamity to the country and its people. She liked beautiful clothes, good food, ostentation, and extravagance.

Under the Qing Dynasty system, there was no fixed funding for the emperors' meals; they were "reimbursed for what they spent." The empress dowager's food expense was 60 taels of silver a day during Qianlong's Reign.

When Cixi took power, she became not only "Her Majesty Empress Dowager," but also the supreme ruler with supreme power. She was the de facto emperor of the Qing Dynasty, and she was absolutely dissatisfied with her daily food expense of 60 taels (1 tael is approximately 30 grams) of silver. It was estimated that her actual food expense may have been double that, or more than 100 taels of silver a day.

Cixi had exclusive kitchens in both the Imperial Palace

and the Summer Palace. Her exclusive kitchen in the imperial palace was called the "Western Kitchen." The Western Kitchen was supervised by the chief managing eunuch. Under him were five sections, each having numerous cooks and *sulas* (laborers who did odd duties). Each section was sub-divided into divisions. The five sections were:

The Meat Section, which specialized in quick-frying, stir-frying, deep-frying, sauteing, steaming, and stewing all meats of land and sea.

The Vegetarian Section, which specialized in stir-frying, deep-frying, and quick-frying vegetarian dishes made of bean curd and gluten.

The Rice, Bun and Noodle Section, which specialized in making rice, porridge, steamed buns, steamed rolls, pancakes and noodles. Each meal included porridges of green bean, meat, millet, the seeds of Job's tears (an Asiatic grass), barley and rice. Sometimes, there were also porridges of lotus leaf, lotus root and lotus seed.

The Snack Section, which specialized in making pastries for the morning and afternoon snacks, and steamed, fried, boiled and baked pastries for the midnight meals.

The Pastry Section, which specialized in making crisp and soft pastries, such as crisp and soft baked buns with stuffings, cream cakes, small fried cakes, and soft cakes.

Each section employed apprentices, eunuchs, and temporary people to do odd jobs. There were hundreds of lower-ranked eunuchs who had the special job of carrying the meal boxes to the Empress Dowager. When Cixi left the Forbidden City on inspection tours, the whole Western Kitchen staff traveled with her.

The eunuchs in the kitchen were each paid a salary. Those cooks with special skills received higher pay and bonuses if Cixi was happy.

Eunuch Xie was the director of the Western Kitchen at that time. His younger brother Xie Er as well as Wang Yushan and Zhang Yongxiang were all famous cooks who toiled to make many new delicacies to please the Empress Dowager and, therefore, were all in her grace.

Xie Er began work at the Palace because Cixi wanted to eat fried cakes filled with sweet mashed red beans. His specialty was making *shaomai* (a steamed dumpling that has the dough gathered at the top). His dough was as thin as paper and his filling was savory and delicious. He was later asked to remain at the palace as a steam and fry cook.

Once, Cixi went to offer sacrifices at the Eastern Qing Tombs. The Western Kitchen sent cooks to go with her, but Xie Er failed to turn up. She ordered *shaomai*, but found it tasteless. When she asked why, she was told that it was made by another cook, Liu Da. Cixi became so angry that she had the cook lashed 40 times for making it poorly, and immediately ordered Xie Er to come to her.

Wang Yushan was famous throughout the Palace for his stir-frying. He created the Four Grabs. These were grab-and-stir-fry: tenderloin, sliced fish, kidney, and shrimp. These dishes were all crisp on the outside but on the inside they were soft and tender with a hint of a sour flavour. They were never greasy. Cixi awarded him the title, "King of Grab-and-Stir-Fry Dishes," and he and the dishes he created became famous throughout Beijing. (In 1925, Wang Yushan joined five others in running the Fangshan Restaurant, which served imitation imperial meals in Beihai Park.)

Besides being exquisite, the dishes Zhang Yongxiang cooked were beautiful and had a fresh, tender, yet distinct taste. His specialties were cooking bean sprouts filled with minced meat and hyacinth beans stuffed with minced meat. He chose big, straight, fat bean sprouts, cut off both ends, used a copper wire to hollow the sprouts, filled them with minced chicken or pork, and then steamed them. Hyacinth beans were prepared in the same way. After they were steamed, both dishes were fragrant and tasty. The bean sprouts were one of Cixi's favorite dishes. It was a labour-intensive dish that took 10 people all day to prepare.

Every year Cixi spent the summer at the Summer Palace, the Three Lakes area (now Beihai Park and the adjoining Zhongnanhai), or the Imperial Palace for Short Stays in Rehe (today's summer resort in Chengde). All the Western Kitchen eunuchs, cooks, and servants went with her. Cixi's private kitchen in the Summer Palace was called the "Longevity Kitchen."

The Longevity Kitchen was located behind the Northern Hall of Benevolence and Longevity. To the east of the theater were eight big compounds with more than 100 rooms. Her entourage and cooking staff totaled as many as 128, one or two dozen more than in Emperor Qianlong's imperial kitchen.

Cixi's private kitchen prepared more than 400 kinds of pastry, 4,000 dishes, and rare delicacies made of bird's nest, shark's fin, bear's paw, chicken, duck, fish, and meat. One of her favorite dishes was small, steamed buns made of fine ingredients that required exquisite workmanship. The main ingredient in the dough was chestnut powder, which was mixed with millet flour, bean flour, broomcorn flour, or corn flour, then sifted through a fine screen. The dough was filled with osmanthus flowers and white sugar, date paste and brown sugar, or preserved fruits. After the dough was well kneaded, it was made into thumb-sized buns and steamed.

Cixi took her meals at fixed times. Breakfast was at 6 a.m., lunch at 12, and supper at 6 p.m., plus there was a nightly snack. Before the meal was summoned, all sections prepared their dishes and stored them in food boxes on tables in the lounge. The wooden food boxes were painted light yellow, and decorated with two blue dragons playing with a red pearl. Beneath the boxes were tin bases of hot water wrapped with cotton-padded cushions to keep the food warm.

Normally, Cixi took her meals in the Hall of Happiness and Longevity, about 100 meters from the Longevity Kitchen. Before the meal, several smaller tables were put together to make a large table in the central hall. Only when the leading eunuch issued the signal to summon the meal could the prepared foods be brought from the kitchen to the Hall of Happiness and Longevity. While waiting for the meal to be summoned, the young kitchen apprentices, dressed in blue robes with white oversleeves, lined up in a long queue to await the imperial instructions.

When the leading eunuch gave the order to ready the meal, the apprentices placed their food boxes on their right shoulders. The eunuch managing the meal and the Director of the Western Kitchen, Eunuch Xie, led the eunuchs as they entered the hall in order and placed their dishes on the table. Then General Director Li Lianying used silver chopsticks to taste the dishes. If the chopsticks turned black, the dish was poisoned and could not be eaten.

When Cixi took her meal, if she looked at a certain dish, the eunuch would put the dish before her and she would eat one or two bites of it. She tasted only a few of the dishes and awarded the rest to the empress, the concubines, and other people in the palace.

Sometimes the extra food was given to families in the

western part of Beijing. Among them were the families of Prince Chun, Prince Gong, Prince Qing, General Director Li Lianying, and Li Baotai, the third younger brother of Li Lianying. The food boxes awarded to these families were slightly smaller than the traditional Chinese meal for eight people, and had the same design of two blue dragons playing with a red pearl on a light yellow background.

The boxes, tied with red and green hemp strings, were carried to the families by two eunuchs. The eunuchs hung the boxes from a long pole carried on their shoulders. Both ends of the pole were painted green; the middle was painted red. The bowls and plates in the boxes were blue or bean green. The eunuchs received rewards when they brought the boxes to the families.

The records from the 10th year of Emperor Guangxu's reign state that 8,080 catties plus two taels of Jade Spring wine were used for food or other purposes in Cixi's private kitchen that year. One story says that when Cixi took a train to Yixian County in Hebei Province to offer sacrifices at the Western Qing Tombs, four coaches were used for her private kitchen, in which "100 cooks made 100 dishes and 100 kinds of pastry and sweets using 50 kitchen ranges." This shows how shockingly extravagant Cixi's meals were.

Every midsummer, people in the palace ate fresh litchi, a delicacy among Chinese fruits. The litchi's skin is as red as fire and its flesh is sweet, juicy, and translucent. Litchis grow in the provinces of Guangdong, Guangxi, Fujian, Yunnan, Sichuan, and Taiwan, but the litchis grown in Fujian are the most famous. The litchis from Fuzhou, Xinghua, Quanzhou, Tanzhou, Funing, and Yongchun are large and rich in variety, but the Zhuangyuanhong litchi, which ripens in June and July, is the best.

It was a difficult job getting fresh litchis to the palace in the hot summer. Since the Qin and Han Dynasties, the Chinese capital cities have all been located in the northern plain regions, which are far from where litchis grow. Because litchis are juicy, they deteriorate and rot quickly so the growing areas mainly dry or preserve them.

According to TCM theory, if litchis are eaten fresh, they help produce saliva, reduce thirst, and strengthen the stomach. People who suffer from high stomach heat, a shortage of saliva, thirst, tooth aches, or sore throats are advised to eat fresh litchis. Fresh litchi juice boiled or cooked with rice porridge helps build the liver and kidneys and strengthen the stomach and spleen. Litchis have long been regarded as a treasured fruit that improves the health. For these reasons, all the feudal emperors of all the dynasties ordered litchis to be shipped to their palaces regardless of the cost.

A story goes that Yang, the most loved concubine of Emperor Xuanzong of the Tang Dynasty (712-756), liked litchis. The emperor sent people on horseback to bring litchis back to the palace. A poem by Du Mu, a poet of the Tang Dynasty, exposed and satirized this palace extravagance. It reads:

"A horse galloped across the land at full speed,
And the concubine laughs.
Who knows it is lichee coming."

According to the list of tributes received during the reign of Emperor Yongzheng (1723-1735), in May of each year naval units in Fujian sent warships to transport 60 barrels of litchi trees to the capital city. The trip took more than 60 days. Whole litchi trees were transported so the fruits would be better preserved. But the expense was shocking. For this reason, the emperor controlled the litchis on each tree. From the day a tree was received, the Office of Internal Affairs daily recorded how many litchis were gathered and to whom they were awarded.

The emperor himself ate only a few litchis every day and awarded the rest to his ministers. This tradition began in the reign of Emperor Qianlong. At that time, only the emperor, his wife and concubines, the crown prince, princes, princesses, and favourite ministers were awarded fresh litchis. Generally, the fresh litchis from the trees satisfied their needs for at least 20 days.

Bowls of refreshing, sweet, cold jelly were made from litchi and other fresh fruits sent to the palace from the various parts of the country. The jelly was made of agar, almond, honey, crystal sugar, and osmanthus flowers, which were boiled into a syrup. Then fresh fruits and litchis were added. After it was chilled, it became translucent like jade and was mottled with the colors of the fruit. It was a great honor for the people who waited on the Empress Dowager to be awarded a bowl of this fruit jelly.

Each year during the Spring Festival Cixi insisted her meals be ostentatious and extravagant. The following story tells how she took her dinner on the first day of the first lunar month. It was so ostentatious and extravagant that there has been no parallel in history.

Cixi required the four "Guardian Gods" and 500 "Buddhist Disciples" to wait on her. Her dinner was usually taken in either the Hall of Tranquility and Longevity or in the Hall of Bodily Peace south of the Hall of Preserving Talents, because these were the two halls where she lived in her dotage.

Three tables, named Heaven, Earth, and the People,

were laid with dishes. The Heaven table was to the east, the Earth table was to the west and the People table was in the center. The People table was solely occupied by the Empress Dowager. This meant that apart from heaven and the earth, she was the arrogant mistress of the world.

Who were the four "Guardian Gods"? They were four old, meritorious eunuchs dressed in official robes who had served previous sovereigns. They were retired and now only served on grand occasions. One of them had been a boy attendant in the study of Emperor Daoguang (1821-1851). Another had been fitted with all the burial clothes made for Emperor Xianfeng before the corpse was dressed for the memorial ceremony. These four old eunuchs stood at the four corners of the hall and were referred to in the palace as the four Guardian Gods.

In addition, 500 eunuchs lined up from the threshold of the hall to the threshold of the Longevity Kitchen. They were known as the 500 "Buddhist Disciples" or arhats. The arhats, all dressed in new silk robes, wore pink and white soled boots, had fresh haircuts, and looked vigorous.

Every light was ablaze both inside and outside the hall. A lantern was positioned every five steps in front of the long queue of 500 eunuchs to form a "dragon of fire." The dragon extended from the Longevity Kitchen to the hall where the Empress Dowager took her meal.

The chosen 500 excluded the very young and very old. Their training began on the eighth day of the last month of the passing year. It included holding plates and bowls but during training, crude bowls and bricks replaced the real plates and bowls. Their only duty was to deliver the bowls quickly and steadily. They used white cloths to hold the bowls and it was said that each training session cost two bolts of cloth.

When the dinner began, the eunuch who was the master of ceremonies shouted, "The dinner is ready," to invite the Empress Dowager to the table. Cixi came to her seat accompanied by Emperor Guangxu and the Empress. She first clasped her hands in tribute to the Heaven table on the east, then to the Earth table on the west. Finally she took her seat in front of the center table.

The four Guardian Gods, with their hands at their sides, immediately paid their respects to the Empress Dowager. Then the 500 eunuchs shouted, "Long live Her Majesty the Old Buddha!" in loud voices that spread to the Longevity Kitchen and all corners of the compound. Simultaneously, firecrackers with swastika designs on their tops exploded in the courtyard, and young trained eunuchs whipped non-stop their three-meter-long whips, made of several strands of twisted sheep intestine. The exploding and whipping produced excitement and crushed evil.

The dishes served at the dinner were divided into three categories. In the first category were dishes of good luck created just for the festive occasion, such as May Your Life Be as Lofty as the Southern Mountain Ranges, Wishing You Good Luck, and Abosolute Authority over the Whole Nation.

In the second category were dishes of tribute from different parts of the country, such as bear's paw, elk, flying dragon (special pheasants that eat pine nuts), preserved venison, lobster, and crabs preserved in wine.

In the third category were regular dishes according to the festive menu prepared in the Longevity Kitchen.

The emperor and empress both waited upon Cixi, one to her east and one to her west. Knowing Cixi was very superstitious, the emperor was clever and first ordered the dishes of good luck while the empress wished their mother a long life and good luck. As the emperor presented a dish to his mother, the empress said its name aloud. The empress was told the names of the dishes when the old eunuch passed them on, for she could never remember the names of so many dishes!

Under the Qing Palace rules, the emperor was never to say: "What I would like to eat" or "What I want to eat today." And, he was absolutely never to let others know which dishes he preferred. The emperor also was never to eat the same dish two days in a row even if it was his favorite, so the kitchen prepared the imperial meals according to regular rules.

An honourable senior eunuch had to wait on the emperor when he took his meals. When the emperor tasted a dish, he was only to eat one or two spoonfuls, never a third. If he did, the eunuch would shout, "Withdraw it!" and the dish would disappear for one or two weeks. This was the family rule: "Don't be greedy for food to avoid being murdered," for there were historical examples where emperors had been poisoned unexpectedly. Such security measures were taken at every meal and became merely a simple, indispensable formality.

When the emperor ate, others waited on him but did not encourage him to eat certain dishes. Eunuchs, the empress, or concubines waiting on the emperor (in the late years of the Qing Dynasty, the emperor had to wait upon Empress Dowager Cixi) could not encourage the emperor to eat because it was forbidden by the palace discipline. The old eunuch who enforced the palace discipline would reprimand them immediately by saying: "Shut your mouth!" and he would slap them on the face using his leather-gloved hand.

For this reason, even the palace maids and eunuchs who

attended the emperors and the Empress Dowager for decades, still did not know what the emperors and the Empress Dowager liked to eat. The emperors and Empress Dowager ate the dishes of tribute today, regular dishes tomorrow, and fresh delicacies the day after that. They would not allow their preferences to be known to others. This was the rule of the Qing Palace.

It is said that the Longevity Kitchen, in the late years of the Qing Dynasty, had more than 100 cooking ranges and about 300 people doing the cooking. Under the rules, each cooking range was tended by three people: the chef, a person who prepared the ingredients for a dish, and someone who did odd jobs. All the ranges were numbered and all the dishes were cooked according to fixed rules. Once the eunuch issued the order to summon the meal, the chefs prepared their dishes one by one in a pre-arranged order.

The work in the kitchen proceeded smoothly, and people without kitchen duties were forbidden to enter. It was clearly recorded in a daily book who did the washing, who prepared the ingredients, and who cooked each dish. If there was a problem, the offender would soon be found out. After each process was finished, the Office of Palace Affairs checked it. Only if it met standards would the work move to the next step.

As the saying goes: "One meal taken by the emperor and empress can feed the common people for several years." If Cixi's daily meals cost 100 taels of silver, that was enough to buy 12,000 catties of rice in those years. If the per capita yearly average were 300 catties, 100 taels would feed one person for 40 years!

In the late years of Cixi's rule, floods and drought frequented different parts of the country. In 1889, the biggest flood in centuries occurred in Northeast China. "Fields and houses were submerged and countless people drowned in the waters along the rivers." Many who survived by sheer luck starved to death. "The land swarmed with famished refugees; it was too horrible to describe."

# Mystery of Using Fire in the Palace

In the Forbidden City, with its circumference of 720,000 square meters, not a single chimney is visible. How did the people in the palace eat and warm themselves?

All palace buildings were wooden structures and, therefore, not fire resistant. For more than 500 years fire was a constant enemy. If there was the slightest carelessness, everything would be burned, so special care was taken when using fire. Ancient people believed charcoal was the ideal fuel because it did not create smoke or dust pollution, so charcoal was closely linked to cooking meals, boiling water and heating the palace. The charcoal-burning stoves used in the palace were specially made. They had big chambers, small openings, no chimneys, and few ashes. Similar stoves were popular with Beijing residents in the early years of the Republic.

The palace had many meal kitchens, and many tea kitchens that also made all kinds of pastry. In addition, stoves were installed in all the halls where the Royal Family lived so they could heat or cook food whenever they wished.

Rong'er, a maid who had waited upon the Empress Dowager Cixi for eight years in the late period of the Qing Dynasty, recalled that more than 300 people worked in the Longevity Kitchen alone using more than 100 numbered kitchen ranges, under rigid rules. The odd-job workers inspected the vegetables and raw materials and passed the ones that met standards to the cooks who prepared the ingredients. Then the cooks cut, chopped, and sliced the raw materials and prepared the flavorings and seasonings. Only materials that met the standards could be given to the chefs. The chefs had to obey the orders from the eunuch who summoned the meals, and had to cook the dishes in a pre-arranged order.

The cooks and laborers were not eunuchs. They lived outside the Forbidden City and were called in whenever they were needed.

In the Qing Palace archives, thousands of records tell of using charcoal everywhere in the palace, and the large quantity of charcoal needed for the palace can easily be imagined. The charcoal was carefully selected hardwood charcoal the length of chopsticks. The pieces had to resonate when struck together and be fire resistant. Such charcoal had a strong flame, burned hot, and produced no smoke, soot or bad smell. It was exceptionally clean and nonpolluting.

The halls in the Forbidden City had floors made of bricks (a special kind of clay brick fired in Suzhou that had a fine texture and was very solid). All the floors were exquisitely polished until they were smooth, level and as reflective as a mirror.

In the backyard halls of all the living areas there were tunnels and fire chambers for burning charcoal under the floorbricks. They were called the "warm pavilions." The palace buildings usually had an odd number of rooms. The middle room was called the open pavilion or main hall; it was where the throne was located. The warm halls (pavilions) were located on the two sides and were called the Eastern Warm Hall and the Western Warm Hall. Under the floors of the warm halls were tunnels where charcoal was burned to heat the buildings. Once the two warm halls were heated, the main hall in the middle also became warm.

There was an open charcoal burner in front of the throne. When the yearly frost season began, charcoal was burned in the fire chambers of the warm halls. The warm temperature spread evenly and softly to all corners of the buildings. The charcoal was first ignited elsewhere, then brought to the fire chambers in the tunnels where it was burned day and night.

Because the halls differed in size, the charcoal burners also differed in size. To prevent burning sparks from jumping out, all the burners were covered with exquisitely made, beautiful wire netting.

# Hot Pot Dishes in the Palace

## Wang Guangyao

The hot pot appeared during the Liao Dynasty (about the 10th century) and was popular throughout the Song, Jin, Yuan, Ming, and Qing dynasties. The emperors and royal families as well as the common people used them frequently.

Every year under the old system in the Qing Palace, "starting from the 15th day of the 10th lunar month, a hot pot was added at every meal, the content varied from mixed ingredients to instant-boiled sliced mutton. People from Northeast China preferred to eat pickled vegetables, blood, intestine, boiled pork without sauce, sliced chicken without sauce, and sliced stomach all mixed together. We ate this hot pot most often. Sometimes, we also ate pheasant. Anyway, we ate hot pot for three months every year. The hot pot was replaced by the earthenware pot on the 16th day of the first month." (*Palace Maids' Memoirs*, by Jin Yi, p. 12)

The hot pot was used during the three winter months every year for "eating hot dishes." With regard to the quality and content of the ingredients used, there were few particulars or rules. Whatever was available could be served as long as the ingredients could be made into hot soup to resist the winter cold. This was a good way for the northern people to cope with the winter cold.

71

In part because she was from the north, the Empress Dowager Cixi created her famous original "chrysanthemum" hot pot. It was prepared roughly in this way:

A small hot pot with chicken extract or pork soup and some other ingredients was brought from the Imperial Kitchen. After the young eunuch uncovered the dish, the Empress Dowager took slices of raw chicken or fish and put them into the dish. The eunuch covered the dish for a few minutes, then uncovered it for the Old Lady to add some chrysanthemum flower petals to the soup. The petals had been specially picked and soaked in vitriol water (water containing alum). When the soup was ready, it tasted fragrant and delicious. It was a treasured dish of the imperial cuisine.

Using a hot pot to make instant-boiled mutton is believed to date back to Kublai, the founding emperor of the Yuan Dynasty (1271-1368). The story goes like this: Mongolian soldiers used to eat beef and mutton as their daily food. One day they were preparing their daily meal and had gotten the mutton and seasonings ready to cook. Enemy troops came by surprise creating a critical situation and allowing them no time to cook the meal in their normal way. The Mongolians simply boiled the mutton before they left for the battlefield so they would not starve to death, if they were not killed fighting the battle.

This solution was meant simply to fill the soldiers' stomachs, but they unexpectedly found it to be a wonderful dish acclaimed by Kublai and his high-ranking men. After continued improvement, instant-boiled mutton became a popular dish among the common people. This story may be false, but it does support the fact that nomadic people in cold regions invented instant-boiled mutton.

By the time of the Qing Dynasty, the hot pot had become indispensable during cold months and was quite popular in the Imperial Palace. The hot pots used in the Qing Palace now reside in the Palace Museum. They show how noble the Royal Family was because the makers and owners of these dishes are clearly identified. No hot pots found among common families could compare with these for the quality of raw materials, exquisiteness of craftsmanship, or perfection of design. The raw materials used included gold, silver, gilt silver, copper, gilt copper, tin, and iron.

The hot pots and their accessories included the pots, lids, chimneys, fire-chamber covers, and bottom bases. The pots were decorated with motifs of animals, plants, the four characters for "wishing you a long, long life," the character for "longevity," the three characters for "good luck, wealth and long life," the "swastika," and the "dragon and phoenix bring prosperity." Some dishes, lids, and bases were inscribed with the dates they were made, the names of the raw materials, or the names of the workshops. It was customary to inscribe the names of the makers during the pre-Qin dynasties. The inscriptions prove the Manufacturing Division of the Board of Internal Affairs did not have a monopoly on the hot pots used in the palace. The hot pots came from two sources. They were either manufactured by the Board of Internal Affairs or bought from independent workshops.

As only one of many drinking and dining sets used in the Qing Palace, hot pots account for an insignificant percentage of the pieces collected in the Palace Museum. However, from the Liao Dynasty to the Qing Dynasty, a period covering several centuries, the hot pot finally attained perfection in its casting, production, shape, raw materials, and the design of its motifs. It evolved from its primitive use for making instant-boiled mutton to become an indispensable cooking utensil for making hot soup and food in the winter months.

# Tea Drinking in the Palace

## Wang Ling

Tea has been the chief drink in China since ancient times, and tea drinking has been a custom for almost as long. Tea was popular in the Tang Dynasty. During the Ming and Qing Dynasties prominent officials and eminent people used tea drinking as an occasion to foster friendships and discuss poetry. Tea drinking was an important part of palace life.

The Forbidden City was the imperial palace of the Ming and Qing Dynasties. The tea drunk by the Royal Family was a tribute from the tea-growing provinces and was stored in the palace for use in all the halls. Its excellence and quality were beyond description. The numerous tea parties held in the palace related directly to civil affairs, education, and court rites.

Most tea parties in the Forbidden City were held in Wenhua Hall (the Hall of Literary Glory), Chonghua Palace (the Hall of Double Glory) or Qianqing Palace (the Hall of Heavenly Purity).

Upon entering the Meridian Gate of the Imperial Palace, one came to the Gate of Supreme Harmony. East of the Gate of Supreme Harmony was an external courtyard that contained three buildings: The main hall, called the Hall of Literary Glory, was in front, the Hall of Main Respect was in the middle, and the Imperial Library was in the back. It was in these buildings that the Qing Dynasty emperors honored Confucius, listened to lectures with their ministers, and kept the Four Collections of Books. They were the cultural center of the Forbidden City, and tea was served whenever the emperors attended lectures.

As early as the Ming Dynasty, it became an important rite for tea to be served in the Hall of Literary Glory when the emperors listened to lectures. The Ming Dynasty emperors and their ministers attended lectures in this hall three times a month. A lecturer spoke first about literature, then about classics, and last about history. After the lecture, the emperor gave tea to the lecturer and his ministers. Tea was served so the lecturer could moisten his throat, but more importantly, as a symbol to encourage education.

The system of lecturing the emperors in the Hall of Literary Glory continued during the Qing Dynasty, but the ceremony became even grander. Emperor Qianlong attended 49 grand lectures, each including a spectacular ceremony. When the emperor arrived, all officials saluted him. The lecture began with four officials of the Manchu and Han nationalities talking on the Four Books (the *Great Learning*, the *Doctrine of the Mean*, the *Analects*, and the *Book of Mencius*). Then the emperor expounded on the books and all officials had to listen on their knees. This was followed by a lecture in the same way on the Five Classics (the *Book of Changes*, the *Book of Songs*, the *Book of History*, the *Book of Rites*, and the *Annals of the Spring and Autumn*).

After the lectures, the emperor asked those present to sit and have tea. Unlike a picnic or a chat in a tea house, tea was served in a solemn atmosphere not only in the palace, but also in the Confucius Temple and in the Imperial Academy.

The emperor also gave tea to officials when he made inspections. This showed that the tea offered by the emperor, apart from his wine and gift giving, was a symbol to promote Confucian doctrine and ethics, and to encourage education.

The emperors also gave a grand "tea banquet" in Chonghua Palace (the Hall of Double Glory) in the Forbidden City almost every year during the Qing Dynasty. Chonghua Palace was located in a compound north of the six Western Palaces.

Tea parties were first described in the Tang Dynasty. Large tea parties were also held in the palace during the Song Dynasty, with the emperor serving the tea. Cai Jing (1047-1126), a prime minister of the Song Dynasty, described how the emperor served tea to him and the princes in the Palace of Yanfu. He said the emperor ordered his personal attendant to take the tea sets, then personally poured boiling water into the cups of his guests. The guests all kowtowed in gratitude.

Zhao Ji, Emperor Huizong of the Song Dynasty, was a tea connoisseur. He poured boiling water into his guests' cups to show his tea expertise and to share in the labor. Although he was a poor administer of national affairs, his personal tea service was a cultured art with a positive message. After that, being served tea by an emperor became a high courtesy; however, few emperors were experts in tea; therefore, few of them personally served tea.

Qing Dynasty Emperor Qianlong was a tea lover and a great tea drinker. It is said that he wanted to retire from his throne in his late years, and some ministers asked: "How can a nation be without an emperor even for a single day?" Qianlong replied with a smile, "How can the emperor be without tea for a single day?" Chonghua Palace was Qianlong's former residence before he ascended to the throne, and was called the palace after he became emperor.

Besides being an avid tea drinker, Qianlong also tried to write poems like a refined, elegant, sophisticated poet. He started giving tea parties in the palace, following the example of literati in ancient times. This was the origin of the annual tea dinner held in the Qing Palace. It was held on a lucky day chosen between the 2nd and 10th days of the first lunar month. Its purpose was to write poems while drinking tea. Initially, the number of people present was not fixed. They were mostly court officials who specialized in literature. Later, the emperor selected a current affairs topic about which the participants wrote poems. Only the long poems were recited.

Finally, it was decided the poems should have 72 rhymes, and only 18 people were invited to attend the tea party. They were divided into eight rows and each person wrote four lines. Qianlong personally chose the topic and made it known beforehand, but he only gave the beginning rhymes when the party began in order to keep the officials on their toes.

When the poems were finished, Qianlong immediately read them one after another, then bestowed cups of tea and awarded prizes. Those who received awards carried the prizes out of the palace themselves to display their glory. Inviting 18 people to attend the tea party followed the example set by Emperor Taizong of the Tang Dynasty, who selected 18 literati from all over the nation to live and work in the Hall of Literature. Additional people outside the palace also composed verses, but they were not admitted to the party.

Following Qianlong, succeeding emperors also gave tea parties in Chonghua Palace, but none matched those given by Qianlong. Most of the poems composed at these tea parties were words of praise and flattery. Moreover, in the depths of the heavily guarded palace and in the presence of the emperor, it was impossible for the literati to mix tea with poetry, man with nature, or their inner world with an objective frame of mind. Nevertheless, the relationship between tea and cultural circles was strengthened through the tea parties, and helped link tea with art.

The biggest tea party ever held during the Qing Dynasty was held in the Palace of Heavenly Purity and was attended by more than 1,000 people. The Ming Dynasty emperors had used the Palace of Heavenly Purity as sleeping quarters, but this changed during the Qing Dynasty. The Qing emperors used it to handle national affairs, summon ministers and officials, meet common people, hold palace ceremonies, receive foreign envoys, read books and memorials, and give comments and instructions.

During their reigns, Emperor Kangxi and Emperor Qianlong (1662-1795) held large banquets for more than 1,000 people in the Palace of Heavenly Purity. These banquets had the largest attendance with the highest ranking officials in the history of tea culture.

The 52nd year of Kangxi's Reign (1713) coincided with his 60th birthday. Local officials throughout the country encouraged their local elders to travel to the capital city to congratulate Kangxi on his birthday. Emperor Kangxi, therefore, decided to give a "1,000 Elders' Banquet." He gave the banquet in the Garden of Flourishing Spring rather than in the palace, and more than 1,800 people attended it.

An important part of the banquet was tea drinking. The banquet began with everyone taking his seat for tea. The band played royal music, and the princes, dukes, and ministers saluted when the officials of the Imperial Kitchen presented cups of black tea with milk to the emperor and his crown prince. After the emperor finished, he asked the princes, dukes, and ministers to drink together. They received the tea sets afterward, and they all kowtowed in gratitude when they received the cups. After the protocol was finished, they began to eat. Ever since the Tang Dynasty there has been a saying in China that tea is above wine. This saying was embodied in the "1,000 Elders' Banquet."

Eight years later, Emperor Kangxi gave a second "1,000 Elders' Banquet" in and outside the Palace of Heavenly Purity in the Imperial Palace. More than 1,000 people 65 or older attended. Qianlong held two other banquets of this kind during his reign. In the first month of the 50th year of his reign, Qianlong gave a banquet in the Palace of Heavenly Purity for more than 3,000 elders. The oldest was 104 years. In order to attend the banquet, many people came to Beijing days ahead of time.

In the 61st year of his reign, Qianlong gave another large banquet for more than 3,000 people in the Hall of Imperial Models. Another 5,000 people were invited but did not have seats. Ministers of the first rank were inside the hall. Officials of the second rank and foreign envoys were under the eaves. Officials of the third rank were on the steps and passage to the throne. Officials of the fourth and fifth rank and Mongolian officials were below and around the steps, and all others were outside the Gate of Peace and Longevity.

There were 800 tables arranged on two sides — east and west — six rows on each side. The shortest row had 22 tables; the longest had 100. There were too many people to receive the emperor's tea service; so tea kitchen officials presented tea to the emperor on behalf of all those present. Those who drank tea received a tea set while those who drank wine received a wine set. Only the Royal Family could afford to host such a tea party, and this party was probably a record in Chinese and world history.

The Qing Palace blended tea drinking with political and cultural activities in five ways:

1. Tea drinking ceremonies were used to honor Confucius, inspect the Imperial Academy, and listen to lectures. The ceremonies were used to link tea with Confucianism, distinguish the emperor from the ministers, and preach ethics, ideology and education.

2. Tea drinking was combined with poetry and cultural affairs meetings to promote culture. As an example, Emperor Qianlong combined tea drinking with writing poetry, compiling the Four Collections of Books, and inspecting the Imperial Academy.

3. Tea drinking was used at birthday celebrations, national festivities, and congratulatory occasions. In the Chinese tea culture, literati, Taoists, and Buddhists stressed poverty, honesty, and retreat from public life while the imperial court and the common people stressed joy, gaiety, and festivity. Tea parties held in the Qing Palace pushed the latter three to new heights.

4. The tea served at the "1,000 Elders' Banquets" in the Qing Dynasty was black tea with milk. The Royal Family drank black tea with milk in their everyday life. "The number of milk cows supplying milk to the Royal Family was fixed. The milk was delivered to the director of the Tea Kitchen. The tea kitchen made milk cakes during the spring and autumn seasons." This passage shows that resi-

dents of the Qing Palace drank both clear tea and milk tea.

Originally, people in the northern parts of China drank milk tea, and the drinking of milk tea in the Qing Palace was at first intended to maintain health. However, at the "1,000 Elders' Banquet", the tea served by the emperor added the color of the northern nationalities to the tea culture. It shows that China's tea culture was synchronized with the blending of China's different nationalities. All of China's nationalities recognized tea as a cultural concept; it was not exclusive to the Han nationality.

5. Tea culture activities in the Qing Palace flourished during Qianlong's reign, the greatest tea lover of all the emperors. Between the 8th and 60th years of his reign, Qianlong gave tea banquets every year for 48 years, except for the funeral service for the empress dowager. During Qianlong's reign, the economy was prosperous, the cultures of the Manchus and the Hans were well blended, and culture was flourishing. This coincided with the law of development of China's tea culture, which is, the tea culture flourished under three conditions: economic prosperity, cultural growth, and peace. The frequent tea drinking activities in Qianlong's reign were proof of this law.

# Tea and Its Healthy Effects

Tea has been drunk in China for five thousand years. Scholars credit the discovery of tea leaves and their medicinal value to Shenlong in the remote ages. *The Materia Medica of Shenlong* is the earliest book in China to mention tea. It says: "Shenlong tasted various herbal plants and was poisoned by 72 herbs one day, but their poison was neutralized after he found tea."

There are two different renditions of this passage: One

is that he tasted all kinds of herbal plants to learn their curative properties so he could cure the ills of the common people. One day he was boiling water when a twig of fresh tea leaves fell into the water. He found the water bitter, sweet, fragrant, and tasty. Afterward, people began using tea as a drink.

Another legend says that when Shenlong was tasting herbal plants to learn their curative effects, he was poisoned while tasting a green plant called *gunshanzhu* and died under the tree. At the right moment, water from the tea shrubs flowed into his mouth and rescued him. This was how tea leaves were found to have a detoxifying effect.

*Chaye* (tea leaf) was called *ming* in ancient times. Shenlong's discovery of tea leaves revealed that tea could cure illness. Over the millennia, tea has been found to contain hundreds of chemicals and is an effective medicine for preventing and curing illness. The evolution from using tea as a sacrifice to using it as a cure for illness and a drink shows we should not underestimate its value.

Ancient Chinese medical books thoroughly discuss tea's medicinal value. The earliest description is found in the *Newly Revised Materia Medica of the Tang Dynasty*: "*Ming* is a bitter tea. *Ming* tastes sweet, bitter, slightly cold, and is nonpoisonous. It is effective in curing fistula and boils, and is a diuretic. It eases expectoration, reduces internal heat, quenches thirst, and makes people alert. It is picked in spring. A bitter tea, it helps control the upward, perverted flow of vital energy, and improves digestion."

This does not contradict the fact that the medicinal use of tea originated in the Shenlong period. Following the continual discovery of knowledge about its properties and a genuine study of its medicinal use, tea was used widely

83

as a drug during the Tang Dynasty. Lu Yu, a scholar of the Tang Dynasty, was among the first to research tea. He has been called the God of Tea since the Song Dynasty.

In his famous writing, *The Book of Tea*, Lu Yu concluded: "The use of tea as a drink started with Shenlong." He also pointed out: "The more you drink tea, the more vigorous and refreshed you are." There are many records and prescriptions for the medicinal use of tea. His book was the world's first book on tea, and described in detail tea's nature, qualities, growing areas, picking, processing, brewing methods, and utensils. Later, people worshipped Lu Yu as the *Tea Sage*

In recent years, tea specialists have discovered that tea contains many chemicals. These can be divided into two categories: Nutrients needed by the human body and non-essential elements that improve the health in some pathological conditions. The latter are referred to as the elements with medicinal effect. Descriptions of some of these chemicals follow:

**1. Alkaloids**. Tea contains purines, among which are caffeine and theophylline. The amount of caffeine varies greatly with the variety of tea. Caffeine dissolves in water. If someone drinks five to six cups of tea a day, about 0.3 grams of caffeine is absorbed. This amount is significant, but caffeine is not accumulated in the human body; it is excreted.

Caffeine and theophylline have similar pharmacological effects; they both stimulate the central nerve system. Caffeine can improve thinking, increase energy, and decrease sleepiness. Stimulation of the spinal cord helps strengthen the muscles and reduce fatigue. The caffeine in tea does not result in secondary depression or bad side effects.

Theophylline works as a muscle relaxant and vasodilator, whereas caffeine is primarily a stimulant and diuretic.

Diuresis. Together, caffeine and theophylline are believed to produce diuresis. They dilate blood vessels in the kidneys so the kidneys excrete unnecessary water, and they stimulate the bladder to increase urine excretion. For these reasons, tea drinking has some effect in curing cardiac edema and pre-menstrual syndrome.

Stimulation of the cardiac muscles. Animal tests have found that tea stimulates the heart and strengthens the systole of the left ventricle, but how the tea is processed affects this ability. Unfermented green tea has the strongest effect, semi-fermented tea is less strong, and fermented black tea is the weakest.

Dilation of blood vessels. Longjing tea used in tests on a rabbit was found to lower serum cholesterol and reduce arteriosclerosis.

Digestion and breathing. Caffeine stimulates the secretion of hydrochloric acid in the gastric juice. Therefore, drinking tea helps improve digestion.

Respiration. Caffeine relaxes the smooth muscle of the bronchus. Therefore, drinking tea helps control asthma.

Hormones. It is reported that theophylline can increase female hormones.

**2. Polyphenols**. Tea polyphenol is also called tannin. The pharmacological effects of polyphenols are:

Amines. Tannin stimulates the adrenal gland thereby increasing energy. It helps strengthen blood capillaries and blood vessels.

Anti-inflamatories. Tea helps improve the metabolism of vitamin C and the resistance and anti-inflammatory properties of blood capillaries. Foods high in vitamin C, together with green tea, have been found to increase the body's ability to resist infection. (Black tea lacks this effect.)

The increased ability to resist infection is caused by the combined effect of tea and vitamin C. Tea protects vitamin C from being oxidized. Tea increases the accumulation of vitamin C in the liver, spleen, kidneys, intestines, brain and blood, and thereby reduces the amount of vitamin C excreted in the urine.

Antibiotic effect. Green tea inhibits the growth of salmonella typhi, dysentery bacilli, aureus staphylococcus, and cholera vibrio. Experiments in China have shown that tea inhibits and kills dysentery bacilli.

**3. Ester polysaccharide**. This is an important component in the cell walls of the tea leaves. Animal tests have shown that tea ester polysaccharides help prevent radioactive injuries, improve blood-building functions, and protect the blood.

**4. Proteins and amino acids**. Tea leaves contain both amino acids and proteins. The protein contained in black tea is 15-30% of its dry weight, but less than 2% dissolves in water. Cow's milk added to tea reduces the astringency of the tea, but does not affect the absorption of protein.

Black tea contains few amino acids, but green tea contains 16 to 24 amino acids, including cystine (a major metabolic sulfur source), serine, and theophyllamine acid. Of these three amino acids, theophyllamine acid is unique to tea, and accounts for 50% of the total amino acids in tea. Almost all amino acids needed by the human body are found in tea.

**5. Sugar**. Tea is low in calories. The sugar obtained from tea made in boiling water is only 4-5% of the solubles. However, drinking tea increases the body's absorption of sugar. If milk and sugar are added to tea, and someone drinks six cups a day, the calories obtained from tea will equal 7-10% of an adult's daily caloric requirements.

**6. Fats**. Fats account for about 2-3% of the weight of processed black tea.

**7. Vitamins**. Tea contains vitamins A, B, C, E, and K, all of which are essential to the human body. Generally, green tea contains more vitamins than black tea. Black tea and green tea contain roughly the same B vitamins, but their composition and content vary by region due to different cultivating and processing conditions.

**8. Minerals**. Tea contains many minerals. Fresh tea leaves and black tea contain about 4-9% minerals, most of which are needed by the human body. The quantity of minerals contained in tea grown in different parts of the world differs. Russian scholars report that tea does not contain much iron and copper, so tea has limited effectiveness in curing anemia. Tea contains little sodium and so is a good drink for those suffering from hypertension. Tea shrubs are apt to accumulate manganese, aluminum, fluorine, and some rare elements.

**9. Aromatic compounds**. Tea leaves contain aromatic matters. These volatile matters account for 0.6% of the dry weight of the tea leaves. Using tea liquid to rinse the mouth helps remove grease, strengthen the teeth, and prevent bad breath.

**10. Selenium**. Selenium was recognized in 1973 as "one of the 14 trace elements indispensable to human life." The amount of selenium in tea varies by region; in some places it is very high. As selenium is a strong antioxidant and protects the cell membranes, it can help prevent cancer and other diseases, and it has no side effects. It "is effective in preventing Keshan disease, which is caused by a selenium deficiency, and Kaschin-Beck disease."

Some people argue that the selenium extraction rate from tea is as low as 20% to 40% and, therefore, is insufficient to make up for a selenium deficiency. However, it is believed that the extraction rate can be raised. Tea bags and instant tea raise the extraction rate to 60% to 80%. Moreover, eating food with tea also helps raise the extraction rate.

# Chinese Food and Health Building

## Guo Feng

Throughout Chinese history people have searched for a way to achieve immortality. Huang Di, the Yellow Emperor, was the legendary forefather of all tribes in the Central Plains. He was well versed in medicine, language, philosophy, and mathematics. There is a Chinese myth that in remote ages Huang Di rode a dragon into heaven.

Emperors of later dynasties, from Shi Huang, the founding emperor of the Qin Dynasty, to Wu Di, the emperor of the Han Dynasty, hoped to turn this myth into reality. They either sent virgins of both sexes to the East China Sea for the elixir of life, or blindly trusted necromancers and worshipped ghosts and gods in search of a way to become immortal.

The Chinese theory of health building developed from efforts to protect and build health, prevent disease, and prolong life. The *I Ching* (*Book of Changes*), a Confucian classic written more than 2,000 years ago, says: "If accustomed to the nature of Heaven and Earth, man can live forever even if he gets sick."

The philosophical writings of thinkers and statesmen from the late years of the Spring and Autumn Period contain many descriptions about health building. These writings include the *Dao De Jing* by Lao Zi, the *Analects* of Confucius and the *Guan Zi* of Guan Zhong. These were the start of Chinese theories on health building.

The Spring and Autumn and Warring States Periods (770-221 B.C.) were a fertile time for multiple schools of thought, and political pluralism provided a rich atmosphere for developing academic thought. Representatives of all schools of thought were concerned with political issues and problems related to life. As life is inseparable from food and drink, scholars of the pre-Qin times contemplated dietetic culture and the relationship between food and health building.

## Taoist Philosophy of Health Building

Lao Zi, the founder of Taoism, advanced his ideas on health building during the Spring and Autumn Period. His ideas laid the groundwork for subsequent doctrines on health building. Lao Zi's birth place, and the date of his birth and death were never specified by historians, but he is believed to have lived during the latter part of the Spring and Autumn Period (722-476 B.C.).

One legend says Lao Zi was Lao Dan, a historian in charge of a library. His family name was Li, his given name was Er, and he was born in the state of Chu (today's Luyi County, Henan Province).

As to why Li Er was called Lao Zi, another legend says he was born with white hair after his mother carried him in her womb for 72 years. He could speak when he was born and said, pointing to a plum tree, "This is my family name." (The Chinese character "li" means plum).

Throughout the dynasties there has been a continuing debate as to whether he authored the book *Lao Zi*, also titled *The Book of Ethics. Lao Zi*, which contains 5,000 Chinese characters, was written in the literary form of poems and odes. It shows a refined style and penetrating thought, but is generally believed to have been written by his followers in the middle of the Warring States Period (c. 381 B.C.)

Lao Zi believed that to stay healthy, people should revert to the primary state by giving up all complex emotions and desires like a newborn baby. He argued for indifference to fame and gain. He believed in nihilism, selflessness, and few desires, and advocated serenity, temperance, and peace. For physical exercise he was devoted to breathing exercises. He held that people should not pursue delicious food; simple food was enough.

Prior to *Lao Zi*, people had thought the Taoists paid minimal attention to health building through food but, in fact, the Taoists believed in simple food, vegetables, and coarse grains. Such a diet actually does help prevent cardiac and cerebral diseases that result from excessive protein and fat.

# Confucian Philosophy on Health Building

Confucianism originated with ancient necromancers and alchemists, who were similar to the witches in later generations that made sacrifices to gods and ancestors. The most important part of the sacrifices was food and wine; therefore, those in charge of sacrificial rites knew protocol and understood cookery.

Confucius (551-479 B.C.) was a philosopher, teacher, and the founder of the Confucian school. He attached great importance to food and described it as one of the three basic conditions, along with an army and trust, for founding a state. He advocated that rulers "practice thrift and love the people."

Confucius spoke highly of Yu the Great (2276-2177 B.C., the founder of the Xia Dynasty). Yu paid little attention to food, but believed few people could abstain from good food and good housing because most people desire delicious food. Yu dedicated himself to the public good.

On the relationship between food and sacrifice, Confucius said animals offered in sacrificial rites should be chosen and cut according to fixed standards or they could not be eaten. He said meats given in sacrificial rites for the head of the state should be eaten the same day and not be kept until the next day. Meat offered in sacrifice at home should not be eaten if it were kept longer than three days.

Confucius advanced many principles of dietetic hygiene and criteria for testing the hygiene of foods. He said foods should not be eaten if they had rotted, if they were not well cooked, if their color had changed, or if the wine and dried meats bought from the market were not clean. He believed foods should only be eaten at mealtime, and if there were many meat courses, people should not overeat. This belief is reflected in the dietetic culture of the Chinese nation; it also conforms to dietetic hygiene because meats are not easily digested.

Confucius said, "Only wine drinking is not limited, but not so much as to make you confused." He meant you could drink as much as you wanted, but should not become drunk. This was because the wine at that time contained little alcohol.

His advice, "Do not eat too much" and "Do not talk at meals," conforms to the principle of building health through diet, as does "Do not take away the ginger." Ginger is pungent, removes dampness, and reduces internal heat and fever, so eating a bit of it before meals aids health and digestion.

Confucius also said: "I do not eat if I do not get the proper soy sauce." In his time meat dishes were unsalted, so they were dipped in soy sauce before they were eaten and different soy sauces were used for different meats. Confucius stressed that the dishes in his meals must be compatible, and did not resign himself to circumstances. "Although they use simple food, vegetables and melons, the three sacrifices must all be offered at the rite." This shows Confucius was serious about meals. Even if simple food were involved, the attitude had to be serious.

In his writings, Mencius said that people's demand for delicious food was reasonable: "Fish is what I like as well as bear's paw." But, he opposed rulers disregarding the desire of common people for good food in order to satisfy their own desires. He exposed the dark reality that "They do not criticize themselves about dogs and swine eating human food, and they ignore the starved people lying on the roads." He believed the emperor should share the joy of life with the people, and his "benevolent government" was the way to achieve this.

With regard to colonies, Mencius believed that only if people were clothed and fed would it be possible to establish harmonious relations and help the common people become cultured. He further believed that people should be vigorous and overcome their natural demands (overcome hunger) in order to shoulder the mission of humankind.

If we judge the history of China's dietetic culture since these times, the Confucianists positively influenced the development of a dietetic culture. As Taoism and Confucianism have since blended spiritually, the two schools have complemented each other in the theory and practice of health building through diet.

## Mohist Philosophy on Health Building

Mo Di, the founder of Mohism, (c. 468-376 B.C.), also called Mo Zi, lived in the State of Song during the Spring and Autumn Period. He first followed Confucianism, but he disliked its elaborate rites so he founded a new school. He advocated arduous practice and obedience to disciplines so that "the starved are fed, the poor are clothed, workers get rest, and disorder is controlled."

Mohist thought and practice reflected the people's urgent demand for food and clothing in the social turbulence of the time. Mo Di said: "The five cereals are what the people rely on and what the emperor wants to grow. Therefore, if there is nothing the people rely on, there is nothing the emperor wants to grow." He also said: "Food is the treasure of the nation."

Mo Zi said: "Why does a farmer leave home early and return late instead of being idle, farming and gardening diligently to accumulate more grain and beans? The answer is: If he works hard, he is sure to get rich; if he does not work hard, he is sure to get poor; if he works hard, he is sure to get fed; if he does not work hard, he is sure to starve. So he dares not be idle."

Driven by their need for food, people had to work hard. However, because of heavy exploitation, "People have insufficient property, and countless people have died of cold and hunger." Mo Zi called for "eliminating unnecessary expenditures," and being moderate in food and drink.

He said the rulers "extort heavy taxes on the common people and eat beef, mutton, pork, chicken, steamed turtle, and roasted fish. A hundred utensils are used in the big states, and 10 utensils in the small states. Delicious dishes are so numerous in a square *zhang* (a little more than 100 square feet) that it is impossible for the eyes to see, the hands to touch, or the mouth to taste all of them. In winter they freeze, in summer they rot. The emperor eats like this, so do his attendants. The wealthy live in luxury and the poor are cold and starved. Although you want no trouble, it is impossible. If Your Majesty really wants peace in the land, you must practice frugality in your food."

When the king was extravagant, his attendants were likewise, causing great waste because a person can only eat a limited amount. When delicious foods were spread over a square *zhang*, it was merely for show and had no actual meaning. Mo Zi stressed the relationship between diet and health and was against pursuing delicacies; it was enough if food could "replenish my energy and vigor, strengthen my muscles, and sharpen my eyes and ears." His ideal daily diet for the king was "either millet or broomcorn, and either a thick soup or a big piece of meat." In other words, one dish of staple food and one dish of non-staple food. The dinnerware should be simple pottery. All this reflected the Mohist school's wish for simple living, but it could not be achieved in reality.

## Buddhist Philosophy on Health Building

To Buddhists, the supreme purpose of life is to become a Buddha; their ideal is to "deliver all beings." They advocate dispelling all private desires and distracting thoughts, doing good deeds, and being altruistic. There is no specific theory on health building in the Buddhist classics. Working, sitting in meditation, eating vegetarian food, and rejecting sexual desire are Buddhism's philosophy on health building.

Ideologically, Buddhism holds that if people sit still with a peaceful mind, concentrate, and persevere, they can achieve a delightful, bright, clear, refreshed state of body and mind. Achieving this state is the purpose of sitting in meditation. From a medical point of view, constant anxiety and worry negatively affect the physiological functioning of the human body and cause pathological changes. The goal of meditation is to free the mind to achieve a natural state of peace.

Buddhists combine chanting with sitting in meditation. Many Buddhists, including lay Buddhists who practice Buddhism at home, live a long life. One reason is because they concentrate on chanting Buddhist scriptures and so have few distracting thoughts running through their minds. They are totally indifferent to personal honor, disgrace, gain, or loss in the physical world.

A Buddhist saying goes: "If I do not work for a day, I will not eat for a day." Monks living in Buddhist temples hidden deep in the mountains farm, fetch water, cook meals, do laundry, and sew. Physical work is an important part of their daily lives, but its purpose is to practice thrift and maintain self-sufficiency, not to improve their health. Their state of mind and physical activity create the foundation for their long lives.

Vegetarianism is not a rule for all Buddhists; it is a unique product of Chinese Buddhism. The rule under which Chinese Buddhists eat vegetarian food dates back to the reign of Emperor Wudi in the Liang Dynasty. Subsequently, Buddhists were prohibited from killing animals and began eating vegetarian food. Vegetables, beans, fruits, and cereals are very nutritious. They contain abundant vitamins, inorganic salts, protein, glucose, sugar, and a little fat.

Rejecting sexual desire is another important part of Buddhist philosophy on health building because rejecting sexual desire can preserve sperm. Chinese emperors in ancient times indulged in sensual pleasures and lost their kidney semen, therefore, they were short-lived; however, Emperor Wudi of the Liang Dynasty, who believed in Buddhism, lived more than 80 years because he had less sex. This was very rare among Chinese emperors.

Buddhists sat in meditation, worked, ate vegetarian food, and rejected sex, not to build their health, but to practice Buddhist doctrine. Therefore, only people outside the Buddhist school thought about whether Buddhist philosophy dealt with health building.

*Nei Jing*, a book by Huang Di that dealt with the theory of traditional Chinese medicine (TCM), appeared during the Warring States Period. It established the belief that medicine and food were identical. It is the earliest existing Chinese medical classic to systematically summarize the achievements of traditional Chinese medicine prior to the Qin and Han Dynasties. Scholars are unsure exactly when the book was completed, but it is believed to have been written in the Warring States Period, then enlarged and revised by medical scientists in the Qin and Han Dynasties. Its author was Huang Di, the Yellow Emperor.

According to legend, Huang Di was born in Youxiong. His family name was Gongsun and his given name was Xuanyuan. He grew up on the Ji River, so his family name was Ji. As an adult, he fought with other tribes, united the

Central Plains people along the Yellow River, and became the forefather of the Huaxia Tribe. Huang Di and his ministers, Lei Gong (the founder of acupuncture) and Qi Bai (his grand doctor and pharmacist), jointly developed TCM. The science of TCM is also called the art of Qi and Huang.

*Nei Jing*, a collection of notes taken during the men's discussions, was written in the name of Huang Di. Because the book was written in different styles, most scholars today believe it was not written by one person, nor was it Huang Di's medical theory. It was merely authored in Huang Di's name.

The *Nei Jing* says: "All illnesses are caused by wind, rain, cold, heat, negative and positive elements, joy, anger, eating, housing, shock, or fright." To strengthen the human body to resist these external changes, the *Nei Jing* says: "The five cereals are staple food, the five fruits are auxiliary food, the five meats are beneficial, and the five vegetables should be taken in abundance. Eat them if they smell good so as to nourish the semen and replenish vital energy." The five cereals are round-grained, non-glutinous rice, wheat, red beans, soy beans, and glutinous millet. The five fruits are peach, plum, apricot, chestnut, and date. The five animals are ox, sheep, pig, chicken, and dog, and the five vegetables are herbaceous plants, leaves of pulse plants (peas, beans, lentils), Allium bakeri (plants of the lily family), onion, and chives.

The *Nei Jing* says: "When the five internal organs are strong,... one can live long... Anyone whose five internal organs are strong is never sick... When the five internal organs are peaceful and the blood and energy are good, the body has vigor."

There are many kinds of foods, but not all of them nourish the internal organs of the human body. TCM purports that animal organs as well as five flavors nourish the organs. The five flavors are: Sour nourishes the liver, bitter nourishes the heart, sweet nourishes the spleen, pungent nourishes the lungs, and salty nourishes the kidneys. Frequent eating of the five flavors improves the functioning of the internal organs.

If the five organs have excessive energy, it will cause disease. The *Nei Jing* says: "Take the five cereals for the five organs as an example: Among the five cereals, broomcorn nourishes the heart, barley the liver, sorghum the spleen, glutinous rice the lungs, and beans (black beans) the kidneys." A story goes that in ancient times a person called Li Shouyu took two to seven black beans with water every morning, describing it as "cereals keeping the five organs strong until old age."

Another way to nourish the internal organs is to eat animal organs, the best being pig and sheep organs because they are most similar to human organs. Medical specialists call this effect "like attracting like." TCM books describe pig and sheep liver as nourishing the liver, building blood, improving eyesight, and curing dizziness, night blindness, and glaucoma. The TCM prescription is: "Take a lobe of pig liver and 10 grams of bat excrement. Powder the bat excrement, put it on the liver, and cook them for 20 minutes. Remove the bat excrement and eat the liver with its soup for seven consecutive days." According to TCM theory, night blindness and glaucoma are caused by weakness of the liver.

In eating food to nourish the internal organs, flavor the food and change the variety. This is as effective as eating organs because many vegetables and fruits also nourish the organs. The big dates produced in Hebei, Shandong, and Shanxi nourish the spleen and increase energy. Chestnuts and walnuts nourish the kidneys. Longan helps the heart and blood; Lily moistens the lungs and improves breathing, and mulberry nourishes the liver. All these foods are neutral and sweet.

Generally, fruits and vegetables should be eaten frequently to improve the health; they either can be eaten alone or together with other foods. For example, dates cooked with lily and then drunk will nourish the lungs and spleen. Chestnuts and mulberry cooked and eaten together nourish the liver and kidneys, and raw chestnuts strengthen the back and knees. Su Che (1039-1112), a Song Dynasty man of letters, wrote a poem in praise of chestnuts. It says that an old man living in the mountains had back and knee trouble. Every day he ate three raw chestnuts morning and evening to ease the pain, but raw chestnuts should not be eaten in excess as they cause digestion problems.

TCM advocates nourishing the energy and blood vessels in the human body. TCM philosophy states, "What man has are vigor and blood." Blood flows in the vessels, promoting *yin* and *yang* to make muscles and bones strong, and joints flexible. TCM theory holds that "qi," or energy, is spiritual matter full of vitality, a formless force and spirit. *Qi*, which exists in heaven, earth, and humans, is an embodiment of the life-force; therefore, a lack of *qi* means the whole body is weak. TCM recommends using ginseng to nourish vital energy.

According to TCM theory, the foods that nourish *qi* and blood are liver, spinach, carrots, and animal blood. This is because the liver is the blood-building organ of animals, especially mammals. The chemicals contained in animal liver are similar to human blood and, therefore, nourish the *qi* and blood of the human body. Modern medical scientists are researching the use of serum from pig blood as the raw material for making substitute human plasma, which shows that animal blood nourishes human blood.

Foods that build semen and bone marrow strengthen the muscles and bones. The "semen" TCM refers to is the natural semen contained in the kidneys. This basic matter makes up and maintains human life. It is also the sperm to procreate. If a man does not have semen, he will be infertile; if a woman does not have semen, she will not become pregnant. The *Nei Jing* says: "Semen is the foundation of reproduction."

Marrow is the soft tissue that fills the bone cavities. It is formed from the overflowing kidney semen that is stored in the bone cavities. According to TCM theory, kidneys produce marrow and the bones are the dwelling places for the marrow. Therefore, both semen and marrow are the most treasured part of the human body, and the Chinese compare the most valuable things in the world to them.

Foods that nourish semen and marrow are called "products of flesh and blood." All animals have flesh and blood and some animals, such as the dog, horse, and ox, even have feelings. If trained, they can understand what human beings mean, so they are said to "have feelings of flesh and blood." Many creatures have such feelings of flesh and blood. In the book *Compendium of Materia Medica*, Li Shizhen recorded 299 animals with hair, feathers, shells and scales. The marrow of pig and ox, and the cartilage of ox, sheep, and pig all contain rich protein, a little fat, and gelatin, which has the same effect as donkey-hide gelatin, a famous and valuable TCM drug that strengthens bones and muscles and nourishes marrow.

Crab also nourishes marrow and semen. TCM prescribes a specific way to eat crabs, the best time being the 9th and 10th lunar months. In his *Compendium of Materia Medica*, Li Shizhen said: "When cooking crabs, add Dahurian angelica root to prevent damage to the crab's ovary and digestive glands, and add onion and Chinese magnolia vine fruits to prevent color change." Both Dahurian angelica root and Chinese magnolia vine fruits are available in TCM pharmacies, 4-5 grams is enough.

The crabs must be alive, and then they must be well cooked. Liquor-saturated crabs should not be eaten because they are served raw. (Liquor is sometimes used to sterilize crabs.) Because crabs eat rotten food and poison-carrying substances, they often cause poisoning if they are not well cooked. Dead crabs should not be eaten.

Yellow croaker, eel, turtle, sea cucumber, and scallops all nourish the semen and marrow. Mix the air bladder of the yellow croaker and the Chinese herb astragali complanati together into balls to improve semen. Sea cucumber and mussels are excellent semen nourishing foods that are highly effective in improving male sexual functioning.

According to scientific analysis, all these foods are nutritious, high in protein, and low in fat. Sea cucumbers contain 55.5% protein and 1.9% crude fat; mussels contain 59.1% protein and 7.6% fat. Both are mild and good for the health.

When eating foods to build health, pay attention to the spleen and stomach. Once food is eaten, the functions of the spleen and stomach digest the food and absorb its nutrients. The spleen and stomach play a vital role in maintaining human life, so it is very important to protect and maintain their normal functioning. This is achieved by paying attention to both internal and external factors. The external factor is the food; in other words, food and drink must nourish the stomach.

Ye Tianshi (1667-1746), a famous Qing Dynasty doctor, wrote the book *On Warmth*, which greatly influenced later generations. He believed that foods must suit the taste, and the stomach must feel good after eating them. He also said, "Food is good if the stomach likes it." Foods the stomach likes contain nutrients needed by the human body and are easily digested. To protect the spleen and stomach, foods should be soft, warm, and chewed carefully.

Even highly nutritious foods will produce the opposite effect if the functions of the spleen and stomach are neglected. In spite of their rich nutrients, chicken, duck, fish, and meat that have been deep-fried or stir-fried in oil are not easily digested. If you eat more of them than you need, they will increase the burden on the spleen and stomach, and cause indigestion.

To ensure the normal functioning of the spleen and stomach, it is necessary to keep a peaceful mind. Because the spleen controls the mind, excessive deliberation and thinking hurt the spleen, and if the spleen is hurt, there is no appetite for food.

The nutrients the human body needs are protein, fat, sugar, vitamins, inorganic salts, and water. There are many foods in the world. Because the nutrients contained in each food vary, people should eat many different foods instead of eating only a few foods. A limited selection of food makes it difficult to obtain all the different nutrients needed by the human body. Many people who maintained good health in ancient times ate vegetarian foods. The *Nei Jing* says: "Excessive eating of fatty meats and fine grains is sure to cause malignant tumors."

Speaking on the advantage of vegetarian foods, Dr. Sun Yat-sen, the great Chinese democratic revolutionary

(1866-1925), said:

"China has invented a great variety of foods and has cooked them in so many ways that no other country can match. However, the eating and drinking habits of the Chinese people, which conform to scientific and hygienic requirements, are beyond the reach of common people in any other country. What the Chinese people drink is very often clear tea, and what they eat is simple food with some vegetables and bean curd...

"Bean curd is, in fact, the 'meat' of plants. It has the same benefits as meat, but does not have the bad effects of meat,... Europeans and Americans have a habit of drinking alcoholic liquors and eating meat and fish... On the question of food and drink, Chinese habits are superior to those in any other country." (*The Chinese Should Stick to Their Own Dietetic Methods*)

In the second year of the Jianyuan Reign of the Western Han Dynasty (139 B.C.), Emperor Wudi (156-87 B.C.) sent Zhang Qian (?-114 B.C.) to the Western Region (Xinjiang in China, and Central Asia) as his envoy. Zhang Qian stayed there for 12 years strengthening cultural exchanges between China and the West, and introducing many new varieties of fruits, vegetables, and soy beans into China. Legend has it that Liu An (or Liu Chang), Prince of Huainan in the Western Han Dynasty, invented bean curd. Emperor Wudi of the Liang Dynasty later invented gluten. These inventions greatly enriched vegetarian foods.

Vegetarianism is not strictly required by Buddhism. Buddhists of the Mongolian, Tibetan, and Dai nationalities in China, who believe in Dacheng Buddhism, all eat meat because meat is more plentiful than vegetables where they live. Some Chinese Buddhist followers are vegetarian because it was advocated by Emperor Wudi of the Liang Dynasty.

Emperor Xiao Yan (502-549), was a wise and versatile monarch during the period of the Southern and Northern Dynasties. When still a child, he learned both Confucian and Taoist classics, and followed Taoism. After many discussions with famous Buddhist monks and literati, Xiao Yan held the Buddhist ideas of "not bringing evil," "doing good deeds," "abstaining from killing animals," "releasing captured animals," "eating vegetarian food," and "maintaining peace and quiet," agreed with the Confucian ideas of "a reputation for benevolence" and "filial piety," so he converted from Taoism to Buddhism. His promotion of vegetarian food had a strong political and religious impact. From that time on, Buddhist followers (mainly in areas inhabited by Han Chinese) equated the idea of not killing animals with vegetarianism.

Buddhist followers contributed greatly to the development of vegetarian food and its own system. Originally, Buddhist followers in India were not required to be vegetarians because, when the monks begged alms door-to-door, they could not choose between meat and vegetarian foods. Neither were Chinese Buddhist monks confined by strict food rules.

Later the pious Buddhist Emperor, Wudi, promoted vegetarianism and prohibited monks from eating meat. He held that eating meat violated Buddhist tenets and he punished monks who drank liquor or ate meat. So, Buddhist temples banned wine and meat. Because the monks then ate vegetarian foods all year, the number of vegetarians increased greatly thereby stimulating the development of vegetarian food. Legend has it that during Emperor Wudi's reign, a monk who cooked in the "Jianye Temple" in Nanjing was skilled at preparing vegetarian food and earned praises from pilgrims and monks in the temple.

To meet the needs of Buddhist followers, the restaurant trade opened more vegetarian businesses and, to accommodate the pilgrims, literati, officials, VIPs, and tourists, Buddhist temples all over China invented many delicious vegetarian dishes. For example, "Fried Spring Rolls" (sliced bean curd, gluten, and wild vegetables wrapped in dried bean milk cream or cabbage leaves) were invented by Great Master Hongren of the Zen Sect of Buddhism after the Tang Dynasty. Spring rolls are a famous vegetarian dish (now also filled with meat) at home and abroad.

After the Han and Jin Dynasties, Buddhist temples were established in all the big mountains and along large rivers. Many had kitchens to cook mushrooms, fungi, vegetables, gourds, fruits, and all kinds of dishes made of bean curd. After the Song Dynasty, up to the Ming and Qing Dynasties, "all vegetarian dinners" including dishes like vegetarian chicken, vegetarian goose, vegetarian duck, vegetarian fish, and vegetarian ham, were served. Even now, the Yufo (Jade Buddha) Temple in Shanghai, the Lingyin Temple in Hangzhou, the Daming Temple in Yangzhou, the Wuzu Temple in Huangmei County, Hubei Province, the Baoguang Temple in Xindu, Sichuan Province, and the Southern Putuo Temple in Xiamen, Fujian Province, are all famous for their vegetarian food.

Buddhist and Taoist cuisines both stress vegetarian food. Ge Hong (281-341), a famous Jin Dynasty Taoist medical scientist, chemist, and health building expert, advocated "the food of five fungi," and stressed food of fungi and flowers. Both Buddhists and Taoists ate fungi and flowers, and the people of China are believed to have been the first to eat flowers as food. Day lily, lily, lotus, plum, osmanthus, cottonrose, yulan magnolia, and chrysanthemum flowers are all used for food. It has since been confirmed that these edible flowers contain amino acids, fructose, vitamins, and trace elements such as iron, potassium, magnesium, and zinc.

Many interesting foods have been made from flowers. The Imperial Kitchen stir-fried lotus and lean meat into a fragrant dish that was refreshing in the summer heat. People in ancient times used plum blossoms in porridge to add a refreshing taste. Cottonrose and bean curd were cooked into a bright moon soup, and scholartree flowers were scrambled with eggs to make a delicious dish. Chrysanthemum and osmanthus make excellent flavorings for cakes.

During the 17th century the Nuzhen, a northern nomadic tribe, came to the Central Plains where they established the Qing Dynasty empire and a preference for vegetarian food. The temples, markets, and palace all had special kitchens that prepared vegetarian food. Vegetarian cooks in the temples were called fragrance-accumulating chefs (cooking monks), and their vegetarian food was called Buddhist food. In the palace, vegetarian food was known as Buddhist food. The emperors and royal family ate vegetarian food when they abstained from eating meat in offering sacrifices to their Gods or ancestors.

The Imperial Kitchen had a special section that prepared vegetarian food using such raw materials as gluten, bean curd, skin of soy bean milk, dried bean curd cream, fresh bamboo, mushrooms, water chestnuts, Chinese yam, day lily, fungi, and fruits. The vegetarian cooks used these materials to prepare hundreds of differently flavored delicacies.

When discussing vegetarian food, it is necessary to mention the rice porridge with nuts and dried fruits that was eaten in the Buddhist temples on the 8th day of the 12th moon. Legend says Sakyamuni ate very simple food in the six years that he practiced Buddhism before he became the Buddha and founded Buddhism. He became enlightened on the 8th day of the 12th moon; to honor this day, later generations began eating rice porridge with nuts and dried fruits. When Buddhist temples fed pilgrims or tourists the porridge, they usually cooked rice with peanuts, dates, chestnuts, longan, lotus seeds, walnuts, red beans, ginkgo, and soy beans. Because it contains so many ingredients, the porridge is very nutritious. In ancient times it was called "Good Fortune and Virtue Porridge" or "Good Fortune and Longevity Porridge" because the porridge can help prolong life and improve health.

From a modern, scientific viewpoint, diet should emphasize vegetarian food but contain a combination of vegetarian and meat dishes. This is because vegetarian food promotes the normal movement of the stomach and intestines. Zhu Danxi (1281-1358), a noted medical scientist in the Yuan Dynasty, said: "If grains, beans, vegetables, and fruits naturally taste mild, they will nourish the human body and improve the male organs."

The *Nei Jing* says, "Vegetables are prescribed for a fear of hunger or if there is too much worry, which hurts the stomach. Vegetables are used to help dredge the stomach and intestines, and improve digestion. This is the benevolence of the Heaven, Earth, and living matters." This passage says vegetarian foods cleanse the stomach and intestines, and their cellulose aids digestion, promotes intestinal peristalsis, and relieves constipation.

The cellulose in vegetables expands in water to form a close network that absorbs inorganic salts, organic acids, and water. This simple process adjusts the digestive and absorptive functions of the intestines, affects the metabolism of the human body, and helps prevent disease. Scientists believe that eating more cellulose-rich foods, such as coarse grains, beans, corn, celery, cabbage, chives, and Chinese cabbage, can help prevent enteritis and intestinal cancers. Some people spit out the "residue" when they eat vegetables, but this is a mistake because that residue is the cellulose that is indispensable to the human body.

Foreign research shows that Europeans and Americans have more than ten times the incidence of intestinal cancer than do Africans. The reason is believed to be diet. Europeans and Americans eat only a fraction of the cellulose that Africans do. Science shows that meat and vegetable dishes should be well blended, preferably with the total quantity of vegetables being two or more times that of meat.

Vegetables have five advantages: They contain vitamins that aid digestion, they prevent nutritional deficiencies, they help prevent obesity, they improve blood circulation, and they prevent and help cure cancers.

Cow's milk, black sesame seeds, and bee honey are also highly nutritious foods. Sun Simiao (581-682), a noted medical scientist in the Sui and Tang Dynasties, noted: "They are far better than meats." The menus from the Ming and Qing palaces show the emperors' daily diets included fruits, vegetables, milk, and foods made of coarse grains, such as cakes made of red beans, bean flour, or corn flour. All of these have been described in earlier chapters of this book.

It can thus be seen that the imperial foods were very effective in building health through diet. Both the Ming and Qing Palaces banned the drinking of strong liquor and greediness, which can negatively affect health.

# Chinese Cuisines

China is a vast country with diverse climates, customs, products, and habits. People living in different regions display great variety in their diets. People in coastal areas eat more aquatic products and seafood, whereas those in central and northwest China eat more domestic animals and poultry. Foods vary from north to south, and typical local dishes may even astonish strangers, such as snake, pangolin, and white rat. Tastes also differ regionally because of the climatic differences.

One popular summary of Chinese food is "sweet in the south, salty in the north, sour in the west, and spicy in the east." People in the different regions have created their own cuisines to suit their tastes, and many chefs and cooks specialize in making these local delicacies. In the past, cooks in the different regions were called the Beijing sect, Shandong sect, Fujian sect, and Sichuan sect, as a way to differentiate the regional cuisines and the cooking specialties of the chefs. After the founding of the People's Republic, the catering trade has referred to the cuisines by the different specialties and regional tastes of the dishes.

There is still no agreement on how many principal cuisines there are in China, but nine major cuisines have influenced Chinese cookery. They are the Beijing, Shandong, Huai-Yang, Jiangsu-Zhejiang, Fujian, Guangdong, Sichuan, Hubei, and Hunan cuisines.

**Beijing Cuisine**. People also call this the Capital City cuisine. Beijing was the capital city for the Liao, Jin, Yuan, Ming, and Qing dynasties. Except for the Ming Dynasty, all the rulers of these dynasties were from northern nomadic tribes. For those 500-plus years, the dishes available from Beijing's catering trade were dominated by meat dishes, which corresponded to the eating habits of the ruling class. The Mongolian rulers of the Yuan Dynasty were especially fond of mutton, and 80% of the dishes in their palace were made of mutton. These mutton dishes still are made today, such as stewed mutton, instant-boiled mutton, quick-fried mutton tripe, and fried dumplings with minced mutton.

The Qing Dynasty rulers ate pork before moving to Beijing from Shenyang in northeastern China. Their cooking methods were stewing, roasting, and boiling. Pork and mutton have been equally represented in Beijing cuisine since the Qing Dynasty as a result of the dietetic influence of the Manchus. Roast and stewed pig, pork dishes, and pig's offal stewed in ceramic pots offered by the Shaguoju Restaurant (ceramic pots restaurant) were the first to be offered to suit the eating preferences of the Manchus. Gradually these dishes were accepted by the residents of Beijing.

Beijing was the gathering place of the literati and officials, and many skilled chefs followed these people to Beijing. These chefs brought the different cuisines to the capital and greatly enriched the flavors of Beijing cuisine. The Shandong, Huai-Yang, and Jiangsu-Zhejiang cuisines all strongly influenced Beijing cuisine. Because Shandong was near Beijing, people migrated from there to Beijing to earn their living, and many worked in the catering trade. Shandong cuisine was similar to Beijing cuisine, so its dishes were quickly accepted. The Shandong people almost had a monopoly on the Beijing catering trade during the Qing Dynasty.

Many famous Beijing restaurants, including the Tongfengtang, Fushoutang, Huifengtang, Guangheju, and Tongheju, were opened by people from Shandong. The quick-frying techniques of the Shandong cuisine and its use of onions greatly influenced Beijing cuisine. For example, quick-fried mutton, a popular, common dish, is a typical Beijing dish that uses the cooking skills and flavoring methods of the Shandong cuisine. Now, people in Beijing quickly fry onions in hot oil before stir-frying the dish because of the influence of the Shandong cuisine.

Being the capital city, Beijing had many cultural and trade exchanges with other parts of the country. Many people came from Huai'an, Yangzhou, southern Jiangsu, and western Zhejiang for business or to seek official posts in Beijing. Literati and officials placed high expectations on restaurant food, and many even created dishes. The chefs in Beijing all boasted of being able to create the dishes of the southern cuisines. Some Beijing residents and businessmen from other areas wanted to eat the dishes of their native cuisines without leaving the city, which stimulated the development of the Huai'an-Yangzhou cuisine in Beijing.

When southern food was introduced in the north, its flavor was changed. For example, Huai'an-Yangzhou cuisine has a sweet and less salty taste, while northern cuisine has salty, rich flavors. Before southern cuisines were accepted in Beijing, they had to adjust their flavors, and dishes had to be created that combined the southern and northern cuisines. For example, Mr. Pan's Fish, a famous dish of quick-fried fish and mutton, was introduced by Pan Zuyin (1830-1890), a member of the Qing Dynasty Imperial Academy. Wu's Sliced Fish, invented by Wu Yansheng of Suzhou, was a Beijing dish that had the flavor of Jiangsu-Zhejiang cuisine.

Manchu and Han banquets, which gradually became popular during Emperor Qianlong's reign, included nearly 200 cold dishes and dozens of refreshments and pastries. The main courses were Manchu style roast dishes, shark's fin, edible bird's nest, sea cucumbers, jellyfish, and abalone served southern style. These were supplemented by traditional Manchu pastries and Huai'an-Yangzhou or Jiangsu-Zhejiang style soups. The banquets were a collection of Beijing style dishes that precisely reflected the cooking skills and flavors of Beijing cuisine. Peking duck, which has become a favorite of people outside Beijing and even with foreigners, is prepared using force-fed ducks. The duck is roasted in Huai'an and Yangzhou style to emphasize the color and taste, then seasoned with fermented flour sauce, and eaten with onions and pancakes baked Shandong style. This typical dish reflects the origin of Beijing cuisine.

Beijing cuisine is famous for its hundreds of dishes with special flavors that are unmatched by any other cuisine. Beijing cuisine does not emphasize strangeness or uniqueness, only delicious food made from common ingredients with tastes that are very agreeable. It is China's most typical cuisine.

**Shandong Cuisine.** As early as the Spring and Autumn Period, more than 3,000 years ago, Shandong was the territory of Qi and Lu. Both states were economically and culturally developed. Because they bordered the sea, and had mountains and fertile plains, they had abundant aquatic products and grains as well as sea salt. The people of the area have stressed seasonings and flavorings since ancient times.

Shandong cuisine was created during the Yuan Dynasty. It gradually spread to north China, Beijing, Tianjin, northeast China, and the palace where it influenced the imperial food. The Shandong cuisine comprises mainly eastern Shandong and Jinan dishes.

Jinan dishes are known for their use of seafood. Sea cucumber, shark's fin, edible bird's nest, dried scallops, mussels, shrimp, and crab are all used to create delicious dishes.

The most typical Jinan dishes are sea cucumber with meat balls; braised shark's fin with shredded chicken; sea cucumber, mushroom, and bamboo shoots; clam in egg white; and fried oysters. Jinan cuisine is known for its soups, quick-frying, stir-frying, deep-frying, and stewing. The most common raw materials are river fish, pork, and vegetables. Some typical dishes are carp in milk soup, Yellow River carp in sweet and sour sauce, stewed pork leg, and quick-fried double crisps.

Shandong cuisine is characterized by quick-frying, stir-frying, braising, and deep-fat frying. Its dishes are crisp, tender, delicious, and greasy with salty and some sweet and sour flavors. Its main condiment is salt, but it also uses salted fermented soybeans and soy sauce.

People in Shandong like to eat onions and use onions as a seasoning. The dishes include braised sea cucumber with onions, cartilage stewed with onions, and meat stewed with onions. Roast meats are also served with onions. The onions are first deep-fat fried before the dishes are quick-fried, stir-fried, stewed, or sautéd so they absorb the onion flavor. People in Shandong also like foods made of wheat flour, such as steamed buns, baked buns, pancakes, crisp cakes, and big cakes stuffed with minced meats.

**Huai-Yang Cuisine**. This cuisine includes dishes from Huai'an, Yangzhou, Suzhou, Hangzhou, and Shanghai. Huai-Yang refers to the cities of Yangzhou, Zhenjiang, and Huai'an in Jiangsu Province along the Grand Canal north of the Yangtze River. Yangzhou was a military fort and a cultural center in ancient times. It was a very busy city as early as the Tang Dynasty, and was the most flourishing commercial city in China after the capital city. Extravagant consumption by rich, important businessmen stimulated the thriving catering trade and the development of cookery.

Every important salt trader employed a skilled cook who specialized in cooking certain delicious dishes or desserts. When a salt trader gave a dinner, he often borrowed cooks from other salt traders, and when every cook prepared his specialty, a lavish dinner was ready. In this way, the cooks exchanged their cooking skills and improved the cooking in Yangzhou.

Yangzhou, located in a region crisscrossed by rivers and lakes, has abundant fish, shrimp, and seafood, which are used in the local cooking. The city's catering trade flourished during the Yuan, Ming, and Qing dynasties. There were also cooks who sold their cooking skills as "external cooks" at festivals, banquets, and weddings. Their different services were evidence of the fierce competition among them, which helped develop the cooking skills in

Yangzhou.

If Shandong cuisine is characterized by stirring and frying over a hot fire, Huai-Yang cuisine is characterized by stewing, braising, and steaming over a low fire for a long time. Famous dishes cooked this way are chicken braised with chestnuts, pork steamed in lotus leaf, duck stewed with eight treasures, pork meat balls Yangzhou style, and butterfly sea cucumber (sea cucumber cut into butterfly shapes and cooked with flavorings).

Yangzhou dishes stress the stock and extract, and require chicken to taste like chicken and fish to taste like fish, with clear distinctions between the primary and secondary ingredients. The dishes are cooked over a low fire and the pots are covered or sealed so the marrow cooks out and the primary taste and form are kept. These traits are unique to cooking over a low fire. Stewing keeps the stock fresh and delicious (this is the main difference between stewing and braising). Stewed dishes are tender, fragrant, and tasty.

Stewing without water in the pot is one stewing method. It is done this way: Put the cleaned meat (preferably a whole chicken or duck) in a sealed vessel and immerse the vessel in boiling water for several hours. Boiling food in its own juice without soy sauce was begun in the Yangzhou cuisine and has since influenced the Beijing cuisine. Yangzhou dishes, which are slightly sweet, are often flavored with both sugar and salt. Sugar makes the dish more delicious and tasty. The Yangzhou cuisine also stresses colors, such as the colors of red sugar, soy sauce, the raw materials, and egg white. Dragon hidden in snow is a good example. The major ingredient is quick-fried eel shreds. Steamed egg white is used as the base color, and when the shining, black-and-yellow, quick-fried, shredded eel is placed on the egg white, it looks like a dragon lying on snow. Other dishes, such as chicken boiled in its own soup without soy sauce, roast Mandarin fish, steamed hilsa herring, and steamed shrimp dumplings look sparkling, lustrous and attractive.

Crystallized dishes made in Zhenjiang are sparkling, transparent, tender, and delicious. They are known for their color, form, and taste. Huai-Yang cuisine also pays attention to color and taste. If a dish is heavy and brightly colored, its taste must be heavy and its soup must be thick. If a dish is simple and light colored, its taste must be light and its soup must be clear.

The vegetarian banquet is a special feature of the Huai-Yang cuisine, and the vegetarian dishes in the Beijing cuisine are mostly variants of the Huai-Yang cuisine. This is not true for the vegetarian foods of the other cuisines. The Huai-Yang snacks and refreshments are exquisite, such as boiled, shredded, dried bean curd; steamed dumplings with minced meat and gravy; steamed meat dumplings with the dough gathered at the top; steamed stuffed meat buns; steamed buns filled with meat, crab roe and gravy; steamed buns filled with meat, bamboo shoots and vegetables; Huangqiao baked sesame cakes; multi-layer cake; boneless fish and noodles; quick-fried eel and noodles; noodles with seasoned topping; and steamed crystal buns from Zhenjiang.

**Jiangsu-Zhejiang Cuisine**. Jiangsu refers to the part of Jiangsu south of the Yangtze River, namely Suzhou and Wuxi; while Zhejiang refers to the western part of the province, namely Hangzhou and Huzhou. The economy in the two provinces began growing after the middle of the

118

Tang Dynasty (around the 5th century). Following the Five Dynasties (907-960), the economic and cultural centers moved south, and literati gathered in these places. If the catering trade in Huai'an and Yangzhou chiefly met the needs of important, rich traders, the cooking skills and features in this area reflected the interests and tastes of the literati.

Jiangsu-Zhejiang cuisine stresses the use of vegetables, bamboo shoots, mushrooms, and water shield, which gives the food a light, fresh taste. Vegetable dishes make up the bulk of the common people's daily meals, but also are popular dishes on the menus of famous restaurants. These dishes include cabbage heart cooked in chicken fat, braised fish slivers, spring bamboo shoots braised in oil, spinach flavored with shrimp sauce, West Lake live fish steamed with vinegar, and water shield soup. Fish or meat dishes are often cooked together with vegetables; and fish, shrimp, crab, and mussels from the rivers and lakes are also served as delicacies. In this area the fish and shrimp are often kept alive until they are cooked, so the foods served in restaurants are very fresh.

The Jiangsu-Zhejiang cuisine has many famous fish and shrimp dishes. For example, Mandarin Fish Shaped like a Squirrel topped with sweet and sour tomato sauce was praised by Emperor Qianlong of the Qing Dynasty as the "the Number One Dish in the World." West Lake fish steamed in vinegar has been famous for centuries, minced perch in Songjiang has been praised for a millennia, and braised shrimp served with Longjing tea in Hangzhou and braised shrimp served with Biluo Spring tea are both very popular.

Jiangsu-Zhejiang dishes are slightly sweet and less salty,

but some dishes are cooked with sweet and sour flavors. The use of distiller's grain is a special feature of the Jiangsu-Zhejiang cuisine. The grains are used to remove unpleasant smells and improve the aroma. According to historical data, crab and goose pickled with grain were among the foods available in Hangzhou during the Southern Song Dynasty. Afterward, distiller's grain was used for flavor in almost all dishes; for example, eggplant was cooked with grain and pork was steamed with grain.

Jiangsu-Zhejiang dishes are cooked in a similar manner to Huai-Yang cuisine, and importance is attached to simmering, stewing, braising, boiling in covered pot, and steaming. Most dishes are served in delicious soup. The shapes and colors are natural, as contrasted with Huai-Yang cuisine. Its cakes and balls, made of glutinous rice stuffed with sweet red-bean paste or with sesame seeds and sugar, are famous throughout the two provinces. Festival delicacies include New Year's cake, gold and silver balls served during Spring Festival, sweet dumplings served at the Lantern Festival on the 15th day of the first moon, green and white dumplings served on the Pure Brightness Day, black rice cake served on the Beginning of Summer Day, cold agar jelly served on July 15, and the sweet cake served on the Double Ninth Festival. Everyday refreshments include stuffed dumplings made of glutinous rice, rice balls, cold cakes, pine-seed cakes, fuling cakes, sponge cakes, crystal cakes, and comb cakes.

**Fujian Cuisine**. Fujian cuisine was a latecomer in southeast China along the coast. The cuisine emphasizes seafood, river fish, and shrimp. The Fujian coastal area produces 167 varieties of fish and 90 kinds of turtles and shellfish. It also produces edible bird's nest, cuttlefish, and sturgeon. These special products are all used in Fujian cuisine.

The Fujian economy and culture began to flourish after the Southern Song Dynasty. During the middle Qing Dynasty famous Fujian officials and literati promoted the Fujian cuisine so it gradually became known to other parts of China.

The most characteristic aspect of Fujian cuisine is that its dishes are served in soup. Its cooking methods are stewing, boiling, braising, quick-boiling, and steaming. The most famous dish is Buddha Jumps Over the Wall. The name implies the dish is so delicious that even the Buddha would jump over a wall to eat it once he smelled it. A mixture of seafood, chicken, duck, and pork is put into a rice-wine jar and simmered over a low fire. Sea mussel quick-boiled in chicken soup is another Fujian delicacy.

Cutting is important in the Fujian cuisine. Most dishes are made of seafood, and if the seafood is not cut well the dishes will fail to have their true flavor. Fujian dishes are slightly sweet and sour, and less salty. For example, litchi pork, sweet and sour pork, soft fish with onion flavor, and razor clams stir-fried with fresh bamboo shoots without soy sauce all have this taste. When a dish is less salty, it tastes more delicious. Sweetness makes a dish more tasty, while sourness helps remove the seafood smell.

In the Fujian cuisine, an important flavoring and coloring material is red distiller's grain. It is a glutinous rice fermented with red yeast. After being kept in a sealed vessel for one year, the grain acquires a sweet and sour flavor and a rose-red color. Chicken, duck, fish, and pork can be flavored with the red grain as well as spiral shells, clams, mussels, bamboo shoots, and even vegetables. When the red distiller's grain is used for flavoring, the dishes can be cooked in many ways, including quick-frying, frying, quick-boiling, and pickling.

Fujian cuisine comprises three branches — Fuzhou, southern Fujian, and western Fujian. There are slight differences among them. Fuzhou dishes are more fresh, delicious, and less salty, sweet, and sour. Southern Fujian dishes are sweet and hot and use hot sauces, custard, and orange juice as flavorings. Western Fujian dishes are salty and hot. As Fujian people emigrate overseas, their cuisine has become popular in Taiwan and abroad.

**Guangdong Cuisine**. Guangdong cuisine is unique among the Chinese cuisines. Its raw materials, cooking methods, and flavorings all differ from the other cuisines. Guangdong is located in southern China. Bordered by the mountain ranges to the north and the South China Sea to the south, it has long been separated from the hinterland. In ancient times the Baiyue people lived there, but many immigrants from the hinterland moved in during the Qin and Han Dynasties. The dietetic culture of Guangdong has retained many eating habits and customs of the ancient people, such as eating snakes. In short, to the people of Guangdong, everything that walks, crawls, flies, or swims is edible. Many of these strange foods no longer appeal to today's refined tastes, and some have been eliminated out of respect for the eating habits of people in other areas, but some strange foods still remain.

The most famous dish, Dragon and Tiger Fight, is a dish of braised snake and leopard. It has even been served as the main course at important banquets. Other famous dishes are dragon, tiger, and phoenix with chrysanthemum (snake, leopard, and chicken), braised phoenix liver and snake slices (chicken liver and snake), and stir-fried shredded snake meat in five colors.

Since the Ming and Qing Dynasties, Guangdong has become more prosperous, and it has developed closer contacts with the hinterland. As Western culture has been introduced, Guangdong cuisine has absorbed the cooking skills of the West as well as the cooking skills of other Chinese regions to develop its own unique methods. The most characteristic cooking methods are cooking in salt, cooking in wine, baking in a pan, and soft-frying.

Cooking in salt means the preserved ingredient (a whole chicken, for example) is buried in heated salt until it is well done. The most famous of these dishes is Salt-Cooked Chicken from Dongjiang.

Cooking in wine means the main ingredient is steamed in alcoholic vapor. The most typical dish is twin pigeons cooked in rose wine. Two cleaned pigeons on two chopsticks are placed in an earthen bowl so as to keep them away from the bottom. Place a cup of rose wine between the pigeons, then put the bowl inside an iron pot and heat the pot until the pigeons are well done. Half a cup of wine will remain without the slightest smell of wine, but the pigeons will have acquired an appealing fragrance of rose wine.

Baking in a pan means the ingredients are put in an iron pan with a cast iron lid. The pan is covered with a red-hot cast-iron lid and heated until the dish is done. A typical dish of this type is baked egg.

Soft-frying is another unique cooking method of the Guangdong cuisine. The main ingredients are liquid or semi-liquid, such as fresh milk and minced chicken. The technique is: heat the pan over a hot fire, then pour some oil in the pan to coat the bottom. Add a little more oil and stir in the ingredients over a medium to low fire. Typical dishes are stir-fried fresh milk and stir-fried eggs.

Guangdong cuisine emphasizes seafood, and unique, mixed flavorings. For example, one flavoring liquid is a mixture prepared from onion, garlic, sugar, salt, and spices. The gravy is prepared from a mixture of peanut oil, ginger, onion, Shaoxing rice wine, crystallized sugar, anise, cassia bark, licorice root, clove, ginger powder, dried tangerine peel, and Momordica grosuvenori. Spiced salt is prepared from refined salt, sugar, powdered spices, and anise. These flavorings, along with other favorite condiments such as oyster sauce, fish sauce, clam oil, and curry, give Guangdong cuisine its unique taste.

Guangdong cuisine is divided into three branches: Guangzhou food is traditional Guangdong cuisine; Chaozhou food is similar to Fujian cuisine because Chaozhou neighbors Fujian Province. It stresses seafood and many dishes are served in soup. Its flavors are thick, delicious, and sweet. Cooks like to use fish sauce, hot sauce and red vinegar. Dongjiang food, which is represented by Huizhou food, emphasizes domestic animals and poultry. Its dishes are slightly salty with simple sauces. Guangdong cuisine has been heavily influenced by foreign cooking cultures.

**Sichuan Cuisine**. People immediately think of Sichuan food as being hot, sour, sweet, and salty; using fish sauce; or having a strange taste. Actually, these flavors were introduced only in the last 100 years, and initially were popular only in the lower strata of society. Hot pepper, an important flavoring in Sichuan cuisine, was introduced

124

into China only 200 to 300 years ago.

During the period of the Three Kingdoms, the Kingdom of Shu was located in Sichuan. According to historical research, the people in Shu liked sweet food. During the Jin Dynasty, they preferred to eat pungent food; however, pungent food at that time referred to food made with ginger, mustard, chives, or onions. As recently as 200 years ago, there were no hot dishes in Sichuan cuisine, and few were cooked with pungent and hot flavorings. Originally, its flavorings were very mild, unlike the popular dishes of today, such as pockmarked lady's bean curd and other hot dishes. Even today, some Sichuan dishes, like velvet shark's fin, braised bear's paw, crisp duck roasted with camphor and tea, sea cucumber with pungent flavor, minced chicken with hollyhock, boiled pork with mashed garlic, dry-fried carp, and boiled Chinese cabbage have kept their traditional flavors.

Sichuan has been known as the land of plenty since ancient times. While it does not have seafood, it produces abundant domestic animals, poultry, and freshwater fish and crayfish. Sichuan cuisine is well known for cooking fish. As a unique style of food, Sichuan cuisine was already famous more than 800 years ago during the Southern Song Dynasty when Sichuan restaurants were opened in Lin'an, now called Hangzhou, its capital city.

The prevailing Sichuan food consists of popular dishes eaten by common people and characterized by pungent, hot, strange, and salty flavors. Although Sichuan cuisine has only a short history, it has affected and even replaced more sumptuous dishes.

The hot pepper was introduced into China from South America around the end of the 17th century. Once it came to Sichuan, it became a favored food flavoring. Sichuan has high humidity and many rainy or overcast days. Hot pepper helps reduce internal dampness, so hot pepper was used frequently in dishes, and hot dishes became the norm in Sichuan cuisine. Sichuan food has become the common food for most people in the area, especially since the dishes go well with rice. In this respect, Sichuan cuisine differs from Beijing cuisine, which was mainly for officials and nobility; Huai-Yang cuisine, which was mainly for rich, important traders; and Jiangsu-Zhejiang cuisine, which was mainly for literati. Typical, modern Sichuan dishes like twice-cooked pork with chili sauce, shredded pork with chili sauce and fish flavor, Crucian carp with thick broad-bean sauce, stir-fried chicken cubes with peanuts and chili sauce, and boiled meat slices are common dishes eaten by every family.

Sichuan food is famous for its many flavors, and almost every dish has its own unique taste. This is because many flavorings and seasonings are produced in Sichuan Province. These include soy sauce from Zhongba, cooking vinegar from Baoning, special vinegar from Sanhui, fermented soy beans from Tongchuan, hot pickled mustard tubers from Fuling, chili sauce from Chongqing, thick, broad-bean sauce from Pixian, and well salt from Zigong.

Sichuan pickles have an appealing smell, and are crisp, tender, salty, sour, hot, and sweet. If pickled elsewhere, even if made the same way using the same raw materials, they still would taste different. This is because the salt, which comes from wells in Zigong, has a unique flavor. In other places, sea salt is often used, which tastes slightly bitter. This example demonstrates that the flavoring materials are very important, apart from the skill of the cooks.

126

In Sichuan food, a single flavor is rarely used, compound flavors are most common. By blending different seasonings, skilled cooks can make dozens of different sauces each with its own flavor, including creamy, salty, sweet and sour, litchi, sour with chili, hot with chili, spicy and hot, mashed garlic, distiller's grain, fish sauce with chili, ginger juice, and soy sauce. The same sauce may be used differently in different dishes. For example, the flavor of the hot with chile sauce for boiled sliced pork is different from the flavor of the hot with chile sauce for pockmarked lady's bean curd.

When flavoring foods, sometimes two or more flavorings are combined, and sometimes a hot fire is used to concentrate the extract from the dish to increase the intensity of the flavor, preserve the primary taste of the dish, remove unpleasant flavors, and increase pleasant flavors. Sichuan cuisine tends to use quick-frying, quick stir-frying, dry-braising, and dry-stewing. In quick-frying and quick stir-frying, the food is fried over a hot fire and stirred quickly without using another pan. For example, it takes about one minute to stir-fry liver and kidney to keep it tender, soft, delicious, and fresh.

The raw materials for dry-braising are mostly fibrous foods like beef, radish, balsam, and kidney beans. These foods are cut into slivers, heated in an iron pot and stirred continuously. Flavorings are added when there is only oil left and the water has disappeared. When the dish is ready, it is dry, fragrant, crisp, and soft.

Dry-stewing is similar to stewing in the Beijing cuisine, but the primary soup or extract in the dish must be condensed over a low fire before the thick broad-bean sauce or hot red pepper is added. No starch is used. When the dish is ready, it looks reddish, oily, and shiny and tastes delicious, crisp and soft. Typical dishes are dry-stewed fish and dry-stewed bamboo shoots.

Sichuan cuisine also has many delicious snacks and desserts, such as Bangbang chicken, chicken with sesame paste, lantern shadow beef, husband and wife's pork lung slices, steamed beef, noodles with chili sauce, and rice dumplings stuffed with sesame paste.

**Hunan Cuisine**. The cooking skills employed in the Hunan cuisine reached a high standard as early as the Western Han Dynasty, giving it a history of more than 2,100 years. Hunan is located in southeastern China along the middle reaches of the Yangtze River, north of the Five Ridges. It contains rivers, lakes, mountains, rolling hills, plains, and pools, which provide abundant delicacies, such as game, fish, shrimp, crab, and turtle. Making full use of these rich resources, local people created a wide variety of delicacies. Hunan cuisine consists of more than 4,000 dishes, among which more than 300 are very famous. Hunan food is characterized by its hot and sour flavor, fresh aroma, greasiness, deep color, and the prominence of the main flavor in each dish. It consists of regional cuisines from the Xiangjiang River Valley, the Tongting Lake region, and the western mountainous area.

Hunan food is hot because the air is very humid, which makes it difficult for the human body to eliminate moisture. The local people eat hot peppers to help remove dampness and cold.

The Xiangjiang River Valley is represented by Changsha, Xiangtan, and Hengyang. The region has good transportation, talented people, and abundant resources. Local dishes require meticulous care of the raw materials and stress cutting skill, length and degree of cooking, color, and appearance. Cooking methods include stewing, simmering, curing, steaming, stir-frying, frying, and quick-frying. The flavors are pungent, chili, fresh and fragrant, and thickly fragrant. Such dishes as fried chicken with hot and spicy sauce, stir-fried tripe slivers, tripe in duck's web soup, dried scallop and eggwhites, and dog meat in hot pot are all typical foods.

The Dongting Lake region, surrounded by Changde, Yiyang, and Yueyang, is a tourist area. *The Story of Yueyang Tower*, written by Fan Zhongyan, a man of letters and a statesman during the Song Dynasty, stressed the beauty of the landscape, and gave a cultural aspect to the making and naming of local dishes. Representative dishes are Xiaoxiang Turtle, Wuling snake in its own soup, mashed shrimp in lotus pod, Tongting wild duck, jade-belt fish roll, and fish fillet in velvet. These famous local dishes are characterized by deep color, hot and salty flavor, aroma, softness, and beautifully shaped and patterned serving dishes.

The western mountainous area is represented by Jishou, Huaihua, and Dayong. Because this area is mountainous, it has abundant game, mushrooms, and fungi. Its dishes are simple, rich, and pure. The mountain dwellers also make smoked, cured meats that are salty, fragrant, hot, sour, and delicious. For example, steamed cured meat, Double Ninth Festival cold fungi, deep-fried loache (a fish similar to a carp), and hot and spicy frog legs all have the rich flavors of this mountainous region. Hunan cuisine stresses a pungent flavor, and dishes made of cured products also make an important contribution to Hunan food.

**Hubei Cuisine**. Hubei used to be the state of Chu in

ancient times. Hubei food began to develop its own unique style during the Warring States Period. Through development and change over the last 2,000 years, it has become today's Hubei cuisine. Hubei food is famous for its freshwater fish dishes since almost every fish available in Hubei can be prepared into different dishes. There are allfish, bream, Mandarin fish, eel, turtle, giant salamander, crab, shrimp, clam, water chestnut, lotus root, wild duck, and preserved-duck-egg dinners. Among the dishes, steamed bream without soy sauce, turtle with wax gourd, instant-boiled fish with tangerine pulp, and braised chicken with chestnuts are all well-known.

An important feature of Hubei food is its blending of fish with other ingredients. The reason why a single variety of fish can be prepared into so many different dishes is that the cooks are very skilled at blending fish with other ingredients. Many of the famous dishes are prepared from two or more raw materials, giving prominence to the major ingredient while attaching importance to the auxiliary materials. For example, stewed turtle is a dish of turtle and pig's spine, sauted three slivers consists of shredded pork tenderloin, shredded chicken and shredded pig's stomach, and dragon and phoenix marriage is a mixture of eel and chicken. The names of the dishes indicate that Hubei dishes are prepared from more than one ingredient.

The main cooking methods are steaming and simmering. Steaming has been well discussed earlier in this book. Simmering is used to cook dishes with soup. It is done this way: First, fry the major ingredients in oil with seasonings, then put them in an earthen pot and heat them over a low fire for a long time. The special features of Hubei dishes are crisp bones, tender meat, and thick, genuine soup that go well with rice.

Hubei food is divided into four schools: Jingnan, Xiangyang, E'zhou and Han-Mian. The Jingnan school is known for its braised and stewed game, Xiangyang is famous for meat dishes, E'zhou is well known for its vegetarian food, and Han-Mian is famous for its seafood, poultry, and meat dishes. The three steamed dishes in Mianyang (steamed with rice flour, steamed with soy sauce and pickles, and steamed without soy sauce) are typical dishes of the Han-Mian school.

# Fangshan Cuisine

Imperial food from the Ming and pre-Ming dynasties has mostly disappeared by today. What has been preserved is the Qing Dynasty imperial cuisine because its cooks passed down their knowledge and skills, and because the palace kept dietetic records.

General Feng Yuxiang (1882-1948) drove Puyi (1906-1967), the last Qing emperor, out of the Forbidden City in 1924 and disbanded the imperial kitchen. Beihai Park, which had been part of the imperial garden, was opened to the public in 1925. Former cooks of the Qing imperial kitchen, Sun Shaoran, Wang Yushan, Wen Baotian, Niu Wenzhi, and Zhao Yongshou, then opened a tea-house in Beihai Park with help from Zhao Renzhai, former chief of the palace vegetable storehouse. Their teahouse was named Fangshan, which means imitation imperial food. They specialized in making and selling the orthodox pastries of the Qing Palace. From making and selling tea, pastries, and refreshments, Fangshan gradually evolved into serving the traditional dishes of the Qing Palace. Many literati and tourists dined at the restaurant out of admiration for their imperial dishes. The restaurant soon became famous throughout the city because of its fresh raw materials, excellent cooking, and unique flavors.

The Fangshan Restaurant is located in Yilantang Hall on the north side of the Jade Isle, where Empress Dowager Cixi (1835-1908) used to take her meals after sight-seeing in the park. The food made in the Qing Palace for the emperors was called imperial food, so a restaurant operating outside the palace making and selling imperial food was only an imitation.

The restaurant's staple food was cooked wheaten products, such as baked sesame seed cakes with fried minced-meat filling and pastries shaped like apple, peach, fingered citron, and lucky rolls. Whatever wheaten food you ate, you received a good luck message: apple — all is well; peach — longevity, you will live a long life; lucky rolls — everything is fine.

The pastries included steamed cornflour cake, rolls of kidney bean flour, and mashed pea cake, which were all favorites of Empress Dowager Cixi. The most sumptuous food at Fangshan Restaurant was their Manchu and Han banquet. These dishes have the flavors of the Beijing cuisine palace dishes.

There is another Fangshan Restaurant at Dongdan, and a Tingliguan (Listening to the Oriole) restaurant at the Summer Palace.

Although imperial food originated with the common people, imperial food uses different raw materials. The rice, flour, meat, vegetables, melon, fruit, poultry, fish, and delicacies from land and sea were carefully chosen tributes from local officials throughout the country. They were unmatched in quality and purity.

The rice used in the imperial kitchen was only grown at Jade Spring Hill and Tang Spring in the Haidian District, west of Beijing. It was known as Jingxi Rice (west of Beijing) or Haidian Rice. Because of its low yield and excellent taste, only the emperors could eat it. Top quality rice tributes from other parts of the country were also eaten only in the palace.

The mutton eaten in the palace came from the Qingfeng Department (Department of Celebrating Good Harvests). The Qing Dynasty Imperial Kitchen did not serve beef, but it did use cow's milk, which came from the same department. All kinds of melon and fruit, and delicacies from land and sea were tributes from different parts of the country. The palace cooking water was brought every morning from the Jade Spring, which Emperor Qianlong named the "Number One Spring in the world." Poultry and seasonal vegetables were bought at the market. Carefully chosen raw materials were a pre-requisite for preparing imperial food.

All cooks in the imperial kitchen were famous. They cooked their dishes to emphasize taste, color, and shape. Besides tasting good, every dish must look as good as a work of art. Many cooks specialized in making one or several dishes during their lives. The more their labor was divided, the better the dishes were. What they created was not so much a dish as a valuable work of art. Their excellent cooking skills were the key to the making of palace delicacies.

Ingredients in the imperial dishes were strictly blended, and the auxiliary ingredients could not be modified. In public restaurants cooks can adjust the ingredients according to whatever ingredients are available as long as they make dishes with appealing color, aroma, and taste. But in the palace, not a single auxiliary ingredient could be replaced. If a cook wished to create a new dish, he had to assume a risk. If the emperor liked his new dish, his bonus would be impressive, but if the emperor disliked it, the cook would be punished or beaten.

Imperial cuisine stresses the original stock and taste of the dishes. Between shape and taste, taste is emphasized. For example, if the main ingredient is chicken, the dish should taste of chicken. Regardless of what auxiliary ingredients and seasonings are used, they should not affect the taste of the chicken. This was also true of venison, aquatic products, seafood, and of hot and cold dishes. Imperial food requires the presence of color, fragrance, and taste. A dish that looks good but does not taste good is not good, and vice versa.

Cold dishes could not be combined on one plate. A plate of boiled chicken should just be boiled chicken and nothing else. A plate of jellyfish salad should be nothing but jellyfish salad, and the same for smoked fish, preserved eggs, and pork cooked in soy sauce. They should all be served on separate plates. There was nothing similar to the assorted cold dishes of today, which are modeled like a work of modern art.

The dragon and phoenix designs were not used in the palace. The dragon and phoenix were the symbols of the emperor and empress, so they could not be eaten. Special dishes were created for display, such as the snow white bird's nest, which was put in four big bowls with four big Chinese characters that meant, "a long life." Other display dishes had characters like "Moon Festival greetings," "many happy returns of the day," "good luck to you for life," and "New Year's Day greetings." The display dishes were prepared especially to flatter the emperors, but they also were delicious in case the emperor wanted to taste them.

Palace dishes were named simply, usually for their cooking methods, main ingredients, or for the major and minor ingredients so the emperors knew what was in the dish as soon as they saw it. For example, quick-fried chicken with fresh mushrooms; balls of pork, shrimp and sea cucumber; stir-fried fish slices; and quick-fried mutton with onion. Looking through more than 200 years of files from the Qing Palace Imperial Diets, we found no dishes with showy names. Maybe this was because the emperors wanted their ministers to think and act consistently. While the imperial dishes were named differently from those in restaurants, they were very similar to dishes eaten by the common people. Palace cuisine can be regarded as a collection of the best examples of Chinese food. The imperial cooks who started the Fangshan Restaurant in 1925 passed along their cooking skills so that today we can taste imitations of the palace dishes.

## Manchu and Han Banquet

The Manchu and Han banquet was introduced during Emperor Kangxi's reign at the government house and official residence of the upper strata. The Manchu and Han banquet derived from changes in the eating and drinking customs of the Manchus before and after the Manchu rulers moved to Beijing. Before they moved, the banquet had been called the "steamed bun banquet." It was cooked simply and there was little variety in the food served. Most dishes were made of wheat flour and served in large quantities, as was typical of the dietetic customs of the nomadic people.

By the middle Qing Dynasty, the eating habits of the Manchus had been greatly influenced by the eating customs and cooking skills of other nationalities, especially the Han Chinese. For example, in the 53rd year of Kangxi's reign (1714), he gave a "1,000 Elders' Banquet" at the palace to celebrate his 60th birthday and the peaceful times under his rule. Actually, he gave the banquet on March 25th and 27th to honor all the elders in the country who were 65 years or older. The Manchu and Han banquet was attended by more than 2,800 people. The emperor dined with his guests and, in a joyful mood, wrote the four big characters, "Man Han Quan Xi" (meaning the Manchu and Han banquet), thus establishing the rare banquet's place in Chinese dietetic culture.

The banquet featured many of the world's edible delicacies from land and sea, famous mushrooms and fungi, and choice vegetables and fruits. Quality was the key selection criteria, and only the best were chosen. For example, the bear's paw had to be the front paw of the black bear in autumn because then it had short sides and much gelatinous protein. Because the black bear has plenty of food to eat, its paws are strong and fat. The paw is delicious when cooked and contains many nutrients. Another example is the preparation of roast pigs. The pigs must weigh 12 to 13 catties and have been fattened with porridge for three to four days before being slaughtered so they would be

136

more tasty. Moreover, Peking duck, roast chicken, and *harba* (pork leg) were requisite banquet dishes.

The Manchu and Han banquet became popular during the late years of the Qing Dynasty. Many restaurants throughout the country served the banquet to attract customers, but the variety, quantity, and quality of the dishes differed by region to accommodate the preferences of the local people. For example, in Guangzhou, a representative city of southern China, the dragon-tiger-phoenix mixture was often served. The dragon was snake, the tiger was cat, and the phoenix was chicken. The dish was prepared from 250 grams of three varieties of snake meat, 150 grams of cat or civet meat, 100 grams of shredded chicken, and 50 grams of fish maw. The minor ingredients were shredded mushrooms, shredded fungi, lard, sesame oil, dried tangerine peels, refined salt, Shaoxing rice wine, liquor, starch, crisp fritter, white chrysanthemum flowers, and lemon squash.

In the ancient capital city of Xi'an, the dumpling banquet was well-known to locals and foreign tourists. The small dumplings, made in various shapes, were stuffed with such fillings as meat, shrimp, dried scallop, dried shrimp, sesame paste, and mushrooms. Each had a fancy name. For example, the dumpling of black and white fungi was called "white silver and black jade"; the dumpling with a cherry on top was called "lone fragrant flower in bloom."

In north China, the Manchu and Han banquet included a hot pot or instant-boiled mutton, while in northeast China it included stewed beef or mutton or roast sheep. In Sichuan, the banquet included shredded pork stir-fried with chili and fish sauce, and stir-fried diced chicken with peanuts. In Shanxi, Pingyao beef was served at the banquet.

In short, the Manchu and Han banquet varied by region because of different cooking skills, the discovery of new delicacies, and people's regional preferences. However, the style and flavor remained the same, and the luxurious Manchu and Han banquet followed a set etiquette, procedure, and pattern. There were strict rules for the location, number of tables, ranks and positions of those invited, seating, and variety and quantity of the dishes, fruits, and alcoholic drinks. All officials had to wear their official robes and a string of 108 beads typically made of coral or amber. Music was played, and a gun salute was fired as the guests took their seats.

After the guests were seated, they used copper basins and clean towels to wash their faces before drinking tea and eating the exquisite dishes. As they ate and drank, they also played chess, recited poetry, painted, or chatted. After the tables were set, the four fruits (oranges, mandarin oranges, shaddock, and apples) as well as pumpkin seeds, almonds, dried litchis, and sugared lotus seeds were served. The four fruits were also used for decoration.

Dinnerware was placed at each seat. After the guests were seated, waiters peeled fruit for them and served cold dishes to begin the wine drinking. This was followed by four hot courses. After three rounds of drinks, shark's fin was served followed by the second course — a hot dish of meats, then the third and fourth courses. The guests ate and drank as much as they could. The fifth course was cooked rice, porridge, and soup. After the dinner, waiters served a small silver tray of toothpicks, areca (betel nut), and round cardamom kernels. To end the banquet, the guests were given a basin of clean water for washing.

The Manchu and Han banquet became very popular during Xianfeng's reign. After Emperor Xianfeng died, Empress Dowager Cixi ordered that the name, Manchu and Han banquet, not be used outside the palace. Later, Emperor Guangxu issued an order that princes, dukes, and generals could serve the Manchu and Han banquet, which caused it to rebound in Tianjin and other cities.

Following the 1911 Revolution, the Manchu and Han banquet became fashionable in more cities, but the content, etiquette, customs, and formalities gradually were simplified, and the number of dishes reduced from more than 200 to about 100. Archived menus show different banquets served 110 dishes, 108 dishes, and 64 dishes. There no longer was any clear distinction between Manchu and Han dishes, so the banquet became known as "the great Han banquet" in Hong Kong and Guangzhou.

After the Republic of China was founded in 1911, the Manchu and Han banquets were stopped because of wars among the warlords and the poverty of the people. The flourishing tourist trade of recent years has caused a new revival of the banquets.

## Officials' Cuisine

Chinese dishes are classified in two ways: One is by region. One of the regional methods defines four major cuisines based on the eating habits of the people in different regions. They include Sichuan, Guangdong, Shandong and Huai-Yang cuisines. Another regional division comprises nine schools. They are the Beijing, Shandong, Sichuan, Guangdong, Fujian, Huai-Yang, Hubei, Hunan, and

Jiangsu-Zhejiang cuisines.

The second classification is based on the origin of the dishes. This system includes the palace, officials', common people's, mountain and forest temples', and ethnic minorities' dishes, and dishes of foreign countries. This second classification is very old. It was based on the rigid stratification of China's feudal society, which lasted for thousands of years and forced different ways of living upon the people. The differences in the stratification of the foods were recorded in the *Unofficial Annals of the States* in the Spring and Autumn Period as follows: "The emperor ate ox, sheep, and pig; princes and dukes ate ox; ministers ate sheep; officials ate pig; scholars ate fish; and the common people ate vegetables." Feudal ethics and different living standards among the differing strata resulted in Chinese food being classified into the palace, officials', and common people's cuisines.

Officials' cuisine, also called the cuisine of the officialdom and literati, included the famous dishes of the wealthy people. The standards for the officials' cuisine were lower than for palace food, but remained far superior to the common people's cuisine. Officials' dishes were created by working people, but were eaten only by feudal bureaucrats, aristocrats, and the rich.

Many bureaucrats and aristocrats ate luxurious food. Huang Sheng of the Tang Dynasty "cooked three catties of venison from dawn to sunset every day, and said with joy: 'It is well done now!' He did this for 40 years." Lu Mengzheng of the Song Dynasty had chicken tongue soup every day, the result being that chicken feathers were piled up like a hill. The family cook of Cai Jing, a prime minister of the Song Dynasty, killed 1,000 quail every day.

Family cooks knew how to make tasty dishes and gradually created their own cooking styles. The luxurious life, rich resources, and abundant raw materials provided important conditions for the creation of officials' cuisine.

Another important condition that aided the creation of officials' cuisine was the combination of famous cooks and gourmets. Famous dishes require cooks and gourmets, and these required education, culture, and a high standard of living. Cooks improved the dishes based on the gourmets' comments so that each dish became better and better. The gourmets helped discard bad dishes and retain dishes with good color, fragrance, and taste.

Gourmets were common throughout history. Most were literati, ministers, or officials, such as Confucius in the Spring and Autumn and Warring States Periods, Su Shi and Lu You in the Song Dynasty, Ni Zan in the Yuan Dynasty, Li Yu in the late years of the Ming Dynasty, and Yuan Mu in the Qing Dynasty. They were food and drink experts who left behind many penetrating remarks and special writings. For example, Dongpo pork, Yunlin goose, Confucian dishes, Sui Garden dishes, and Tan family dishes were all famous officials' dishes that have been passed down to later generations.

The special features of the officials' dishes are that the materials are carefully selected and the cooking is exquisite. Yuan Shikai, the first president of the Republic of China, had many family cooks with excellent skills. He liked to eat duck, especially steamed duck. In winter, he ate duck steamed without soy sauce at every meal. To make sure the duck was more nutritious and tasty, he ordered the farmers to powder pilose antler, mix it with sorghum, and feed it to the ducks.

Pan Zuyin, minister of the board of works during Xianfeng's reign in the Qing Dynasty, had a profound knowledge of how to eat well. In his home, bean curd was braised together with the brains of live ducks to make a delicious dish.

Great attention was paid to cooking methods and careful preparation. For example, Dongpo Pork was named after Su Dongpo (or Su Shi) who described it thus: "Clean the pan, put a little water into it, and cook the pork over a low fire. Don't hurry, but wait until it is well done. It tastes natural and good when it is ready."

Diced chicken with peanuts stir-fried with chili sauce was a dish created by the family cook of Ding Baozhen, an imperial inspector for Shandong Province and the Governor of Sichuan Province. The main ingredient is the breast meat of roosters several months old. The meat is fried over a medium to hot fire. When the chicken cubes separate, add the mixed gravy and salted peanuts. Then shake and turn the ingredients several times.

The Tan Family cuisine in Beijing and the Confucius Family cuisine that now exist reveal their careful choice of materials, preparation of ingredients, and cooking.

Officials' cuisine stresses a family atmosphere during meal times. At that time, there was no etiquette to make people overcautious at meals as there was in the palace, nor was there interference from neighboring tables as in a restaurant. It was similar to common family life, where there is no restraint and diners concentrate on eating.

In the feudal society, the literati and officials always enjoyed food and drink as a fruit of the culture. They liked natural tastes, cleanliness, beauty, and sought benefit from their food. They were interested in tasting the deliciousness of their food and they treated good food as a work of art. Tan Zhuanqing, founder of the Tan Family cuisine, was a connoisseur of cultural relics as well as a gourmet. The Tan Family cuisine stresses both the original juices and taste of the ingredients. Both Tan Zhuanqing and his father, Tan Zongjun, preferred their food to have a natural taste.

Pan Zuyin was a man of letters and a gourmet. Toward the end of the Qing Dynasty, the Guangheju Restaurant had many renowned cooks and was famous throughout Beijing. Pan Zuyin was a frequent customer of the restaurant. He taught the cooks how to cook fish, then had them cook it for him using this procedure: Boil the cleaned carp for a few minutes, then use your hands to break the fish into two parts. Add the minor ingredients and flavorings and steam the fish until it is done. The special features of this dish are that neither a cutting tool nor cooking oil are used. The fish is steamed to keep its original flavor. It is tender and both the meat and soup are delicious. The cook found it satisfactory and guests spoke highly of it. This Pan Family dish was later introduced in restaurants as "Pan's fish" or "Pan's steamed fish."

There are many other dishes that were originally created for officials' families, then later became popular in restaurants. Their common feature was to preserve the original taste and stock.

Exquisite dinnerware serves as an accent to tasty dishes and adds glory to banquets. Today, people can see the exquisite dinnerware from Confucius' mansion, including silver and porcelain sets. Many sets are uniquely shaped and are very beautiful. Some dinnerware was especially designed and made for special dishes. The Tan Family

Food Restaurant in Beijing has many specially designed sets, such as the plates for shark's fin, which are slightly higher in the center to make the shark's fin more appealing.

The shape of dishes should not affect their natural taste and flavor. Loss outweighs gain if the taste of the dish is lost for the sake of shape. Yuan Mei in his *Sui Garden Menu* said, "Good food should be matched by good dinnerware." Officials' cuisine stresses taste foremost, then uses good dinnerware to accent the good taste.

Many dishes were named after the literati who invented or especially liked them. For example, Dongpo pork, stir-fried diced chicken with peanuts, and Pan's fish. Many years ago some Beijing restaurants that were frequented by literati and officials, served dishes named for famous people. For example, Wu's dishes in the Sansheng Restaurant, of which the most famous was Wu's fish slices: Cut fresh fish into long slices and cook the slices with good quality soy sauce and water from Yao's family well in the south. Wu here referred to Wu Junshe or Wu Yansheng, an imperial cook.

Hu Shi's fish in the Chenghuayuan Restaurant: Cut fresh carp into small cubes and cook it into thick soup with three fresh delicacies, such as abalone, sea cucumber, shrimp, chicken cubes, mushrooms, or bamboo shoots. The dish was invented by Dr. Hu Shi and prepared for him by his cook.

The Guangheju Restaurant was known for its wide variety of famous dishes. Most of these were officials' dishes. When these literati and officials met in restaurants, they taught the cooks how to make their family delicacies. Apart from Pan's fish, the restaurant also served Jiang's

144

bean curd, a soft bean curd prepared with shrimp roe, fermented soybeans, and bamboo shoot cubes. It was taught by Jiang Yuntao, magistrate of a prefecture, hence the name. Other dishes were Han's pork leg, a dish prepared from the top part of a pig leg along with five flavorings. It was taught by Han Xinshe. Tao's dish was taught by Tao Fu, a vice minister in the Qing Dynasty; Hu's fish was taught by Hu Guqing, a vice minister in the Qing Dynasty, and Zeng's fish was taught by Zeng Guofan.

Today, the Beijing Television Station has a special program on Chinese cooking that invites famous chefs to demonstrate their cooking skills and literati and artists to teach their own specialties.

# Chinese Stir-Fried Dishes

## Guo Feng

The invention of Chinese stir-fried dishes greatly influenced Chinese cooking. Stir-fried dishes use a wide range of ingredients and are cooked quickly so they retain the nutrients of the meats and vegetables. Stir-fried dishes can be meat dishes, vegetable dishes, or meat and vegetable mixtures. Popular dishes found in the north include fried bean curd with minced meats, fried pork with shredded ginger, and quick-fried mutton with onion. These popular dishes are known throughout China.

Those Chinese families who eat cereals as their staple food often serve stir-fried mixtures of meat and vegetables. Stir-fried dishes first appeared after the Han Dynasty and were common even in the palace and in officials' residences. In the Han and pre-Han dynasties, most dishes were thick soups and uninspired boiled, deep-fried, or roasted dishes without seasonings.

The character "chao" for the word "stir-fry" does not appear in the book *Explanatory Notes for the Ancient Classics*, which was completed in the 12th year of Yongyuan's reign in the Eastern Han Dynasty (100 A.D.). In a rhyming dictionary compiled in the 6th century, the ancient form of "chao" was first seen, but it meant to stir cereal in a pot without oil to dry it. In cooking dishes, "chao" means to stir-fry meat or vegetables with seasonings in a small amount of oil or fat at the proper temperature until they are done.

When stir-frying Chinese dishes, the Chinese wok must be used. If a flat-bottom pan was used, the taste would be different. The temperature of the oil in the pan is very important. For example, when stir-frying hot pepper powder, a skilled chef can make it as red as blood. In Sichuan, stir-fried bean curd with minced meat is a dish of white bean curd in red oil, which is very appealing to the eye. If the temperature of the oil is not well controlled, the fried hot pepper powder turns burnt ochre and loses its appeal.

Ingredients for stir-fried dishes are mostly meats and vegetables cut into small sizes by mincing, dicing, slicing, shredding, slivering, and forming into balls. Even though the cooking time is short, the flavors of the seasonings permeate the dishes.

The term "stir-fry" includes stir-fry without soy sauce, stew-fry, half-fry, grab-fry, stir-fry for a shorter or longer time, stir-fry with raw meat, stir-fry with boiled meat, fry without water, soft fry, hard fry, and quick-fry. Broiling, stewing, braising, and boiling in a covered pot are all cooking methods developed based on stir-frying.

The stir-fried dish was invented at the latest during the Southern and Northern Dynasties (420-581). Jia Sixie, an outstanding agronomist in the late years of the Northern Wei Dynasty (386-534), wrote the *Essential Points for the Common People* in 544. It is the earliest and most complete agricultural encyclopedia still in existence in China. In it he described a "duck frying method" that was done this way: "Use a fatted duck, as big as a pheasant, with its head cut off and its internal organs and tail gland removed. Wash it clean and chop it up like minced meat. Cut green onion bulbs into thin shreds. Add salt, fermented soybean sauce, and stir-fry it until it is well done. Add minced ginger and Chinese prickly ash."

The process exactly describes the stir-frying method used today. Jia Sixie does not say whether oil is used, but his smooth writing style and the words "duck frying" indicate that oil should be used, otherwise the chopped green onions would burn. It could not be called "frying" if no oil was used; therefore, the "duck frying method" he describes exactly duplicates the method now used to stir-fry minced meat.

Another cooking method, the "pickled Chinese cabbage cooking method," is also similar to the stir-frying method used today. It is done this way: Choose fatty pork (or mutton and venison) and cut it into thin shreds. Put the meat in a wok together with fermented soybean juice and salt and stir them, then add pickled Chinese cabbage with its juice. This dish is similar to fried pickled Chinese cabbage with shredded pork.

The menus of the Tang and Song Dynasties included stir-frying, but they often called the method "stewing." The "five animal dish" eaten in early spring during the Tang Dynasty was a dish in which slices of mutton, beef, rabbit, bear's meat, and venison were stir-fried without soy sauce until they were well done, then cut into thin slivers and mixed with dressings.

The *Forest of Recorded Affairs* from the Song Dynasty describes "Dongpo fish" like this: "Cut the fish meat into long slivers. Preserve them with salt and vinegar for a short while, then dry them with paper. Mix spices and starch. Coat the fish slivers with the mixture, spread the slivers and rub them with sesame seed oil, then stir them in the frying pot." This is the same dish we eat today. Many stir-fried dishes were popular in the Northern Song Dynasty, but they became even more common in the Ming and Qing Dynasties.

Stir-frying can be used for all kinds of ingredients, such as vegetables, including eggplant, cucumber, cabbage, spinach, potato, taro, celery, and bamboo shoots; wild game; seafood; domestic animals; poultry; gluten; bean curd; cooked rice; and rice cakes.

Tender meat should be grab-fried (coat the shredded or sliced meat with a thin paste of flour, fry it in oil slightly, then remove it. Heat the oil in the wok, add cornstarch mixed with water and flavorings, and boil the mixture. Then return the fried meat and stir it quickly). Tender meat can also be quick-fried (fried quickly over a hot fire) or stir-fried (sauté with thickened, starchy gravy slightly burned in deep oil, and stir-fry with thin starchy gravy boiled instantly in water).

Tough meat or large pieces of meat can be stewed or braised until they are well done after they have been stir-fried with flavorings. Some materials can be dry-fried before stewing, such as pea sprouts and beef, some are fried after they are cooked, such as twice-cooked pork with chili sauce, or fried together with a fixed amount of juices. Some dishes are fried with mixtures of raw and cooked materials (the peanuts used in the diced chicken with peanuts and chili sauce are fried in advance). Mixtures of meats and vegetables fried together are common.

In most cases flavorings are added in the course of stir-frying, but in some cases, the major ingredients are preserved and their flavors fixed before they are stir-fried. Many flavorings are mixtures, such as sweet and sour sauce, sweet and chili sauce, spicy and chili sauce, five-flavored sauce, and fish and chili sauce.

In stir-fried dishes, ingredients of different flavors are blended so that the flavors mix together in the course of heating to produce a new, delicious taste. This is true for stir-fried pork shreds with ginger, fried garlic shoots with pork, shredded pork stir-fried in soy sauce of Beijing flavor, and shredded pork stir-fried with fish and chili sauce. Cooks add garlic, ginger, and onion in the course of heating the ingredients so that they permeate each other to produce a new taste that stimulates the diner's appetite.

More attention was paid to naming dishes, blending colors, and cutting skills after literati became involved in Chinese cooking. Su Shi, a famous man of letters in the Song Dynasty, Ni Zan (1301-1374), a famous painter in the Yuan Dynasty, Xu Wei (1521-1593), a famous painter and literati in the Ming Dynasty, and Yuan Mei (1716-1798), a famous man of letters, were all gourmets and good cooks. Through their influence, Chinese stir-fried dishes were made more artistic and colorful. For example, "five-willow twig fish" is a dish of fish stir-fried with shredded onion, ginger, winter bamboo shoots, red pepper, and winter mushrooms. Stir-fried chicken with chestnuts and shredded chicken stir-fried with winter bamboo shoots are also delicious.

There are many ways of cutting the ingredients, such as shredding, dicing, lumping, and slicing. The knife should follow the grain of the meat while cutting. Pattern cutting is a very artistic cutting method. For example, stir-fried kidney is a common dish, but the meat can be cut into many different shapes such as wheat ears, litchi shapes, or the Chinese character for longevity. The differing shapes not only give the dish a pleasing appearance, they also help the dish cook evenly, remove bad odors, and absorb flavors.

Temperature should be strictly controlled when stir-frying, because the taste of a dish will differ as a result of the duration and degree of heating. Temperature is more easily adjusted with deep-fried foods because there is more oil in the pot. Stir-fried dishes depend entirely on the heat of the oil and the wok surface because the ingredients are cut in small pieces, little oil is used, and the cooking time is short. This is a crucial test of the chef's cooking ability.

In his book *The Story of Chef Wang Xiaoyu*, Yuan Mei of the Qing Dynasty described a scene of Wang's cooking like this:

He stood by the cooking range on one leg, the other leg raised. He kept his eyes on the cooking range to observe the temperature. He heard nothing when others called him. He shouted "Big fire!" one moment, and the stoker instantly made the fire blaze like the red sun. The next moment, he shouted: "Small fire!" and the stoker immediately took away some of the burning firewood to reduce the heat. Another moment, he shouted: "Stop for the moment!" and the stoker instantly took away all firewood to stop the burning. He commanded with perfect ease like a general commanding his army.

In *Sui Garden Menu*, under the title "Instructions on

Temperature," Yuan Mei wrote: "The most important point in cooking food is temperature. A hot fire is preferred when stir-frying a dish. If the fire is too low the dish will become tasteless. A low fire is used when stewing or simmering foods. If the fire is too hot, the food burns. When a hot fire is used before a low fire, it reduces the juice of the food." Controlling the temperature accurately requires much cooking experience in using different temperatures for different dishes. One can only gain this knowledge by sense; it is very difficult to explain in words.

This book includes an appendix with instructions on how to prepare and cook imperial dishes. However, when you cook the dishes using the recipes in this book, you will find the dishes differ from the orthodox dishes served in the Fangshan Restaurant in terms of color, flavor, and taste because of the temperatures you use and other factors.

# How Chinese Dishes
# Were Named

China is a country that attaches great importance to names, honor, and prestige. The set phrase, to "achieve both fame and wealth," gives the true meaning of the word "fame." Only when people are famous worldwide have they laid the foundation to achieve great wealth.

The owners of many famous restaurants throughout the dynasties won praise from their customers for their good service and became famous. This, in turn, brought them more customers and still better business. Among them are the Donglaishun, Quanjude, and Hongbinlou restaurants in Beijing, the Songhelou Restaurant in Suzhou, the Louwailou Restaurant in Hangzhou, the Laozhengxing Restaurant in Shanghai, the Goubuli Restaurant in Tianjin, and the Juchunyuan Restaurant in Fuzhou. Of course, the pre-requisites for the restaurants being well known were their delicious food, fair prices, and honesty, or they would not have been famous.

During the period of the Qin and Han Dynasties dishes were named for their major ingredients and cooking methods. During the Southern and Northern Dynasties, some dishes received fancy names.

When ordinary dishes were given beautiful names, it

raised the attractiveness of the dishes and made diners happy. For example, sliced fish mixed with orange was called "powdered gold and minced jade," camel's foot simmered with hearts of rape was called "desert boat sails on green," quail and its eggs cooked together was called "mother and children get together," chicken cooked with bear's paw was called "palm controls the land," a dish of shrimp, sliced tender bamboo shoots and mushrooms was called "leaves of wind, frost and snow," a dish of sea cucumber, prawns, chicken breast, white fungus, and water chestnuts was called "butterflies swarm the peonies," and a dish of chicken and soft-shelled turtle was called "Xiang Yu the Conqueror says goodbye to his concubine." Fancy names reminded people of other things during the banquets and created a pleasant dining atmosphere.

Naming dishes is an artistic expression of the inventors' ideas. Often, dishes are named for natural phenomena and things that exist in nature: The four seasons, wind, flowers, snow, plants, gold, jade, gems, animals, and the moon have all been used in naming dishes to add beauty and appeal, to attract customers, and to increase diners' appetites. Some examples are the "wind lulling cake" (a pancake first baked on a pan, then deep-fat fried before eating), "snowflake shortcake" (similar to the sweet and salty square available in Beijing today), "snow-box vegetable" (a green vegetable steamed with milk cakes), "snowflake bean curd" (stir-fried minced bean curd), "lotus flower sliced chicken" (a chicken dish made of quick stir-fried egg white, sliced chicken breast and corn starch), "100-flower chess pieces" (flat noodles cut into pieces and served with soup), "squirrel-shaped croaker," and "black dragon spitting pearls" (sea cucumber braised with quail eggs). These names stress the taste, bright color, flavor, thick aroma and shape of the dishes.

The colors used in naming dishes are red, yellow, white and green. Psychometric tests show these colors help stimulate the appetite while blue and azure colors cause disgust. Moreover, bright colors produce a pleasant sensation and stimulate the appetite while dark colors have the opposite effect. The naming of dishes follows this principle.

People sometimes use names with lustre rather than color to give the dishes a sense of quality, as in the dish "powdered gold and minced jade." Gold and jade are both expensive, have a shining lustre, and produce a pleasant sensation. Also used are jadeite ("jadeite shrimp and jadeite thick soup"), amber ("amber pork and amber peanuts"), crystal ("crystal pork leg" and "crystal shrimp cake"), pearl ("pearl turtle" and "pearl meatballs"), and brocade ("brocade ribbon soup"). If there are dark colored foods, people sometimes use lustrous terms to describe them.

Some dish names tell interesting stories. For example, the dish "five duke mixture of fish and meat" is described in the *Miscellanies of the Western Capital* as: "Lou Hu was an eloquent speaker and a frequent visitor of the five dukes, where he received delicious food. He blended the foods into a mixture of fish and meat, a rare delicacy later known as the 'five-duke mixture'." The five dukes refer to the five brothers of the mother of Emperor Chengdi of the Western Han Dynasty, who all received the title of 'duke' on the same day. The story tells that when Lou Hu visited these families, they all gave him cooked mixtures of fish and meat, but each had a different flavor. He blended them all together and cooked them again to produce a new flavor. His dish was later known as the five-duke mixture.

Hangzhou was the capital city of the Southern Song Dynasty. It was also the burial place of the famous general Yue Fei who led the army of resistance against the invading troops of the Jin Dynasty. To express their hatred for the treacherous court official Qin Hui, people in Hangzhou called the deep-fried twisted dough sticks, which are a breakfast delicacy, "deep-fried Hui." The people in Beijing called them "deep-fried devils" during the period when Japan occupied Beijing, because they called the Japanese invaders "devils." During the same period, people in Sichuan, a rear base for resistance against the Japanese, called their local dish of rice crust with mixed dressings "bomb Tokyo."

Some dishes were named to honor their inventors. The dish, "husband and wife sliced lung," was invented by Guo Chaohua and his wife who lived in Chengdu. Pockmarked lady's bean curd was a special dish invented by a pockmarked woman named Chen who owned a small restaurant near the Happiness Bridge in a northern suburb of Chengdu, Sichuan Province.

The "Duke of Pei's dog meat," a popular dish in northern Jiangsu Province, is said to have been invented by Liu Bang, the founding emperor of the Han Dynasty. He had been awarded the title, Duke in Pei, which is today called Peixian County.

"West Lake fish with vinegar" is also called "brother and sister-in-law's fish with vinegar." The younger brother of a fishing family and his sister-in-law, who both lived near West Lake in Hangzhou, were both good at cooking fish with vinegar. They ran away after killing a despot who tried to blackmail the fishermen. The neighbors continued making their special dish in honor of them, and the fish dish has been a local delicacy for centuries.

"Dongpo Pork" is said to have been invented by Su Dongpo, a famous man of letters in the Song Dynasty, when he was an official in Hangzhou. He once mobilized the local people to dredge the lake, and he served stewed pork in Shaoxing rice wine with special flavor instead of water to reward them. The pork dish was praised as Dongpo's number one dish.

The dragon and phoenix mixture tells a story from the period of the Three Kingdoms (220-265 A.D.). General Zhao Yun escorted Liu Bei, who was newly married to Sun Shangxiang, a sister of Sun Quan, duke of Wu, to Jingzhou. They were greeted by Zhuge Liang and his civilian and military officials. A grand banquet was held outside the southern gate of Jingzhou City, and the first course served was the dragon and phoenix mixture. The chef used eel for the golden dragon and chicken for the colorful phoenix to form a flying dragon and dancing phoenix on the plate. It implied good luck and beauty. The sweet and sour dish is golden yellow. The meat melts in your mouth and the skin is crisp. It is a delicacy in the Hubei cuisine that is often served at wedding dinners.

"Thong eel" tells a story about the 8th year of the reign of Emperor Daoguang of the Qing Dynasty. Zhu Caizhe, who had been born in Jianli County, Hubei Province, was appointed magistrate of Yilan County in Taiwan. Shortly after taking office, he had to decide a case where eels had destroyed the boundaries between paddy fields. The paddies in Taiwan seethed with eels, which lived in holes they dug in the ridges of the fields. Their holes destroyed the boundaries between the paddies and caused many civil disputes.

The local people did not eat eels, so such cases were extremely common. After investigating the cause of the boundary dispute, he ordered his family chef to cook an eel dish. He then asked both the plantiffs and the defendants to taste it, and they all thought it was delicious. From then on, the people in the county caught eels for food and no longer filed suits before him. It is said that the dish was invented by a cook named Gou'er (the Chinese word for dog), which the local people called "thong," hence the name "Thong eel." Thong eel, which is crisp, soft, sweet and sour, is a famous dish in the Hubei cuisine.

There are many stories and allusions behind the names of Chinese dishes, which add to the mystique of the Chinese dietetic culture. There are elegant names, vulgar names, and farfetched names, but they all were intended to stimulate the appetite. The names of the dishes were mostly related to the status of the customers. At banquets attended by businessmen, the dishes were named to promote their business and their profitability, while palace dishes were named to wish the rulers good luck and a long life.

# 54 Imperial Dishes

## Brooding Phoenix

**Major ingredients:**

1 chicken, 15 quail eggs.

**Minor ingredients:**

50 g each of water-saturated mushrooms, bamboo shoots, and fish maw.

**Seasonings:**

20 g cooking wine, 10 g soy sauce, 600 g light broth, 50 g onion chunks, 25 g ginger, 15 g corn starch dissolved in water, 2 g salt, and 15 g chicken fat.

**Cooking method:**

1. Cut open the chicken vertically along the spine. Remove the internal organs, wash the chicken, then remove the leg bones from inside its belly. Boil the chicken for a short time in water, then put it in an earthenware pot. Add small amounts of cooking wine, salt, onion, and ginger. Stew the mixture over a low fire for about two hours, then pour it into a big bowl and steam it with its own gravy in a steamer.

2. Shred the mushrooms, bamboo shoots, and fish maw. Boil them for 1 to 2 minutes in hot water, then remove them. Put them in a pot with the light broth and a small amount of salt and cooking wine. Simmer them for three minutes. Remove them and put them on a plate.

3. Put the quail eggs in a pot of water and boil them for about 5 minutes. Remove the eggs, shell them, wash them, and put them on the plate half burying them in the mushroom, bamboo, and fish maw shreds. Remove the steamed chicken from the soup and place it breast upward on top of the shreds.

4. Pour 250 g of stock from the steamed chicken into a pot. Add a small amount of soy sauce and cooking wine, then add the moistened starch to thicken the soup. Drip the chicken fat into the soup. Pour the thickened soup over the chicken.

# Goldfish-Shaped Duck's Webs

**Major ingredients:**

12 duck's webs.

**Minor ingredients:**

100 g chopped chicken, 30 g each of water-saturated mushrooms, bamboo shoots, and fish maw, 450 g light broth, 2 egg whites, 25 g cucumber skin, some cherries and sliced carrot, and small amounts of cooking wine, salt, soy sauce, wheat flour, chicken fat, moistened corn startch, and moistened corn flour.

**Cooking method:**

1. Pour water into a pot and cook the duck's webs for about 15 minutes; remove them when they are about half cooked. Cool the webs in clean water, then remove the bones and tough tendons from the back. Put the webs on a plate, sole up. Spread some wheat flour on the heels of the webs.

2. Shred the mushrooms, bamboo shoots, and fish maw. Bring them to a boil in water then remove them and simmer them in 250 g light broth for two minutes. Remove them and put them on a plate. Put the egg white in a bowl and whip it until it is frothy. Shred the cucumber skin.

3. Add the minced chicken to the broth, then add a small amount of cooking wine, table salt, moistened corn flour, and chicken fat and stir everything well. Pour in the whipped egg white and mix everything into a paste (mashed chicken).

4. Mould the mashed chicken by hand into 5 cm 'goldfish,' and place them by the heels of the webs. Halve the cherries and place a cherry half on both sides of the fish heads for eyes. Cut the carrots into the shape of dorsal fins and place them on the backs of the fish. Place the shredded cucumber on both sides of the carrot fins as scales. Make 12 goldfish in all. Steam the duck webs and goldfish in a steamer for 6-8 minutes. Take them out and place them on a plate.

5. Pour 200 g light broth into a wok and add a small amount of cooking wine and salt. Boil the mixture, skim off the floating foam, thicken it with a small amount of moistened corn starch, and pour the chicken gravy over the dish.

# Fish with Hidden Swords

**Major ingredient:**

1 grass carp.

**Minor ingredient:**

1 cucumber.

**Seasonings:**

20 g cooking wine, 1.5 g salt, 100 g sugar, 70 g vinegar, 10 g ketchup, a little chopped onion and ginger, 100 g moistened corn starch, 2 egg whites, 200 g peanut oil, and 250 g broth.

**Cooking method:**

1. Remove the scales, gills, and internal organs from the carp, then cut off the head and tail and set them aside. Skin and de-bone the fish, then slice the meat into 20 rectangles, each 5 cm x 3 cm x 0.3 cm. Put the slices in a bowl, add small amounts of cooking wine and salt, and set them aside for 10 minutes.

2. Cut the skin of the cucumber into 20 pieces, each 5 cm long, and preserve them with small amounts of salt and cooking wine for 5 minutes.

3. Lay the fish slices flat on a cutting block. Put one piece of cucumber on each fish slice and roll up the fish slice. Make 20 rolls in all. Put the egg white and moistened corn starch in a bowl and mix them into a paste.

4. Put the peanut oil in the wok and heat it to medium hot. Dip the fish head, fish rolls, and fish tail in the egg white paste, then deep-fat fry them until they turn golden yellow. Remove them and drain off the oil. Place the fried fish head and tail on two sides of a plate and place the fish rolls between them in the shape of a fish.

5. Pour out most of the oil from the wok leaving just enough to stir-fry the chopped onion and ginger for a few seconds. Add small amounts of cooking wine, salt, sugar, vinegar, and ketchup, and bring everything to a boil. Mix in a small amount of moistened corn starch and peanut oil, then pour the mixture over the fish head and rolls.

# Taiji Bird's Nest

**Major ingredient:**
200 g water-saturated bird's nest.
**Minor ingredients:**
200 g water-saturated hairlike fungus, 300 g pork broth, 50 g chicken stock, 1 red cherry, and 1 green cherry.
**Seasonings:**
Small amounts of cooking wine, salt, onion, ginger, light broth, moistened corn starch, chicken fat, and oyster oil.
**Cooking method:**
1. Simmer the water-saturated bird's nest in 300 g of boiling pork broth, then place it toward the edge of a large plate.
2. Put the water-saturated hairlike fungus and small amounts of pork broth, onion, and ginger, and 50 g chicken stock in a bowl and steam them in a steamer for one hour. Drain the soup and put the fungus on the opposite side of the plate to form the *yin-yang* symbol. Place a red cherry in one side and green cherry in the other side of the symbol.
3. Use two woks. Heat small amounts of the moistened

corn starch, light broth, and chicken fat in one of the woks to make gravy and pour it over the bird's nest. Mix small amounts of moistened corn starch, light broth, and oyster oil in the other wok and pour it over the hair-like moss.

# Duck Rolls with Three Delicacies

**Major ingredient:**
250 g cooked duck meat.
**Minor ingredients:**
50 g bamboo shoots (tender part), 50 g water-saturated mushrooms, and 4 eggs.
**Seasonings:**
50 g bread crumbs, 50 g wheat flour, small amounts of onion, ginger, salt, cooking wine, pepper, coriander, moistened corn starch, and sesame oil.
**Cooking method:**
1. Cut the duck meat into 3-cm-long slivers. Cut small amounts of onion and ginger into thin slivers. Cut a small amount of coriander into chunks and place everything in a bowl. Add the bread crumbs and a small amount of salt, cooking wine, pepper, and sesame oil, and mix the ingredients into a stuffing.

2. Whip the eggs and mix in a small amount of salt and moistened corn starch. Pour the batter into a heated, oiled wok and make 10 thin, round wrappings each with a diameter of 9 cm.

3. Mix the wheat flour and water into a paste. Spread a small amount of the paste over an egg wrapping, then place the duck stuffing on top of the wrapping and roll it

into a cylinder. Make 10 rolls in this way. Dip the rolls in the remaining paste, then coat them with the bread crumbs. Deep-fat fry the rolls in medium hot oil until they become golden yellow. Remove the rolls and let the oil drain off.

# Buddha Prawns

**Major ingredient:**

12 whole prawns

**Minor ingredient:**

100 g chopped shrimp, 1 egg white, 5 g chopped rape, and 5 g chopped ham.

**Seasonings:**

Small amounts of cooking wine, salt, white sugar, moistened corn flour, chopped onion, and ginger, 250 g peanut oil.

**Cooking method:**

1. Remove the heads from the prawns, clean them of sand and intestines, and set them aside. Fry the heads in a small amount of peanut oil until they become red, then add small amounts of cooking wine, salt, white sugar, light broth, onion, and ginger and simmer the heads over a low fire for 3-5 minutes. Remove the heads when the soup has thickened and place the heads on one side of a plate.

2. Shell the body of the prawns but leave the tails intact. Cut open the prawns at the back and de-vein them. Add salt and cooking wine to them.

3. Combine the raw egg whites with the chopped shrimp and add small amounts of salt, cooking wine, corn flour, and oil. Mix everything into a paste.

4. Spread the paste over the prawns, put a small amount of chopped rape and ham on the prawns and then deep-fat fry the prawns in peanut oil. Remove the prawns when they turn golden brown and let the oil drain off. Place the prawn bodies on the plate next to the heads to make a complete prawn.

# Black Rice Porridge

**Ingredients:**
200 g black rice, 500 g water.
**Cooking method:**
Wash the black rice clean. Put the rice in a pot with the water and cook it over a hot fire until it boils. Skim off the foam and reduce the heat to low. Cook the rice for two hours. Use more water if you want a thinner porridge, use less water for a thicker porridge.

# Chicks to Be Fed

**Ingredients:**
160 g dough made from flour and oil, 150 g mashed red beans, 100 g egg yolk, a few black sesame seeds, and a small amount of sugar water.
**Cooking method:**
1. Put the egg yolk in a bowl and whip it with a whisk. Put the wok over a medium fire. When the wok is slightly heated, slowly pour in the whipped egg yolk and vigorously stir it in only one direction for 5 minutes using a

long spoon. Drain off the oil and the "egg down" is ready.

2. Separate the oil dough into 12 balls and press them into 7-cm-flat wrappings. Stuff each wrapping with the mashed red beans and mold the wrapping into the body of a chicken with a head and beak on the top. Place a black sesame seed on each side of the head for eyes. Bake the chickens in a medium hot oven until they turn golden brown. Brush the chicken bodies with a small amount of sugar water and cover them with the "egg down."

# Mandarin Duck-Shaped Crisp Cake

**Ingredients:**

150 g wheat flour, 50 g lard, 75 g mashed red bean filling, 75 g of osmanthus-sugar filling, and 750 g peanut oil (actual comsumption 40 g).

**Cooking method:**

1. Sift the wheat flour and separate it in half. Use one half of the flour and a small amount of water to make a dough; then use the other half of the flour and the lard make a dough. Divide the dough into 15 balls. Flatten each of the water-dough balls. Wrap one water-dough wrapping around an oil-dough ball. Round the ball and then roll it out long. Roll the dough up, gently press it flat, and then roll it out again. Then start at one edge of the dough and roll it up leaving a 5-cm flap unrolled.

Roll the 5 cm flap of dough very thin, then cut it in half starting at the middle of the roll to the opposite edge. Pull one of the flaps of dough around to the side and stick it to the end of the roll. Do the same with the other flap of dough. Cut the roll in half at the middle. Press each half into two round doughs. Stick the layered side on the block, and make 15 round wrappers from each dough (a total of 30 wrappers).

2. Divide each of the two fillings into 15 parts. Stuff one part into a wrapper and shape them like dumplings. Pair a dumpling of each filling and stick the edges together. Flute the edges of the dumplings to look like feathers. Deep-fat fry the dumplings in moderately hot peanut oil until they become golden yellow. Remove them and let the oil drain off.

# Birthday Peach

**Ingredients:**
225 g raised dough, 25 g white sugar, 100 g mashed date filling, a few coriander leaves, some baking-soda water, and a small amount of red food coloring.

**Cooking method:**
1. Mix the raised dough with a small amount of baking-soda water and white sugar. Knead the dough well, then let it stand for 10 minutes. Divide the dough into 15 pieces and flatten each piece by hand into 10 cm wrappers.

2. Divide the mashed date filling into 15 parts. Stuff one part into each wrapper and form the dumpling into the shape of a peach. Score a slight dimple on the side of the peaches and place two coriander leaves under each peach. Let the peaches stand for 10 minutes, then steam them for 8 minutes. Remove the peaches from the steamer and apply a bit of red food coloring to make a rose blush on the peaches.

# Sweet Snow Lotus

**Ingredients:**

100 g lotus seeds and 200 g white sugar.

**Cooking method:**

1. Remove the green skins and green hearts from the lotus seeds saving only the white flesh. Wash them in warm water.

2. Put the seeds in a bowl, cover the seeds with water, and steam them for 20 minutes. Remove the seeds, drain off the water, and put the seeds in a soup bowl.

3. Put 500 g water in a pot, add the white sugar and bring the water to a boil. Pour the syrup on the lotus seeds.

# Sesame Cakes Stuffed with Fried Minced Pork

**Ingredients:**

500 g raised dough, 50 g white sugar, 25 g sesame seeds, 50 g sesame oil, and some sugar water.

**Cooking method:**

1. Thoroughly mix the raised dough with the white sugar. Use part of the dough and separate it into 15 pieces. Flatten each of the pieces into 10-cm round wrappers. Separate the remaining dough into 15 balls. Take a dough ball, dip it in the sesame oil, and place it in the middle of one of the wrappers. Enclose the wrapper around the small ball, knead the dough between the thumb and forefinger until it closes up. Press the round ball into a 5 cm flat cake. Make 15 cakes in all.

2. Dip the top of the cakes in sugar water and then in the sesame seeds. Put the cakes on the baking sheet sesame side upward. Bake them in a medium hot oven until they turn golden brown.

# Opening Crabapple Flower

**Ingredients:**
250 g oil dough, 150 g mashed red bean filling, 1 beaten egg, and a small amount of red food coloring.

**Cooking method:**
1. Divide the dough into 18 pieces and roll them into 10-cm round wrappers. Distribute the mashed red bean filling on top of the wrappers. Fold the wrappers around the beans and make 5 vees of dough on the top. Score each vee on the top and bottom using a pair of scissors. Place a small amount of the beaten egg on the center of the vee. Pull the end of each vee towards the center and use the egg to stick the dough together. Put a big dot of red food coloring at the center of each cake.

2. Deep-fat fry the cakes slowly over small fire until the turn golden brown.

# Coined Mushrooms

**Major Ingredients:**

75 g dried mushrooms.

**Minor ingredients:**

50 g minced fish, 3 water chestnuts, 75 g cooked ham, 12 fresh peas, a little water-saturated hairlike fungus, and 1 egg white.

**Seasonings:**

15 g cooking wine, 1.5 g refined salt, 200 g light broth, 20 g moistened corn flour, and 10 g chicken fat.

**Cooking method:**

1. Put the dried mushrooms in a basin, pour in warm water, and soak the mushrooms for about one hour. Change the water and clean the mushrooms of any mud and dirt. Cut the stems off the mushrooms with a pair of scissors, then choose 12 round mushrooms each with a diameter of 3 cm. Pour clean water into the pot and boil the water. Stir the 12 chosen mushrooms into the boiling water and cook them for about 1 minute. Drain the water off the mushrooms. Place the mushrooms on a plate, top down, and spread some corn flour over the bottom side of the mushrooms.

2. Put the minced fish in a bowl. Add a small amount of cooking wine, salt, moistened corn flour, and chicken fat and mix them together well. Whip the egg white into a froth, then pour it over the minced fish and mix them together into a paste. Mince the water chestnuts and mix them into the paste.

3. Cut the remaining mushrooms into 24 cm x 3 mm strips. Slice the ham into (48) 1.5 cm x 6 mm x 3 mm

strips; then mince the remaining ham.

4. Form the minced fish into 3 cm diameter balls and place them on the mushrooms. Symmetrically place the mushroom and ham strips on top of the fish balls in the shape of ancient coins and place a fresh pea in the center. Spread minced ham on the outer side of the mushroom strips and some hairlike fungus on the outer side of the sliced ham. Steam the coined mushrooms in a steamer until they are well done, then remove them and place them on a round plate.

5. Pour light broth into a pot. Add the remaining wine, salt, and chicken fat and boil the mixture. Skim off the foam. Add the remaining moistened corn flour to thicken the mixture, then pour the thickened gravy over the mushrooms. Pour the chicken fat over the gravy.

# Embroidered Balls with Dried Scallops

**Major Ingredients:**
200 g water-saturated scallops and 150 g mashed fish.
**Minor ingredients:**
25 g water-saturated mushrooms, 2 egg whites, 8 rape hearts, a small amount of minced ham and rape, and 200 g light broth.
**Seasonings:**
10 g cooking wine, 25 g melted lard, 15 g chicken fat, 20 g moistened corn flour, a small amount of MSG (optional), and a little salt.

**Cooking Method:**

1. Steam the scallops in a steamer, then separate them into strips and put the strips on a plate.

2. Whip the egg white into a froth. Mix the egg white, mashed fish, a little salt, 5 g cooking wine, MSG, and melted lard into a paste. Form the paste into 2 cm diameter balls, and roll them in the scallop strips so that the balls are completely covered by the scallop strips.

3. Cut the mushrooms into 28 slivers. Cross the mushroom slivers on the balls and top them with a small amount of chopped rape and minced ham. Steam the balls until they are well done.

4. Cook the rape hearts in boiling water, then stack them on the plate with the stems toward the center. Place the scallop fish balls on top of them.

5. Boil the light broth and add the remaining cooking wine, MSG, a small amount of salt, and the moistened corn flour to make a thin gravy. Pour the gravy over the dish, then pour the chicken fat over the gravy.

# Grab-Fried Sliced Fish

**Major ingredients:**

200 g fish meat (preferably Mandarin fish meat).

**Minor ingredients:**

500 g peanut oil (actual consumption 40 g), 25 g white sugar, a small amount of MSG (optional), 10 g rice wine, 10 g soy sauce, 25 g melted lard, 10 g vinegar, a small amount of chopped leek and ginger, and 100 g moistened corn flour.

**Cooking method:**

1. Skin and debone the fish. Then slice the meat into 5 cm x 3 cm x 1 cm rectangles and mix them with the moistened corn flour.

2. Pour 500 g peanut oil in the wok and put it on a hot fire. When the oil starts to smoke, put the fish slices into the wok one at a time to avoid their sticking together. If the oil is too hot, reduce the heat and fry the fish strips for 2 minutes. Remove the fish strips when they are yellow and well done.

3. Put the soy sauce, rice wine, vinegar, white sugar, and a small amount of MSG, leek, ginger and corn flour in a bowl and mix them together well. Put a pot on a hot fire and pour in the melted lard. When the lard is heated, stir in the mixture from the bowl. When the mixture is stirred into a paste, put in the fried fish and stir everything quickly for about 1 minute.

# Chicken Breast with Peas Simmered in White Sauce

**Major ingredients:**

100 g Deboned chicken breast with the skin removed.

**Minor ingredients:**

5 Egg whites, 100 g fresh peas and 1,000 g light broth.

**Seasonings:**

A small amount of MSG (optional), 15 g cooking wine, 35 g moistened corn flour, a small amount of salt, 10 g chicken fat, 500 g melted lard (actual consumption 75 g)

**Cooking method:**

1. Pound the chicken breast into mash. Mix it with the five egg whites and 5 g moistened corn flour into a paste (stirring instead of beating). Add 5 g wine, MSG, and a small amount of salt.

2. Put the frying pot over a hot fire and pour in the melted lard. Quickly push the chicken paste through a strainer into the oil. Fry the paste into white pea-like balls. If there are large balls, break them. Take the chicken balls out and let the oil drain off.

3. Use another pot and put in the light broth. Add 10 g cooking wine, a little MSG and salt, and 30 g corn flour to make a thin gravy. Pour the peas into the pot, then add the chicken balls and drip in the chicken fat. Pour the dish into a bowl.

# Fried Minced Pork

**Major Ingredients:**

500 g fatty and lean pork.

**Seasonings:**

A small amount of MSG (optional), 5 g cooking wine, 10 g white sugar, 10 g soy sauce, a small amount of onion, ginger, sesame oil and salt.

**Cooking method:**

1. Remove the skin and sinews from the pork and mince the remainder.

2. Heat the wok without adding oil, then put in the minced meat and stir it. Use a strainer to move the meat aside, and add the soy sauce, white sugar, and a little salt

to the pork juice. Stir the pork in its juice until the meat is flavored. Add cooking wine, MSG, sesame oil, chopped onion, and ginger and continue stirring until the meat is dry.


# Fried Fingered Citron

**Major ingredients:**
200 g minced lean pork.
**Minor ingredients:**
2 eggs.
**Seasonings:**
50 g dry corn flour, 10 g wheat flour, 5 g cooking wine, 5 g sesame oil, 100 g peanut oil, and a small amount of MSG (optional), chopped onion, chopped ginger, and salt.
**Cooking method:**
1. Mix the minced pork with the MSG, cooking wine, sesame oil, salt, chopped onion and ginger, and a little corn flour.

2. Break the eggs into a bowl and whip them. Add a little water, 50 g corn flour, and the salt and mix them well. Very lightly oil the wok. When the wok is heated, pour in half of the egg mixture. Rotate the wok so that the egg mixture forms a large, thin piece. Turn the wok upside down and heat the inside over the fire to cook the inside (the egg should adhere to the pan). When the egg mixture is thoroughly cooked, use a ladle to loosen and remove the egg pancake. Make a second pancake using the remaining egg mixture.

3. Cut the cakes in half. Divide the minced pork into four parts. Mix the 10g wheat flour with a small amount of water to form a paste and spread the paste over the cakes. Place one portion of the pork on each pancake and roll the pancakes into long sticks about 3 cm in diameter. Slice the roll four times in a row every 0.7 cm. then leave 0.3 cm and make a fifth cut completely through the roll. The meat roll looks like a fingered citron.

4. Put the peanut oil in a wok and when it is hot, fry the rolls for about 10 minutes. Remove the rolls and let the oil drain off.

# Golden Frogs Look at the Moon

**Major Ingredients:**

12 abalone in the shell with their own juice.

**Minor ingredients:**

50 g mashed fish, 30 g water-saturated mushrooms, water-saturated bamboo shoots, 25 g cooked ham, 40 g water-saturated fish maw, 24 fresh peas and 5 g hairlike fungus.

**Seasonings:**

15 g cooking wine, 1.5 g refined salt, 1 egg white, 400 g light broth, 25 g moistened corn flour, 10 g chicken fat and 10 g melted lard.

**Cooking method:**

1. Cut the abalone shells open two-thirds of the length making sure not to tear them entirely apart.

2. Pour water into a pot and bring it to a boil, then add

the mushrooms, bamboo shoots, and fish maw and cook them for about 1 minute. Take them out and cool them in clean water. Cut them and the ham into 1-cm strips.

3. Whip the egg white into a froth. Put the 50 g mashed fish into a bowl and add a small amount of cooking wine and salt, 20 g light broth, melted lard and 1 g corn flour. Mix these ingredients well, then add the egg white and mix it all into a paste.

4. Put the mixed paste into the openings of the abalones and use a table knife to spread it smoothly. Press a pea on each side of the fish paste for eyes, adorn it with some hairlike fungus, and put it on a plate. Position the rough edges of the abalones in front as the feet, and the frogs are ready. Make 12 frogs this way. Steam them in the steamer.

5. Pour 150 g light broth into a pot. Add the shredded mushrooms, bamboo shoots, fish maw, and ham, and simmer them over a low fire for two minutes. Remove the ingredients, drain the water, and spread them on the plate. Stack the steamed frogs on top of the shreds to form a circle, with their mouths facing outward.

6. Pour 250 g light broth into a pot, add 1 g cooking wine and a small amount of salt and boil the broth. Skim off the foam. Mix a small amount of water with 1 g corn flour to make a thin paste, and pour it into the broth to make gravy. Drip a small spoonful of chicken fat into the gravy, then pour the gravy over the dish.

# Black Dragon Spits Pearls

**Major ingredients:**

250 g water-saturated sea cucumber and 6 pigeon eggs.

**Seasonings:**

20 g cooking wine, 1.5 g refined salt, 15 g soy sauce, 150 g light broth, 50 g onion, 15 g moistened corn flour, 150 g peanut oil (actual consumption about 20 g), 40 g chicken fat.

**Cooking method:**

1. Place the sea cucumbers in water and clean them, then cut them vertically into two halves. Cut the onions into one-cm chunks. Pour water into a pot and bring it to a boil. Add the sea cucumbers and boil them for about 1 minute, then scoop them out.

2. Pour cold water into a pot, put the pigeon eggs in, and cook them for about 5 minutes. Shell the eggs and wash them. Pour the peanut oil into a wok and when the oil is hot, put in the eggs. Fry the eggs until they become golden yellow. Remove the eggs with a strainer and let the oil drain off.

3. Pour the chicken fat into a wok and heat it. Then fry the onion chunks. Remove the onions when they turn golden yellow. Pour off half of the onion oil into a small bowl and leave the other half in the wok. Return the wok to the fire and put in the sea cucumbers and fry them quickly. Then add the cooking wine, salt, soy sauce, light broth, and eggs. Simmer them over a low fire for about three minutes. Mix in the moistened corn flour to thicken the soup and add the onion oil from the small bowl. The dish is ready.

# Shredded Dragon and Phoenix

**Major ingredients:**

250 g deboned, skinned fish meat, and 250 g chicken breast.

**Minor ingredient:**

50 g winter bamboo shoots.

**Seasonings:**

1 egg, 2-3 g sesame oil, and small amounts of salt, MSG (optional), cooking wine, moistened corn starch, light broth, chopped onion, and chopped ginger.

**Cooking method:**

1. Cut the fish and chicken meat into 5 cm long shreds. Add the salt, cooking wine, and egg white. Thicken them with the moistened corn starch. Shred the winter bamboo shoots.

2. Heat the wok and put in 2-3 g of oil. When the oil is medium hot, put in the shredded fish, chicken and bamboo shoots. Instantly fry them and then pour them out.

3. Put a small spoonful of oil in the wok and add the chopped onion, ginger, light broth, salt, MSG, and cooking wine to make gravy. Pour in the shreds and stir them. Adding some sesame oil and the dish is ready.

# Dried Scallop and Wax-Gourd Balls

**Major ingredients:**
500 g wax gourd.

**Minor ingredients:**
50 g water-saturated dried scallops.

**Seasonings:**
100 g light broth, and small amounts of salt, cooking wine, onion, ginger, moistened corn starch, and chicken fat.

**Cooking method:**
1. Use a spoon to scoop out balls from the wax gourd.

2. Heat the wok and pour in the broth. Add small amounts of salt and cooking wine, then put in the wax-gourd balls and dried scallops. Cook them well and set them aside.

3. Put small amounts of onion, ginger, light broth, salt, moistened corn starch, and cooking wine in the wok and boil them to make gravy. Put in the wax-gourd balls and scallops, then drip some chicken fat over the dish.

# Richly Seasoned Steamed Pork

**Major ingredients:**
500 g uncured bacon with skin.

**Minor ingredients:**
Mashed chicken and lettuce leaves.

**Seasonings:**
Small amounts of salt, cooking wine, soy sauce, leek, ginger, MSG (optional), moistened corn starch, light broth, liquid chicken fat, and oil.

**Cooking method:**

1. Fry the bacon slightly in hot oil. Put small amounts of soy sauce, salt, MSG, wine, leek, and ginger over the bacon and cook them until they are well done. Put the bacon on a plate, skin upward, and use the mashed chicken to make the Chinese character "Fu" for good fortune. Steam it in a steamer for 2-3 minutes.

2. Add a small amount of oil in the wok and stir in the leek, ginger and lettuce leaves. Fry them until they are well done and place them around the bacon.

3. Put small amounts of light broth, soy sauce, salt, MSG, moistened corn starch, and cooking wine in the wok and boil them to make the gravy. Drip in some chicken fat, then pour the gravy over the dish.

# Sail the Desert Boat on Green

**Major ingredients:**

1 camel's foot.

**Minor ingredients:**

500 g rape hearts, and small amounts of sliced winter mushrooms and winter bamboo shoots.

**Seasonings:**

Salt, MSG, light broth, cooking wine, soy sauce, pepper, moistened corn starch, and leek-flavored oil.

**Cooking method:**

1. Cut the sole of the camel's foot into slices. Place the sliced foot, winter mushrooms and bamboo shoots in a bowl together with the light broth, salt, wine, pepper, MSG, and soy sauce. Steam it in a steamer for around one hour.

2. Put a small amount of broth, salt, cooking wine and leek-flavored oil in a wok together with the rape hearts. When they are well cooked, scoop them out and place them on a plate. Put the steamed camel's foot on the rape hearts.

3. Heat two woks, one with small amounts of salt, moistened corn starch, and cooking wine to make white gravy for the rape hearts, and the other with soy sauce to make red gravy for the camel's foot.

# Duck Squares with Walnuts

**Major ingredients:**
Half a cooked duck.
**Minor ingredients:**
Small amounts of mashed shrimps, water chestnuts, walnuts, chopped rape, and chopped ham.
**Seasonings:**
Peanut oil and small amounts of salt, cooking wine, moistened corn starch, and wheat flour.
**Cooking method:**
1. Put the cooked duck on a plate, skin downward, and spread some flour over the duck.

2. Mix the mashed shrimps, salt, moistened corn starch, cooking wine, and peanut oil into a paste and spread it over the duck. Put walnuts, chopped rape and chopped ham on top of the paste.

3. Put peanut oil in the pot and when the oil is heated, put in the duck and deep fry it until it turns golden yellow.

Remove the duck and let the oil drain away. Cut the duck into squares on a cutting block and put the squares on a plate.

# Pork Leg with Rape Hearts

**Major ingredients:**
1 clean pork shoulder and upper leg.
**Minor ingredients:**
250 g rape hearts.
**Seasonings:**
Small amounts of salt, soy sauce, cooking wine, sugar, moistened corn starch, oil, onion, MSG (optional), water, light broth, and ginger.
**Cooking method:**
1. Fry the pork shoulder and leg slightly in oil and remove it with a strainer. Stew the pork leg with a small amount of onion, ginger, soy sauce, cooking wine, sugar, and water until the meat is well done. Put it on a plate.

2. Put small amounts of light broth, salt, MSG, and cooking wine in a wok and boil them. Add the rape hearts and fry them until they are well cooked. Stack them around the pork leg.

3. Heat a wok and add small amounts of light broth, salt, MSG, moistened corn starch, and cooking wine to make white gravy for the rape hearts. Make red gravy for the pork leg.

# Bean Curd with Mixed Stuffings

**Major ingredients:**

250 g bean curd.

**Minor ingredients:**

Small amounts of pork, mashed shrimps, water-saturated dried scallops, water-saturated winter mushrooms, water chestnuts, winter bamboo shoots, cucumber skins, water-saturated hairlike fungus, carrot, and rape hearts.

**Seasonings:**

4 egg whites and small amounts of salt, MSG (optional) cooking wine, moistened corn starch, chicken fat, sesame oil, and light broth.

**Cooking method:**

1. Soak the bean curd in water to remove the yellow liquid, then drain the water from the bean curd. Combine small amounts of salt, MSG, cooking wine, moistened corn starch, chicken fat, and the 4 egg whites, and mix them into a paste.

2. Mince the pork, mashed shrimps, scallops, mushrooms, water chestnuts, and bamboo shoots. Add small amounts of salt, MSG, cooking wine and sesame oil and mix them well.

3. Spread a small amount of chicken fat on two molds and pour in the bean curd paste and spread it flat. Steam them until they are done. Put one bean paste mold on a 9-inch plate. Spread the mixed stuffing on top of it and cover it with the other steamed piece of bean curd. Spread a thin layer of bean curd paste over it.

4. Cut the mushrooms into shreds using a pair of scissors, cut the cucumber skin into the shape of bamboo leaves and stems, and slice the carrot into diamonds.

5. Form a tree from the shredded mushrooms, form a bamboo plant with the cucumber skin, and form small flowers with the carrots. Garnish them with the hairlike fungus to make a beautiful design.

6. Steam the prepared bean curd in a steamer for a dozen minutes. Remove the bean curd and put it on a plate. Place the cleaned rape hearts around it.

7. Put small amounts of light broth, salt, moistened corn starch, and cooking wine in a wok and cook them to make a gravy. Drip some chicken fat into the gravy and pour the gravy over the bean curd.

# Mashed Pea Cake

**Ingredients:**
500 g white peas, 375 g white sugar, 10 g freezing powder and 2 g baking soda.

**Cooking method:**
1. Use a mortar and pestle to crush the peas and remove their skins. Wash the peas in cold water three times. Put enough water to cover the peas into a bronze pot and add the peas and baking soda when the water boils. Simmer the peas until they become mushy. Push the peas and their juice through a sieve.

2. Put the sieved peas into a pot. Add the white sugar and melted freezing powder. Cook them for 30 minutes over a low heat being sure to stir them occasionally so they don't burn.

3. Pour the cooked mashed peas into a 36 cm x 16 cm x 2 cm galvanized iron mould (or cake pan), and let the peas cool at room temperature for three to four hours. The cake is ready when it has throughly cooled. Cut the cake into pieces and place the pieces on a plate.

# Kidney Bean Rolls

**Ingredients:**
500 g kidney beans, a small amount of baking soda, 250 g mashed red beans.
**Cooking method:**
1. Use a mortar and pestle to crush the kidney beans and remove their skins. Put the beans in a bowl, cover them with boiling water, and let them soak overnight to make any unremoved skins puffy. Use lukewarm water to remove the remaining skins. Simmer the kidney beans in boiling water with a little baking soda until they are soft. Remove the beans with a strainer when they are done, wrap them in a piece of cloth, and steam the beans in the cloth in a steamer for 20 minutes. Strain the water off the beans, crush the beans into mash, and push the mash through a sieve to make vermicelli.

2. When the vermicelli is cooled, put it on a piece of wet cloth and squeeze it into mash. Spread a 50 cm x 50 cm piece of wet, white cloth on a cutting board. Place the bean mash on the cloth and roll the mashed beans into a long cylinder with a diameter of 3 cm. Position the cylinder in the middle of the wet cloth and use the blade of a cutting knife to spread the beans into a 3 mm x 17 cm x 7

cm rectangle. Layer the mashed red beans over the mashed kidney beans, roll the rectangle up from both sides together with the cloth and join the two edges of the rectangle together to form a cylinder. Use both hands to hold the edges together tightly and press the edges gently from outside the cloth. Remove the cloth and place the cylinder on a cutting block. Cut off and discard the two ends. Cut the remainder of the cylinder into 2 cm thick segments.

# Gold and Silver Venison

**Major ingredient:**
  500 g venison.
**Seasonings:**
  2 eggs, 5 g Shaoxing rice wine, 5 g corn flour, 5 g chicken fat, 500 g peanut oil (actual consumption about 50 g), and small amounts of salt, onion, wheat flour, and ginger.
**Cooking method:**
  1. Wash the venison, then cook it in a pot with water. When it is half done, remove the meat and cut it into 7 cm thick pieces. Put the venison pieces in a bowl and add a small amount of Shaoxing rice wine, salt, onion, ginger chunks, and chicken fat. Steam the venison pieces until they become soft. Strain the venison and divide it in two.

  2. Separate the egg whites from the yolks into two bowls. Mix each with corn flour, wheat flour, and a little salt to make a paste. Heat a pot and add the peanut oil. When the oil is heated, dip half the venison pieces in the egg yolks and then deep-fat fry them. Remove them when

they turn golden yellow. Dip the remaining venison in the egg whites and then deep-fat fry them. Remove them when they are well done. Cut the venison pieces separately into slivers and place them on a plate together with their egg batter.

# Lantern Bean Curd

**Major ingredient:**
Two pieces of bean curd, 800 g total.
**Minor ingredients:**
50 g minced pork, 25 g water-saturated mushrooms, 25 g water-saturated bamboo shoots (preferably fresh bamboo shoots), and 100 g peanut oil.
**Seasonings:**
2 water chestnuts, 2 pea sprouts, 250 g light broth, 5 g Shaoxing rice wine, 5 g white sugar, 10 g chicken fat, 10 g sesame oil, 1 egg, small amounts of soy sauce, onion, salt, and ginger.
**Cooking method:**
1. Cut the bean curd into 5 cm x 2.5 cm pieces, and fry them in peanut oil until they become yellow. Mince half of the mushrooms, bamboo shoots and 1 water chestnut and stir-fry them in sesame oil together with the minced pork. Add small amounts of the Shaoxing rice wine, salt, and soy sauce.
2. Cut a round hole in the bean curd, fill the hole with the fried minced meat. Whip the egg white and yolk together into paste and spread some of the egg paste on top of the bean curd and minced meat.

3. Deep fat fry the bean curd in moderately hot peanut oil. Cut the remaining half of the mushrooms and bamboo shoots into diamond slices and boil them in water. Cook them together with 1 water chestnut, pea sprouts, and light broth, Shaoxing wine, soy sauce, salt, onion, ginger, and white sugar for two or three minutes. Make a gravy and drip a few drops of chicken fat into the gravy.

# Bamboo Shoot with Mashed Chicken

**Major ingredient:**
1 bamboo shoot (about 20 cm long).
**Minor ingredients:**
150 g mashed chicken meat, 3 water chestnuts, 25 g minced ham, 25 g chopped rape, 2 egg whites, 200 g light broth.
**Seasonings:**
10 g Shaoxing rice wine, a little salt, 15 g moistened corn flour, and 10 g chicken fat.
**Cooking method:**
1. Peel the bamboo shoot, cook it in water for 10 minutes, and cut it into 14 cm long by 7 cm wide slices.
2. Mince the water chestnuts and mix them with the egg whites and mashed chicken into a paste. Add half the Shaoxing rice wine, a little salt, and the chicken fat.
3. Spread the bamboo slices flat on top of a piece of white cloth, and spread the chicken paste on the narrow ends of the bamboo slices. Put some chopped ham and rape on top of the paste. Roll up both ends of the bamboo slices into a cylinder. Wrap the cylinder in the white cloth

and steam it until it is well done. When the bamboo shoots have cooled, cut them into 7 cm wide slices shaped like fish scales, and stack the slices in a bowl. Heat the slices in a steamer, then turn the bowl upside down onto a plate.

4. Use the light broth, Shaoxing rice wine, corn flour, and salt to make a thin gravy. Drip the chicken fat into the gravy, then pour the gravy over the dish.

# Egg Dumplings with Meat Filling

**Major ingredients:**

50 g pork fillet.

**Minor ingredients:**

3 eggs, 25 g water-saturated mushrooms, 25 g water-saturated bamboo shoots, 5 g chopped ham, and some rape leaves.

**Seasonings:**

5 g Shaoxing rice wine, 25 g moistened corn flour, 1.5 g salt, 25 g fatty pork, 100 g peanut oil, and 25 g wheat flour.

**Cooking method:**

1. Mince the pork fillet, mushrooms, and bamboo shoots. Add the Shaoxing rice wine and a small amount of salt and mix them into a filling.

2. Break the eggs into a bowl. Add the moistened corn flour and a small amount of salt and mix them well.

3. Heat a small frying pan. Rub the inside of the pan with the pork fat to coat the inside of the pan. Put a spoonful of the egg mixture into the pan. Rotate the pan over the heat so that the egg mixture makes a pancake with a dia-

meter of 8 cm. Repeat this step until all the egg mixture has been made into pancakes.

4. Roll the pork filling into 1 cm balls. Put a ball in the center of each pancake. Fold the pancakes in half. Use chopsticks and press the cakes gently to evenly distribute the filling and make a dumpling. Spread a little flour-water paste on the outside of the dumplings and put some chopped ham and rape on them. Deep-fat fry the dumplings in medium-hot peanut oil until they turn yellow. Remove the dumplings and allow the oil to drain off, then place them on a plate.

# Stuffed Mandarin Fish

**Major ingredient:**
1 mandarin fish (1,000 g).
**Minor ingredients:**
250 g light broth, 50 g water-saturated mushrooms, 50 g water-saturated bamboo shoots, 50 g water-saturated sea cucumber, 50 g water chestnuts, 50 g ham, 50 g egg whites, and 2 rape hearts.
**Seasonings:**
15 g Shaoxing rice wine, 15 g moistened corn flour, 10 g chicken fat, 25 g melted lard, 50 g onion, 50 g ginger, and a little salt.
**Cooking method:**
1. Remove the internal organs of the fish through the gill. Scale the fish, then quick-boil it. Gently scrape the black residue off the fish body from head to tail with a knife — make sure not to scratch the fish skin. Score cuts diagonally on the fish body.

2. Set aside three mushrooms and four slices of bamboo shoot. Shred the water chestnuts and the remaining mushrooms and bamboo shoot slices.

3. Dice the sea cucumbers. Mix the mashed fish meat, egg white, Shaoxing rice wine, melted lard, and a small amount of salt into a paste. Stuff the paste into the fish belly through the gills. Rub a little rice wine and salt on the outside of the fish body. Place the reserved mushrooms and bamboo shoot slices on the fish body along with chunks of onion and ginger. Steam the fish until the meat and bones separate. Drain the fish soup and discard the onion chunks.

4. Quick-boil the ham and place it on the fish body. Combine the light broth, moistened corn flour, rice wine, and a little salt to make a thin gravy. Pour the gravy over the fish and drip the chicken fat into the gravy. The fish is ready. Place the two rape hearts parallel to the sides of the fish, one facing toward the head, the other facing toward the tail.

# Braised Four Treasures

**Major ingredients:**

1 tin of abalone in its own juice and 225 g fresh asparagus spears.

**Minor ingredients:**

6 leaf-mustard roots, 100 g ham, 100 g mashed chicken meat, 2 egg whites, 24 peas, and 500 g light broth.

**Seasonings:**

15 g Shaoxing rice wine, 25 g melted lard, 10 g chicken fat, 15 g moistened corn flour, and a little salt.

**Cooking method:**

1. Mix the mashed chicken meat and egg white into a paste. Use the paste and 12 abalone pieces to make frogs.

2. Peel the asparagus spears and cut them in half lengthwise. Add the rice wine and a little salt, then steam the spears for 10 minutes.

3. Peel the mustard roots and score them with crosses. Cook them in 250 g light broth with half of the seasonings until they are done.

4. When the dish is ready, lay the asparagus spears in the center of a plate and place the abalones around them to make a rectangle. Place the mustard roots and sliced ham at the four corners. Use the remaining broth and seasonings to make a thin gravy. Pour the gravy over the dish and drip the chicken fat over the gravy.

# Lotus Flower Shredded Fish

**Major ingredients:**

250 g raw fish meat, 1 fresh lotus flower.

**Minor ingredients:**

150 g winter bamboo shoots, 50 g egg white.

**Seasonings:**

15 g Shaoxing rice wine, 100 g melted lard, 5 g sesame oil, and small amounts of moistened corn starch, shredded ginger, and salt.

**Cooking method:**

1. Debone the fish. Wash the fish meat and shred it. Shred the bamboo shoots.

2. Wash the fresh lotus flower petals and put them

around the edges of a lotus flower plate. Mix the egg white, half the rice wine, and the moistened corn starch.

3. Dip the shredded fish meat into the egg white mixture and fry the fish meat in the melted lard until it is done. Drain the grease off the fish. Add the ginger, remaining rice wine, and a small amount of salt and fry everything quickly until it is done. Drip the sesame oil onto the dish, then pour the dish onto the lotus flower plate. Leave the edges of the lotus petals exposed.

# Powdered Gold and Minced Jade

**Major Ingredient:**
200 g of the middle section of a black carp.
**Minor ingredients:**
150 g fresh tangerines without seeds and 50 g winter bamboo shoots.
**Seasonings:**
5 g cooking wine, 1.5 g salt, 50 g wheat flour, 50 g chicken soup, 2 egg whites, 25 g onion, 25 g ginger, 10 g white sugar, a small amount of sesame oil and 15 g moistened corn starch, and cherries for garnish.
**Cooking method:**
1. Debone the fish. Wash the fish meat and cut it into 6.5 cm by 2.5 cm slices. Marinate the fish in a small amount of cooking wine and salt for a short time.

2. Mix the moistened corn starch and egg white together. Separate the tangerines into segments. Slice the onion and bamboo shoots.

3. Heat the pot and add enough oil to deep-fat fry the

fish slices. Remove the fish slices and let the oil drain off.

4. Pour most of the oil out of the pot leaving just enough to fry the ginger and onion. When the ginger and onion are fried, remove and discard them. Add the bamboo shoots and tangerines and stir them. Immediately add the salt, cooking wine, white sugar, chicken soup, and moistened corn starch and make a thin gravy. Add the fried fish slices and mix everything well. Drip a few drops of sesame oil into the dish, then put the dish on a plate decorated with tangerine segments and cherries.

**Allusions:**

When Emperor Yangdi of the Sui Dynasty (605-617) went to Jiangdu (now called Yangzhou), he ordered the local official to feed him the local delicacies. The official presented Minced Perch Meat. The emperor tasted it and said: "Powdered Gold and Minced Jade is the delicacy of the southeast." Lu You, a famous poet in the Song Dynasty, also praised the dish in one of his poems.

# Spring on Chopsticks

**Major ingredients:**

5 live quails (preferably 3 months old).

**Minor ingredients:**

Mushrooms, winter bamboo shoots, and egg whites.

**Seasonings:**

Small amounts of onion, ginger, cooking wine, moistened corn starch, salt, pepper, and melted lard.

**Cooking method:**

1. Kill the quails, pluck their feathers, drain their blood,

and remove their internal organs and bones. Dice the quail meat into small pieces the size of the top of a chopstick. Dice the mushrooms and bamboo shoots into even smaller pieces.

2. Boil the mushrooms and bamboo shoots for 1-2 minutes.

3. Make a paste from the egg white and small amounts of cooking wine, moistened corn starch, and salt. Coat the diced meat with the egg white paste and quick-fry them in the melted lard. Remove the meat when it is well done and put it in an earthenware pot. Add milk soup and small amounts of onion, ginger, salt, cooking wine, and pepper, and simmer everything for about 30 minutes, then add the bamboo shoots and mushrooms. The quails are done when the flavors are well blended.

# Crisp Vegetable Eel

**Major ingredients:**
250 g water-saturated mushrooms.
**Minor ingredients:**
50 g ginger and 500 g peanut oil (actual consumption 75 g).
**Seasonings:**
50 g dry corn starch, 125 g white sugar, 50 g vinegar, 25 g soy sauce, and a small amount of moistened corn starch.
**Cooking method:**
1. Cut the mushrooms into eel-like shreds and pat some dry corn starch on the shreds. Peel the ginger and cut it into shreds. Heat the wok and add the peanut oil. When

the oil is hot, put in the mushrooms. Fry the mushrooms until there are no air bubbles in the pan, then remove them.

2. Heat the wok and put in 75g water, white sugar, and soy sauce. When the mixture boils, add the moistened corn starch and vinegar to make a gravy. Pour the gravy over the crisp eel slices and drip the juice from the ginger into the gravy.

# Chinese Cabbage with Golden Edges

**Major ingredient:**
500 g Chinese cabbage.
**Seasonings:**
7.5 g dried red hot pepper, 6 g salt, 20 g soy sauce, 25 g vinegar, 10 g white sugar, 5 g chopped ginger, 75 g rapeseed oil, 5 g sesame oil, 15 g moistened corn starch, and a small amount of chicken fat.
**Cooking method:**
1. Discard the outer leaves of the cabbage. Clean the tender inner leaves and dry them. Put the cabbage leaves on a cutting block and hit them with a cleaver to soften them, then cut the leaves into slivers 2.6 cm by 1 cm.

2. Cut open the hot peppers, remove their seeds, and cut them into 2.6 cm pieces. Heat a wok. When it is hot, add the rapeseed oil. When the oil is hot, put in the red hot peppers and fry them until they emit a pungent odor.

3. Add the ginger and cabbage when the peppers turn brown. Quick-fry them over a hot fire. Add the vinegar and stir the mixture quickly. Add the soy sauce, white

sugar, and salt and continue frying until the cut edges of the cabbage turn golden yellow.

4 Add the moistened corn starch to make a thin gravy, then drip a few drops of chicken fat into the gravy. Turn the cabbage over and put it on a plate.

# It Tastes like Honey

**Major ingredient:**

150 g mutton fillet.

**Seasonings:**

5 g sweet fermented flour sauce, 10 g soy sauce, 40 g white sugar, 2.5 g vinegar, 25 g moistened corn starch, 2.5 g Shaoxing rice wine, 1.5 g ginger juice, 60 g sesame oil, 500 g peanut oil (actual consumption 50 g).

**Cooking method:**

1. Wash the mutton fillet, then cut the fillet diagonally into slices 3.3 cm long, 1.6 cm wide, and 0.16 cm thick. Add the sweet fermented flour sauce and 15 g moistened corn starch and mix them together well.

2. Mix the ginger juice, soy sauce, vinegar, Shaoxing rice wine, white sugar, and 10 g moistened corn starch together to make a gravy.

3. Pour the peanut oil into a pot. When the oil is hot, put the mutton fillet slices into the pot, stirring them quickly so they do not stick together. When the slices become white, remove them and pour out the oil.

4. Replace the frying pot over a hot fire with 10 g sesame oil and heat the oil. Add the mutton slices and the gravy and stir them quickly until the gravy completely

covers the slices. Drip another 10 g sesame oil over the dish.

## Sea Cucumbers Cooked with Onion

**Major ingredients:**

1,000 g water-saturated small sea cucumbers and 105 g onion.

**Minor ingredients:**

15 g green garlic stems, 5 g chopped ginger, 27 g ginger juice, 10 g moistened corn starch, 200 g chicken stock, and 50 g burned onion oil. (Burned onion oil is obtained by cooking 500 g fatty pork. Then add 100 g green onion, 75 g sliced ginger, and 50 g sliced garlic to the extracted pork fat. When the vegetables are fried golden yellow, add 100 g coriander. After the vegetables become burned, remove them and save the oil.)

**Seasonings:**

27 g white sugar, 12 g soy sauce, 15 g Shaoxing rice wine, 2 g salt, 2 g MSG (optional), 150 g melted lard (actual consumption 75 g).

**Cooking method:**

1. Clean the water-saturated sea cucumbers, then cover them with cold water in a pot. Boil the sea cucumbers for five minutes. Remove them and drain off the water.

2. Cut 100 g onion into 5-cm-long chunks. Mince the remaining 5 g onion. Cut the green garlic stems into 3.3 cm chunks. Pour 125 g melted lard in a wok. When the lard is hot, add the onions and fry them to a golden yellow. Put the onions in a bowl and add 50 g chicken stock, 5 g

rice wine, 2 g ginger juice, 2 g soy sauce, 2 g white sugar, and 1g MSG. Steam the onions over a hot fire for 1-2 minutes. Drain off the soup and set the onions aside.

3. Put 25 g melted lard in a wok and heat it over a hot fire. Add 5 g white sugar and fry the lard to a golden yellow color. Add the chopped onion, ginger, and sea cucumbers and stir them quickly for a few seconds, then add 10 g rice wine, 150 g chicken stock, 10 g soy sauce, 25 g ginger juice, a small amount of salt, 20 g burned onion oil, and 1 g MSG. When the soup has boiled, cook it over a low heat until the soup is reduced by two-thirds.

4. Make the fire hot again. While turning over and stirring the dish in the pan, drip in the moistened corn starch to make a gravy. Cover all the sea cucumbers with the gravy, then pour them onto a plate.

5. Put the wok over a hot fire and pour 30 g onion oil in it. When it is hot, add the green garlic and onion chunks. Stir-fry them slightly and spread them over the sea cucumbers.

# Fried Ringing Bells

**Major ingredients:**
15 soy-bean milk skins (Produced in Sixiang near Hangzhou in East China — or produced elsewhere. The skins are as thin as cicada wings, yellow, and transparent) and 50 g pork fillet.

**Seasonings:**
A quarter of an egg yolk, 1 g white onion, 1 g Shaoxing rice wine, 1 g salt, 1.5 g MSG (optional), 50 g sweet flour

sauce, and vegetable oil.

**Cooking method:**

1. Remove the sinews from the pork fillet, then wash the fillet and mince it. Put the minced meat in a bowl and add the onion, salt, rice wine, MSG, and egg yolk. Mix everything together. Divide the mixture into five parts.

2. Soak the circular milk skins in water for 2 to 3 minutes. Remove the skins and make sure they are folded exactly in half. Cut off and discard the outside edges of the skins. Cut off the the curved sides of the skins to make the skins rectangular; set the cut-off pieces aside.

3. Take three of the rectangular skins, open and flatten them, and pile them three high. Take one portion of the meat filling and place it on one of the narrow ends of the top skin. Use a knife blade and spread the meat filling into a 3.5 cm wide sliver across the end of the skin. Place the arcs from the three skins on top of the meat filling. Roll the skins into a cylinder (neither too tightly nor too loosely) beginning at the end with the meat filling. Use water to seal the opposite end of the skins onto the rolls. Repeat the process four more times to make five rolls. Cut the rolls into 3.5 cm long sections and set them aside.

4. Put a wok over medium heat and add enough vegetable oil to deep-fat fry the rolls. When the oil is medium hot, place the rolls into the wok one at a time stirring continuously so they do not stick together. Use a strainer to remove the rolls when they become yellow, shiny, and crisp. Let the oil drain off, then put the rolls on a plate. Eat the rolls with sweet flour sauce and onion chunks.

# Cooked Duck

**Major ingredient:**

1 force-fed duck (2,500 g).

**Minor ingredients:**

2,000 g duck broth and 1,000 g peanut oil (actual consumption 55 g).

**Cooking method:**

1. Cut the duck in half vertically along the spine and remove its internal organs. Wash the duck clean, then cook it in boiling water until it becomes soft and tender. Remove the duck from the water and cook it in duck broth for 5 minutes. Wipe the broth off the duck.

2. Deep-fat fry the duck halves in hot oil until they become purplish red. Remove the duck and let the oil drain off. Put the duck on a cutting block and cut it into pieces. Put the wings and legs on either side of the plate, the bones at the bottom of the plate, and the breast at the top.


# Walnut Duck

**Major ingredients:**

1 force-fed duck (2,500 g).

**Minor ingredients:**

100 g mashed chicken, 200 g walnut kernels, 150 g water chestnuts, 100 g egg white, and a small amount of chopped rape.

**Seasonings:**

10 g Shaoxing rice wine, 50 g moistened corn flour, 150 g peanut oil, and a small amount of onion, ginger, and salt.

**Cooking method:**

1. Cut the duck in half vertically along the spine and remove its internal organs. Wash it clean, boil it for about 10 minutes in water, then add the onion, ginger, and half the rice wine and salt. Steam the duck in a steamer until it is done. Remove the bones and skin when the duck has cooled.

2. Mix the mashed chicken, egg white, corn flour, and the remaining rice wine and salt into a paste. Mince the walnuts and water chestnuts and mix them into the paste. Spread the paste on the insides of the duck breasts.

3. Fry the duck in medium hot oil until it becomes crisp. Remove the duck and let the oil drain off. Cut the duck into long pieces, stack the pieces on a plate, and place the chopped rape around the duck.

# Stir-fried Carrot Sauce

**Major ingredients:**

200 g lean pork and 100 g carrots.

**Minor ingredients:**

1 piece of dried bean curd, 25 g dried shrimp, 50 g melted lard, and 500 g sesame oil (actual consumption 50 g).

**Seasonings:**

10 g salted, fermented soy sauce, 5 g soy sauce, 5 g Shaoxing rice wine, 5 g moistened corn starch, and a small amount of chopped onion, chopped ginger, and light broth.

**Cooking method:**

1. Dice the lean pork and carrots. Put the diced carrots and sesame oil in a frying pan and fry the carrots until

they turn red. Dice the dried bean curd into pieces the same size as the carrots.

2. Soak the dried shrimp in boiling water to remove their salty flavor. Heat the wok, pour in the melted lard, and stir-fry the diced pork. When the juice has come out of the meat and it sizzles loudly, reduce the heat to low. When there is little sizzle and the juice has evaporated, increase the heat again.

3. When the meat color changes from dark to light, add the onion, ginger, and the salted, fermented soy sauce. Cook the meat stirring it constantly for another 2-3 minutes. When the meat smells of soy sauce, add the diced bean curd, shrimp, carrots, wine, and soy sauce.

4. When the juice in the pan has evaporated, add the light broth and moistened corn starch to make a gravy. When the gravy has thickened, drip in 25 g sesame oil and stir the sauce for a short time.

**Allusions:**

The four sauces have a long history. When the Manchu troops entered the hinterland in the 17th century at the beginning of the Qing Dynasty, battles were fought continuously. The soldiers often had little time to prepare meals, so they cooked meat directly over a fire, then diced the meat and put it in bowls together with chopped green vegetables and salted, fermented soy sauce.

After the Qing Dynasty was founded, some Manchus remained fond of the dish. The cooks in the imperial kitchen improved the dish, changed the mixing to stir-frying, and made the dish even more delicious. Thereafter, it became a common dish in the Qing palace and remains a popular local dish among the old residents of Beijing.

# Rice Rolls

Rice rolls are a mixture of rice, wheat flour, and hot water that is steamed. There are many varieties of rice rolls and they can be made from old rice, non-glutinous rice, or glutinous rice. The rolls are either sweet or salty. Salty rolls are mixed with Chinese prickly ash and salt, or with spiced prickly ash salt. The sweet rolls are stuffed with mashed dates, mashed red bean paste, white sugar and walnuts, or white sugar and pine nuts.

# Deep-Fried Cake

The kneaded cake dough is made from oil and wheat flour. The cakes, which are as big as sesame cakes, are filled with white sugar, sesame, or haws with a little cream. The sweet, tasty cakes are deep-fat fried so they are crisp outside, but soft inside.

# Shaomai Dumpling

The kneaded dumpling dough is made from top-quality wheat flour. Shaomai dumpling skins are bigger than those used for cooked dumplings. The filling is made from minced pork and chopped mushrooms. The dumplings, whose tops are left open, are steamed for 20 minutes.

# Yellow Sponge Cake

Yellow sponge cake is made from whipped eggs, wheat flour, white sugar, osmanthus flowers, and preserved fruits. The soft, sweet, delicious cake is steamed in molds.

# Fried Triangles

Water is added to sesame paste and then mixed with wheat flour. Chopped meat, dried shrimp, mushrooms, and ham are used as seasonings, and are mixed with corn starch to make a moist filling. Small pieces of dough are rolled into thin skins that are slightly larger than those used for cooked dumplings. The dumpling skins are cut into two halves. The halves are pressed together and filling is stuffed between the skins. Then the skins are closed by pressing the edges together into triangles. The dumplings are fried in oil until they turn yellow. They are crisp outside and soft inside. Usually they are eaten together with porridges.

Porridges can be made from many different ingredients, such as lotus leaf, lotus root, mung beans, pork, preserved fruits, millet, Job's tears, barley, and old rice. Some porridges are seasonal. When the Empress Dowager Cixi felt ill, she ate porridge made of yellow rice, which is nonglutinous.

## Vegetable rolls

Vegetable rolls are made of stir-fried bean curd, mutton fat, and salted and fermented soy sauce. Vegetables are stir-fried, then mixed with bean curd. Tender, cleaned Chinese cabbage leaves are used to roll the bean curd mixture into cylinders.

## "Monk Jumps over Wall"

Crisply fried meat and four cooked, shelled duck eggs are steamed together until they are well done. Because half of the glossy, slippery eggs are exposed like bald heads beside the brown meat, the Empress Dowager Cixi named the dish "Monk Jumps over the Wall." The imperial kitchen frequently prepared this dish.

# 宫廷餐饮与养生

上官丰　编

中国文学出版社

# 引　言

　　中国传统饮食习俗对美食和营养一直是非常重视的。约在周朝，宫廷中即有食医出现，用现代的话说，就是营养医师，且居于医之首位。汉、唐以后的历代王朝，也都在宫廷中设有专门负责膳食的医生。在浩如烟海的中医书籍中，几乎均有"医食同源"、"食药同源"的论述。中医药学起源于人类对食物的寻觅，古代中国部族先民在长期的实践中，逐步认识到许多动物、植物，诸如谷类、果蔬、禽蛋、兽肉、鳞介等不仅是美味佳肴，还有健身益寿的功能。在人体发生病变时，食用某些动物、植物得当，还有去病强体的功效。人类由于地区、季节、体质、年龄、性别及所患疾病的不同，在饮食的选择上，也都有严格的讲究。在中国长期的封建社会中，一直是中国精神传统支柱的儒学体系，在饮食方面的讲究，又使中国历代宫廷在饮食方面精益求精。中国宫廷餐饮可以说是集天下之美食，敛世间之珍馐、役名厨之高手，使民间饮食文化再度升华。其实不少宫廷佳肴出自民间，只不过宫廷厨师把美食本着美学和养生的法则进行更精到的加工，把食品加工当作美术创作来进行。中国伟大的民主革命家孙中山先生（1866—1925）有云："夫悦目之画，悦耳之音，皆为美术，而悦口之味，何独不然?! 是烹调者，亦美术之一道也（《建国方略》）。"

中国人的饮食生活体现了中国文化的一些特性，而中国宫廷饮食则是研究中国饮食文化的一把钥匙。目前，饮食文化这个概念还十分模糊，有人笼统地认为是讲吃、讲喝；或是怎么吃，怎么喝，怎么做。也有人认为饮食文化孕育出六门科学，即烹调学、食品制造学、食疗学、饮食民俗学、饮食文艺学、饮食资源学等。宫廷餐饮与养生学、饮食美学、饮食用具学都有密切的联系，可惜明代以前这方面的史料已如凤毛麟角。本书主要讲述明清以来宫廷餐饮的概况，由于宫廷菜肴源于民间，编者为了使读者能较清楚地认识这一源流，还介绍了中国传统菜系、宫廷茶事及有关典故。在《明代的宫廷餐饮》及《清宫御膳述闻》的文中及文后附有数十道宫廷菜点的做法，以增添情趣并供爱好烹饪的读者尝试。

由于成书仓促，疏漏不妥之处恳请读者指正。书中有的篇目，系编者根据多方资料汇撰，非一家之言，故未署名。本书在编辑过程中得到故宫博物院研究室徐启宪老先生、紫禁城出版社林京先生和方大药业集团主治医师张洪宽先生的帮助与支持，谨此鸣谢！

编者

1997.8

# 目　　录

# 中国宫廷菜肴的形成与发展

中国宫廷菜肴始于奴隶社会，自有朝廷皇宫之时，就有宫廷菜肴。宫廷菜的供食对象主要是帝王后妃及其家属。他们凭政权之威、横敛天下美食、役人间之名厨、精烹细饪，创造出那个时代最美的菜肴。可以说宫廷菜肴代表一个朝代最高的烹饪水平。虽然宫廷菜肴自古以来为帝王将相、达官显贵所独享，但它却靠农、牧、渔民提供原料，工匠提供制造厨具、厨师提供技术服务、文官斟酌菜名、礼仪官员设计规制，而构成了中国宫廷的饮食文明，它是中华民族的宝贵文化遗产之一。

宫廷菜肴是从民间菜肴升华而来，其创造者从来不是王公将相，而是厨役百姓，在此要向读者申明，所谓宫廷菜肴的原始模特，可能就是您曾亲手烹制过的菜肴。

饮食制作，离不开厨师，古代帝王对手艺高超的厨师也十分重视。据《史记．殷本纪》载，曾辅佐商汤（约前1766—前1760在位）灭夏桀（约前1818—前1766在位）的历史上首位名相伊尹就是一位名厨，他原名阿衡，本是有莘氏家奴，欲游说于汤而无缘由，于是带了全套厨具，凭自己高超的烹饪术赢得了汤的信任。汤称他擅调五味、做"鹄鸟之羹"有治国安邦之才并任其为相。

被厨师尊为祖师的彭祖，是尧帝（约活动于公元前21世纪初）的厨师，据说夏朝的第七位国王少康在夏朝建立之前曾是"有虞氏"的"疱正"（负责厨役的官员）。

后来也有厨人参与政治的，如春秋时期齐国的易牙善于辨味与烹饪而得到桓公的信任。春秋末期还有一位刺客，他是吴国的专诸，为了帮助公子光取得王位，他曾向名厨学习"炙鱼"绝技，靠自己的厨艺接近吴王僚，最终将吴王刺死。

商朝后期，宫廷吃喝之风盛行，朝政腐败，特别是商纣王（前1154—前1122在位）时期"以酒为池、悬肉为林、使男女倮（裸）、相逐其间，为长夜之饮（《帝王世纪》）。"这样荒淫无耻的生活，导致商朝的灭亡。

中国的宫廷菜约形成于周朝（前11世纪—前256），可以说周朝以前是饮食文化的产生和初步发展期，而周秦两汉（前1122—220）则是饮食文化的形成和昌盛阶段。春秋（前770—前476）时期是中国思想史上空前活跃的时期。诸子百家的思想涉及宇宙、社会、人生各个方面，务实的中国思想家们对于人们天天接触的饮食问题，自然十分关注。随着医学的发展，食疗思想产生了，饮食卫生受到普遍重视。中国的饮食习惯与西方有很大差异，西方人肉食比例很大，而中国人以植物食品为主（即中国传统食物五谷，据说是上古先民的首领神农氏所发现并倡耕种），华夏民族以种植五谷为食的稳定时代，是从周朝开始的。

周朝是奴隶社会最兴旺发达的时期，社会政治、经济和文化全面发展，是夏商周三代中最为强盛的一个朝代。

周朝的宫廷御膳在夏商两代发展的基础上更为完善。夏朝从帝王宫廷建立开始，设立膳食官员与机构，帝王开始追求生活上的享受，宫廷御膳处于萌芽状态。商朝宫廷御膳虽然比夏朝有了新的发展，天子与诸侯膳食开始分等并实行"鼎食制"，但在宫廷膳食管理上还没有一套健全的机构与膳食制度。周朝的宫廷御膳从膳食机构人员配备，天子及诸侯等官员膳食内容与等级，宫廷膳食的制作与管理等方面，都有一套较为完整的制度，并按照"食礼"所规定的顺序进行。宫廷膳食水平亦高于夏商时期，而且名菜、各种宴会相继出现。周朝是我国宫廷御膳全面形成和发展的时期。

周朝主副食品较为丰富，宫廷菜点众多，名菜相继出现。

西周由于经济较为发达，谷物、蔬菜和各种肉食比较丰富。当时食用的谷物有稻、黍、稷、菽、麻栗等七种。据《诗经》记载，各种植物已有130余种。其中常用的蔬菜就有葵（葵菜又名胭脂菜）、藿（豆叶）、芹、茆（莼）、采（油菜）、蒲笋、菖蒲、荷、薇、芥、葑（蔓菁）、菲（萝卜）、韭、薤（藠头）、葱、蒜、蘋、繁（白蒿）、莪（萝蒿）、藻、蕨、荇菜、堇、藜、荠、荼（苦菜）、芑（似苦菜）、卷耳、芝、瓠、芋等30余种。水果已有桃、李、杏、梅、枣、棘（酸枣）、栗、榛、梨、甘棠、沙棠、山樆（野生梨）、柿、瓜、樱桃、杞、桑椹、菱茨（即鸡头米）、柑、桔、柚等。动物已有牛、羊、犬、猪、马、鹿、熊、狼、象近百种。鸡、雉、雀、雁等禽类有数十种。鱼类已有鲤、鲂、鲔、鲂鱼、嘉鱼、鳖、蛇、鳢、鲨等近20种左右。所以宫廷食用的荤素菜点众多。

217

除了上述菜肴外，宫廷中还有各种腌菜和酱菜，如用醋浸制的各种腌菜。

宫廷食用的饮料有"六清"、"五齐"、"三酒"。

"六清"，即水、浆（酢浆、酸汁酒）、醴（煮米成干饭所酿成的甜酒）、醇（凉水渗淡的酒）、医（用米煮成的粥，加曲、蘖酿成的酒）、酏（音移，即用薄粥酿成的酒）。

"五齐"，指用稻、粱、黍三米制成五种有滓未澄清的酒。泛齐：一种酒汁有些浊，泛浮的甜酒。醴齐：酒已制成，酒汁和酒滓相半的醴酒，它酿造一宿即成，有酒味，但很淡的甜酒。盎齐：一种浊而微清的甜酒。缇（音题）齐：酒色赤红，比盎齐更清些。沈齐（又名沉齐）：酒酿成后，浊滓沉下，清汁在上。

"三酒"，是三种已经渗漉糟滓的酒，它和五齐不同，齐酒多用于祭祀，三酒供人饮用。三酒是指酒的种别。事酒：有事临时酿造的酒。昔酒：是陈酒，此酒因时间长，要求酿才熟，故用"昔"为名，它是冬酿春熟、酒液清醇。清酒，它比昔酒酿造的时间更长。冬酿夏熟，酒色更清于昔酒。

"四饮"：一日清，指将五齐中的醴齐经过滤去糟渣后的清汁之酒。二日医，将米煮成了粥，然后加曲，酿之成酒。三日浆，有酢浆汁的酸酒。四日酏，用薄粥酿成的酒。有的史书说它是取用黍米之粥，酿成的黍酒。

制订了天子、诸侯、大夫等主要官员的膳食制度。《周礼》规定："王日一举，鼎十有二，物皆有俎，以乐侑食。"这是西周最初沿续商代"鼎食制"的规定。所谓王日一举，指皇帝的朝食，一天三次进餐盛器与饮食。鼎是用来盛肉的。鼎十有二，即用十二只鼎食，谓：牛一、羊二、猪三、鱼四、腊五、肠胃六、肤（切小的熟肉）七、鲜鱼八、鲜腊九；又有陪鼎三只：膷（牛）一、臐（羊）二、膮（猪）三，合为十二鼎。物皆有俎，俎为盛肉盘，鼎有十二，盛食俎也要十二盘。所谓以乐侑食，指天子吃饭时必奏乐来助食。后来又作了调整，据《礼记·礼器》记载："天子之豆（食具）二十有六，诸公十有六，诸侯十有三，上大夫八，下大夫六。"将天子、诸公、诸侯、上大夫、下大夫、吃饭时分别分为五个等级，每天都依照这个规定办理。

天子、上大夫和下大夫宴请也有规定。《周礼》记载："凡王之馈，食用六谷，膳用六牲，饮用六清，羞用百有二十品，珍用八物，酱用百有二十瓮。"就是说：凡是皇帝设宴用稻、黍、稷、粱、麦、苽（水生食物，现今称茭白）六谷。膳用马、牛、羊、豕、犬、鸡六牲。饮用六清，指水、浆、醴、醇、医、酏。羞用一百二十品，是指天子所食的各种珍味。据郑玄注：凡是与禽兽及牲有关的食物均称为庶羞。酱用百有二十瓮，即指皇帝宴请时，醢人要供醢（酱）六十瓮，以五齑、七醢、七菹，醢（音"希"）人共齑菹醢物六十瓮。

上大夫和下大夫之食礼，据《仪礼·公食大夫礼》记载："上大夫庶羞二十，加于下大夫，以雉、兔、鹑。"根据郑玄在《礼记·内则》注中所说："上大夫之食：饭有黍、稷、稻、粱、白黍、黄粱。"膳有膷（牛）、臐（羊），（豕）醢（酱）、牛炙、牛胾（牛肉块）醢、牛脍、羊炙、羊胾（羊肉块）醢、豕（猪）炙、醢、豕（猪）胾，芥酱、鱼脍、雉、兔、鹑、鷃。

下大夫之食：饮食同上。膳有膷、醢、牛炙；牛胾醢、牛脍、羊炙；羊胾醢、豕炙、豕胾、芥酱、鱼脍。

第三，周朝宫廷御膳机构齐全，人员众多，分工明确。宫廷膳食机构与人员配额和各部门具体职责分工如下：

膳夫：上士二人，中士四人，下士八人，府二人，史四人，胥十有二人，徒百有二十人。膳夫掌王之食饮膳羞，以养王及后、世子。凡王之馈，食用六谷，膳用六牲，饮用六清，馐用百有三十品，珍用八物，酱用百有二十瓮。王日一举，鼎十有二，物皆有俎，以乐侑食。

庖人：中士四人，下士八人，府二人，贾八人，胥四人，徒四千人。庖人掌共（供）六畜、六兽、六禽、辨其名物；凡其死生鲜槁之物，以共（供）王之膳与其荐馐之物，及后、世子之膳馐。共（供）祭礼之好馐，共（供）丧俎之庶馐，定额之禽献。

内饔：中士四人，下士八人，府二人，史四人，胥十人，徒百人。内饔掌王及后，世子膳馐之割亨煎和之事，辨体肉物，辨百品之物。王举，则陈其鼎俎，以牲体实之。选百馐、酱物，珍物以俟馈。共（供）世子之膳馐。

外饔：中士四人，下士八人，府二人，史四人，胥十人，徒百人。外饔掌外祭祀之割亨，其（供）其脯、脩、刑、朊、陈其鼎俎，实之牲体、鱼、腊。凡宾客之飧饔、飨食之事，亦如之。

亨人：下士四人，府一人，史二人，胥五人，徒五十人。亨人掌供炉镬，以给水火之齐。职外，内饔之亨者，辨膳馐之物。祭祀，共（供）大羹、铏羹，宾客亦如之。

食医：中士二人。食医掌和王之六食、六饮、六膳、百羞、百酱、八珍之齐（剂）。

酒正：中士四人，下士八人，府二人，史八人，胥八人，徒八十人。酒正掌酒之政令，以式法授酒材。凡为公

220

酒者，亦如之。辨五齐之名。辨酒之物，一日事酒、二日昔酒、三日清酒。辨四饮之物，一日清、二日医、三日浆、四日酏。其掌厚薄之齐，以供王之四饮、三酒之馔，及后、世子之饮与其酒。

此外，还有一些部门，总共22个部门，二千三百余人。可见，周朝宫廷膳食机构之庞大，各种部门齐全，人员众多，分工非常具体而明确，从而保证了宫廷御膳、国宴、节日祭祀等各项食事正常有序地进行。上述这些人员中，膳夫，是官名，主管周王饮食的长官。上士、下士，属爵位称号，为一般官员。府、史是膳夫选用的属员，没有爵位。府，掌管财务帐目。史，负责记帐，写菜单。胥、徒及其以下均为平民百姓，调进膳房当杂务工人员。

由于统治阶级把宫廷餐饮扩及到祭祀、天子与诸侯会晤时的宴会，这样宫廷餐饮就把饮食与政治联系起来。中国春秋时期著名思想家老子曾说："治大国若烹小鲜"，译意是治理大国像烹制小鱼，不可翻来复去；政策方针应具有稳定性。在五十余年前，旧中国政府的公文中还把负责行政的首脑职责称为："调和鼎鼐"。"鼎鼐"在古文中就是大大小小的菜锅，"调和鼎鼐"也就是调和锅中菜肴的味道，使之适口。饮食与政治的关系在周秦两汉（约公元前11世纪—220）时期尤其显得重要；天子与诸侯、诸侯与诸侯会见都离不开宴享。

两汉（公元前206—公元220）以后是中国饮食文化的昌盛时代，这个时代有许多共同点，体现了"昌盛"的特征。饮食文化进入自觉，出现了一系列有关饮食文化的专著。如北魏的崔浩所著的《食经》、贾思勰《齐民要术》的饮食部分等。这些著述不仅表现了这一时期的饮食观点，

221

而且还记录了许多菜肴的做法，使饮食开始走向专门化。

在这一时期的汉魏（前206—265）时期，宫廷餐饮沿用周礼之制，其时，由于生产发展，中外文化交流加强，烹馔原料来源扩大，炊具也有所改进，普遍使用铁器，烹饪技术提高很快，宫廷菜肴水平高于前代。西汉（前206—公元8年）枚乘《七发》写吴客说楚太子，有关美馔的描写，虽有文学夸张因素，但仍可反映出当时宫廷饮食的一隅：牛犊嫩肉，蒲笋鲜蔬，肥狗羹汤，石耳盖浇，苗地好米，菰米做饭，手抓成团，到口即散。简直象伊尹掌灶，易牙烹调，烂烹熊掌，调以香酱，烤里脊片，切生鱼片，秋香茄子，露后蔬菜，兰花香酒，饭后漱口，山上野鸡，家养豹胎，少吃饭，多喝粥，如同热汤浇雪，容易消化。

汉代（前206—公元220年）宫廷中已有温室培植的蔬菜，打破了蔬菜受时令限制的状况。东汉末年宫中尚食蜜渍甜食。

三国（220—265）时期，据说陈留王曹奂曾制驼蹄为羹，一瓯千金，号七宝羹。那时的曹氏父子大权在握，挟天子令诸侯，他们的餐饮习俗实际上已是宫廷饮食习俗的代表。他们十分注重饮食的花样、口味并特别讲究餐具的精美。那时宫中流行饮茶或赐茶以当酒。

到了南北朝（420—589）时期，作为中国菜肴最主要的烹饪方法——炒已经出现，炒菜成为人们日常佐餐最富中国风格的菜肴。这一时期，佛教传入我国，随着佛教习俗的影响，素肴随之出现，寺院宫廷中均尚食素肴，为适应素肴发展的需要，梁武帝首创了面筋。两汉以后，羹在人们眼中只是汤，它在副食中的地位大大降低了；至于用炙、炮、烤等方法制出的熟肉，汉族人并不常食，即使食用也多借以下酒，并非作为佐餐下饭之常品。南北朝时已出现一些名肴佳馔，这些肴馔有着特殊的命名方法，往往体现出丰富的历史文化内涵；而以前人们只依据制作方法命名肴馔（如"熬"、"捣珍"等）。关于菜的命名，将在"中国菜肴的命名"中详述。这期间发酵技术已进入主食的制作。现在通行的面制食品，如馒头、包子、蒸饼等在汉末都已产生，其它如饼（烤制的）、面条（也称汤饼）等也都步入主食行列。两汉以前通行的分餐制逐渐起了变化，变成今日通行的圆桌、方桌或条桌的合餐。这一变化非常缓慢，伴随着胡床（类似今日的活动椅子）的使用而开始。这一时期长达一千七百余年。

隋唐两宋（581—1279）时期，宫廷饮食规制仍沿袭前朝，在菜肴品种花色上、进食程序方面都有不少发展。隋炀帝（605—618在位）时期，海味水产大量涌入宫廷食单。

隋唐（581—907）时期，宫廷菜比前期品种增多，讲究菜的造型工艺，在菜名上花样翻新，故隋唐宫廷菜既讲究美味也讲美色、造型。其中著名的宫廷菜留传至今者有：炸响铃、油爆大虾、蟹花卷、水晶龙凤糕、清蒸桂鱼等。

如果把饮食特点、习俗细细分别，南北朝与隋唐（581—907）更接近一些，可划为一个时期。宋元（960—1368）则一脉相承，明清（1368—1911）则与近代相似。这期间中国饮食方面及食疗养生方面的专著越来越多，如南北朝（420—589）时期崔浩的《食经》、陶弘景的《名医别录》，隋朝（581—618）谢讽的《食经》、虞世南（杰出书法家，558—638）的《北堂书钞》（酒食部），唐朝（618—907）的孙思邈《备急千金要方·食治篇》、娄居中的《食经通说》、杨晔的《膳夫经手录》，宋朝（960—1279）

郑望之的《膳夫录》、司膳内人《玉食批》、苏轼的《物类相感志》(饮食部分)、《格物粗谈》(兽、禽、鱼类)、黄庭坚的《士大夫食时五观》,元朝(1280—1368)倪瓒(杰出画家1301—1374)的《云林堂饮食制度集》、忽思慧的《饮膳正要》。明朝(1368—1644)宋诩的《宋氏养生部》、陈继儒(著名画家)的《饮食绅言》、刘若愚《明宫史．饮食好尚》。清朝(1644—1911)朱彝尊《食宪鸿秘》、李渔《闲情偶寄》(饮馔部分)、袁枚《随园食单》等等不下数百部。上述有关饮食及食疗养生的数百部著述中,多是当时的文人、士大夫、医药学家、文学家、书画家、史学家完成的,因而中国饮食烹饪及食疗养生是中国古代文化的重要组成部分,它广泛汲取了文学、美学、医学和厨艺的营养。

作为一个民族,从广义上来说就有某种程度的封闭性,正是由于这种封闭性,才能构成一个民族。它们对外来的东西往往采取犹豫或拒绝的态度,但各个民族从不拒绝吸收其它民族的优长特别是食物。许多历史学者认为自明朝以后,中国逐渐走上自我封闭的道路,可在这个时期,大量的产于南洋、西洋的食品传入我国。它们不是被西方人用坚船利炮送来的,而是我们自己主动从外边"拿来"的,有些食品在引进过程中还曾冒过危险。例如番薯是明中叶从南洋传入我国的,据考,吴川名医林怀芝到交趾(越南)一带行医,以高超的医术治好了许多病人,国王赐给他甘薯吃。林想把这生熟皆可食的甘薯引入中国,于是要求吃生甘薯,国王赐给他一块,林咬了两口,便把剩下的藏了起来。当时交趾国严禁甘薯外传,林携薯离开交趾时被一关将查出,此将也曾得重病被林治好,为酬谢林之恩,遂允许他携薯出境。

玉米原产于美洲，在明代已传入我国，不过那时尚未普及，而被视为珍异美味。

这一时期传入中国的粮食作物还有原产于非洲的高粱。

大豆原产于中国，但豆类中有些品种是引进的，如绿豆原产于印度，北宋期间传入中国。

介于主食与蔬菜之间，从西洋引进的是马铃薯。传说明代有海盗将它携入中国，最初只在福建、浙江一带种植。明中叶画家徐渭（1521—1593）有《土豆》一诗，末四句为：配著人犹未，随饈箸亦知。娇口嬾非不赏，憔悴浣纱时。"写出了它味美而不为世所知。

两汉以后，植物油逐渐取代了动物脂肪的地位，在烹饪活动中逐渐成为主要的导热介质和调味起香的佐料。日常食用的植物油有胡麻油（北方称香油）、菜籽油、花生油、豆油、葵花籽油等。除胡麻（即芝麻）为西汉时传入，大豆为中国所产外，其它油料作物均为南北朝后传入中国。

调料中最重要的甜味原料——糖，唐代（617—907）已出现。战国时期，楚人已懂得从压榨的甘蔗浆中获取甜味。唐太宗派遣使臣到西域摩揭陀国学习熬糖法，使臣学成回国后用扬州进贡的甘蔗制糖，其颜色、味道比摩揭陀国所产的还要好。这样制出了沙糖。糖后来在烹调中发挥了很大效用，它易溶于水，味道纯正，便于食用，是获取甜味和提鲜的重要佐料，不仅可用汤羹，还可用于炒菜、拌菜乃至炸、烹、炮、烤之中；而两汉以前用于调味的麦芽糖、蜂蜜则大多用于羹汤。

辣椒在今日食用是如此广泛，湖广、四川等地人食之成癖，并有"辣椒是穷人的肉"、"辣椒当盐"的说法，言其如肉和盐一样下饭。它开胃醒脾，促进食欲，还能除湿祛寒。辣椒原产于美洲，明末清初（约15世纪前后）从南洋传入中国。

从外域传入历史最久、声名较著的蔬菜是菠菜，原名波斯菜，系唐太宗时由波斯（今伊朗）传入，因其根赤红，又有赤根菜之名。菠菜质地脆嫩，不耐久炒久煮，在江南一年四季都有，被视为凡品。北方较为普通的外来蔬菜是胡萝卜，原产欧洲，据《本草纲目》说"元时自胡地来，气味微似萝卜，故名。"它营养丰富，有假人参之称，不仅能做菜，还可当水果生吃。苏北东台、泰县、大丰一带，有午间生吃胡萝卜的习俗。

茄子原产于印度，南北朝时随佛教流入中国，在南方宿根成树，可高达五、六尺。在北方则多作草本，一年一种，又名"落酥"、"酪酥"、"昆仑瓜"。

另外还有一些原产于中国，但在上古声名不彰，两汉以后才逐渐被人重视起来的蔬菜，如菘，南北朝时有"春韭秋菘"之称。菘就是近世北方冬季的当家菜——白菜。又如莼菜，自西晋张翰因见秋风起，乃思吴中菰菜、莼羹、鲈鱼脍，曰"人生贵适志，何能羁官数千里以要名爵乎"之后便身价倍增。其它如笋、菌类、冬瓜、各种菜豆，也都是宋代之后才显于世。这些再加上以前已屡见于记载的韭菜、萝卜、大葱、黄瓜、葵菜、苋菜、蔓菁等，就是这一时期的主要蔬菜了。至于晚近才传入中国的甘蓝（洋白菜）、番茄（西红柿）、菜花等，其风行不过数十年光景。

为清人所珍视、现代高档筵席上不可缺少的鱼翅、燕窝，明初已从南洋传入，据说是三保太监（郑和）下西洋携回。清中叶后有了以燕窝、鱼翅制成的以大菜领头的

226

"燕窝席"、"鱼翅席"等名贵筵席。海参、大虾等海产品虽产于中国，却是在以后才较为普遍地进入宫廷肴馔。

这一时期随着城镇的增多和日益繁荣，烹调活动大量涌入商业领域，许多城市酒楼食馆林立，厨人摆脱了为君王贵族个人服务的奴隶地位，逐渐转变为出卖烹调技艺的独立劳动者，他们中间涌现出了许多著名的烹调家，享大名于一时，如南宋的宋五嫂、清代的王二余等。

此时士大夫也介入了烹饪领域，厨人们的智慧与劳动的结晶大多通过他们的记述而流传后世。而且他们凭着自己的文化教养和细腻的审美感觉，促使厨人烹饪的肴馔更富于情致，能够更大限度地满足人们在视觉、嗅觉、味觉、触觉上的要求。他们是精通饮食、烹调之道的美食家，与历代厨师共同创造着饮食文化。他们是厨师作品的鉴定者、评判者，是烹调进步的推动者和烹调经验的总结者。

随着中外文化的交流，许多根本不产于中国的食品逐渐成为人们日常生活中的常食，如玉米、白薯、花生、辣椒。由于地域的差别，各地的饮食风味在扩大交流的基础上形成了具有独特风味的菜系。

人们的饮食生活不仅受地域的影响，更受到其经济状况、文化教养、宗教信仰等因素的制约，因而形成了具有阶级和等级差异的宫廷饮食文化、贵族饮食文化、士大夫饮食文化、市井饮食文化和寺庙饮食文化。特别是到了明朝时代宫廷餐饮与饮食养生密切配合，形成了独具特色的宫廷御膳。

# 明代宫廷餐饮

明朝的开国皇帝朱元璋定都南京，明初宫廷尚食南味。1403 年燕王朱棣（朱元璋四子）称帝，年号永乐。他于永乐 18 年 9 月（1420 年）迁都北京，南京宫廷厨役高手北上，但原料多用北京当地产品，宫食兼有南北两味。那时各地贡品繁多，宫中肴馔四方皆备。北京为元朝故都，昔宫中饮食受元蒙影响，明代宫廷以汉食为主，改变了昔元蒙宫食之风。

元代宫廷虽以蒙食为主，习嗜肉食、兽禽兼用，羊肉比重较大，水产海味甚少，宫廷御食荤腥与蔬菜配用，兼有回、汉及域外风味，这是由于元朝京城——大都（今北京）一直是交通要道和汉族人居多的城市。在这里，元蒙统治者的饮食必然受到汉族及其他民族的影响。

元、明两朝宫食有一点是共同的：重视饮食保健，讲究养生之道。元世祖忽必烈（1215—1294）很重视饮食保健。天历（1328—1330）年间，元太医院饮膳太医忽思慧写了《饮膳正要》一书献给皇帝，论述了饮食营养与饮食卫生方面的问题及各种汤、羹、浆、膏、油、茶以及各种

228

烧饼、包子、馒头、粥、面等膳食的制做及其营养作用。对元代宫廷饮食产生了很大的影响。宫中提倡养生避忌、重视胎教、讲究妊娠食忌、饮酒避忌、提倡四时食宜，防止五味偏走，特别注重食疗养生。

明太祖朱元璋（1328—1398）即位不久，即召见海宁百岁老人贾铭，查询长寿之要诀，贾铭献《饮食须知》给朱元璋。元太医院医忽思慧所撰《饮膳正要》一书亦受到明朝皇帝重视，景泰年间明代宗朱祁钰亲为此书作序，重刊于世。

明宫饮食与历代宫食一样，按节令供食，追求时新果品肴馔。明宫餐饮中素蔬水果比荤食要多，荤腥中主要有鸡、雉、鹅、鸭、鲤、鲫、鳜、鳊、兔、鹿。

明代宫廷饮食，每日排换食单，变换口味，菜肴不重复，点心也有异，这种每日饮食翻新的做法，一直延续到清代。

明代中叶，宫廷饮食品种更为丰富，质量精益求精，并出现了一些新的烹调方法。朝廷有逢节日、祭日、庆典等活动时，还赐食给朝臣和官员等。如端午节赐朝官于门外吃粽糕，逢典礼时，赐晋见者红绫饼等。逢国子监太学生晋谒孔子时，也赐食。不过所赐食品品种不多。明宫中重视食用黄鼠，黄鼠蒙古语名塔剌花，又名土拨鼠，秋高肥美，是山西每年的贡品，食用黄鼠是元蒙食尚的遗风。但从整体看，明代宫廷汉食习俗占绝对优势，按节令供食，据孙承泽《典礼记》云：

"正月：韭菜、生菜、鸡子、鸭子；二月：芹菜、薹菜、冰菱蒿本、鹅；三月：茶、笋、鲤鱼；四月：樱桃、杏子、青梅、王瓜、雉鸡；五月：桃子、李子、来禽、茄子、大麦仁、小麦面、鸡；六月：莲蓬、甜瓜、西瓜、冬瓜；七月：枣子、葡萄、鲜菱、苋实、雪梨；八月：藕、芋苗、茭白、嫩姜、粳米、粟米、稷米、鳓鱼；九月：橙子、栗子、小红豆、沙糖、鳊鱼；十月：柑子、橘子、山药、兔、蜜；十一月：甘蔗、荞麦面、红豆、鹿、兔；十二月：菠菜、芥菜、鲫鱼、白鱼。"这些荐新之物素蔬水果占很大比重，荤腥中鸡、雉、鹅、鸭均有，鳊、白、鲤、鲫、鳜齐备，畜兽类丰富。

明宫中所食南味居多，汉食占主导地位。

奢侈豪华，饕餮成风，是明宫饮食的一大特点。据刘若愚记载："凡宫眷所用饮食，皆本人所关赏赐置买，雇请贫穷官人，在内炊爨烹饪。其手段高者，每月工食可须数两，而零星赏赐不与焉。凡煮饭之米，必拣簸整洁，而香油、甜酱、豆豉、酱油、醋一应杂料，俱不惜重价自外置办入也。凡宫眷内臣所用，皆炙煤煎熯厚味。遇有病服药，多自己任意胡乱调治，不肯忌口。总之，宫眷所重者，善烹调之内官；而各衙门内官所最喜者，又手段高之厨役也。"

由于性生理受到摧残变异，太监们特别重视强肾壮阳食品。"内臣又最好吃牛驴不典之物，曰'挽手'者，则牡具也。又'羊白腰'者，则外肾也。至于白马之卵，尤为珍奇贵重不易得之味，曰'龙卵'焉。""烂煮老雄鸭，功效抵参耆。"太监们喜食上文提到的雄鸭腰子，原因也在此。

明宫菜点特别讲究餐具，超过前代。柴、汝、官、哥、饶窑器之外，内府又有宣德、成化、嘉靖、万历瓷珍品。角、玉之外，还有景泰蓝器皿。至于纯金、纯银或镶宝金

230

银器其形制之巧者，亦不可胜数。严嵩（1480—1567）家截藏的贡品中，即有大量的高档餐具。

明宫菜点并无专谱。仅参考有关史料，将明宫部分有代表性的菜点列举制法如下：

**炙羊肉**　用肉为轩，研酱末、缩砂仁、花椒屑、葱白，熟香油揉和片时，架少水锅中，纸封锅盖，慢火炙熟。或熟者复炙之。（《宋氏养生部》）

炙羊肉片：生羊肉切片，炭火上用铁网炙，不时蘸盐水、酱油，俟反正俱熟，乘热用。

**爆炒羊肚**　将羊肚洗净，细切条子，一边大滚汤锅，一边热熬油锅。先将肚子入汤锅，笊篱一焯，就将粗布扭干汤气，就火急落油锅内炒，将熟，加葱、蒜片、花椒、茴香、酱油、酒醋调匀，一烹即起，香脆可食。如迟慢，即润如皮条，难吃。（《遵生八笺》）

**爆羊肚**　生肚切骨牌块，滚水略余，入熟油锅连翻数次，澄去油，加豆粉、葱段、蒜片、酱油。炒羊肚：羊肚切小片，入鸡油、酱油、酒、姜、葱花炒。又，切条，入滚水上一余即起，用布挤干，用熟油炒微黄，加酒、酱油、葱炒。（《调鼎集》）

**蒸羊肉**　肥羊治净，切大块，椒盐擦遍，抖净。击碎核桃数枚，放入肉内外，外用桑叶包一层，又用捶软稻草包紧，入木甑按头，再加核桃数枚于上，密盖，蒸极透。（《食宪鸿秘》）

**蒸牛乳白**　每用牛乳三盏，配鸡蛋、胡桃仁一枚（研极细末）、冰糖少许（亦研末），和匀蒸用，兼能补益。（老人气燥、有痰者加姜汁一茶匙）（《调鼎集》）

**冷片羊尾**　羊尾蒸烂，冷透切片，蘸糖。（《调鼎集》）

**灌肠**　大肠实肉醢料，缚两端，水烹。（《宋氏养生部》）

**水龙子**　用猪精肉二分，肥肉二分，剁极细。入葱、椒、杏仁酱少许，干蒸饼末少许，和匀。用醋着手圆之，以真粉作衣。汤汤下，才浮便起。清辣汁任供。（《云林堂饮食制度集》）

**烧猪肉**　洗肉净，以葱、椒及蜜少许，盐、酒擦之。锅内竹棒阁起。锅内用水一盏，酒一盏，盖锅，用湿纸封缝。干则以水润之。用大草把一个烧，不要拨动。候过，再烧草把一个。住火饭顷，以手候锅盖冷，开盖翻肉。再盖，以湿纸仍前封缝。再烧草把一个。候锅盖冷即熟。（《云林堂饮食制度集》）

**糟猪蹄**　糟猪头、蹄爪法：用猪头、蹄爪煮烂，去骨，布包摊开，大石压扁，实落一宿。糟用甚佳。（《遵生八笺》）

**清蒸肉**　用好猪肉煮一滚，取净方块，水漂过，刮净，将皮用刀界碎。将大小茴香、花椒、草果、官桂用稀布包作一包，放汤锣内，上压肉块，先将鸡、鹅清过好汁，调和滋味，浇在肉上。仍盖大葱、腌菜、蒜椰，入汤锅内，盖住蒸之。食时去葱、蒜并包料，食之。（《遵生八笺》）

**白煮肉**　凡要煮肉，先将皮上用利刀横立刮洗三四次，然后下锅煮之。随时翻转，不可盖锅，以闻得肉香为度。香气出时，即抽去灶内火，盖锅闷一刻捞起，片吃，食之有味。（《又云：白煮肉，当先备冷水一盆，置锅边，煮拨三次，分外鲜美。（《醒园录》）

**暴腌肉**　猪肉切半斤大块，用炒盐，以天气寒热增减椒、茴料并香油，揉软，置阴处晾着，听用。（《食宪鸿

232

秘》）

**套肠** 猪小肠肥美者，治净，两条套为一条，入肉汁煮熟，斜切寸断，伴以鲜笋、香蕈汁汤煮供。风味绝佳，以香蕈汁多为妙。煮熟，腊酒糟用亦妙。（《食宪鸿秘》）

**炒肉丝** 切细丝，去筋祥皮骨，用清酱，酒郁片时，用菜油熬起白烟变青烟后，下肉炒匀，不停手，加蒸粉、醋一滴、糖一撮、葱白、韭、菜之类。只炒半斤，文火不用水。又一法：用油炮后，用酱水加酒略煨，起锅红色，加韭菜尤香。

**炒肉片** 将肉肥精各半，切成薄片，清酱拌之，入锅油炒；闻响即加酱、水、葱、瓜、冬笋，韭菜，起锅火要猛烈。（《随园食单》）

**荔枝肉** 用肉切大骨牌片，放白水煮二三十滚，撩起，熬菜油半斤。将肉放入泡透撩起，用冷水一激，肉皱，撩起。放入锅内，用酒半斤。清酱一小杯，水半斤煮烂。（《随园食单》）

**炸铁脚雀** 铁雀干捋净毛，一手捏雀脯，一手以刀从雀尾处划小开口，挤出内脏，刀从尾沿脊骨剖开，剔净胸骨，拍断脊骨、腿骨，斩掉嘴尖、爪尖，去眼，洗净沥干，入绍酒、盐、姜、葱汁碗中浸渍片刻，染糯米粉，入沸花生油锅略炸，沥油停冷，重油再炸，至酥脆金黄，勾蒜末糖醋芡加麻油，浇雀装盘。（《中国菜谱》）

**烧鹅** 用烧肉法。亦以盐、椒、葱、酒多擦腹内，外用酒蜜涂之，入锅内。余如前法。但先入锅时以腹向上，后翻则腹向下。（《云林堂饮食制度集》）生鹅加三香盐擦透，锅烧。（《调鼎集》）

**鸡醢** 肥鸡白水煮半熟，细切。用香糟、豆粉调原汁，

233

加酱油调和烹熟。鹅、鸭、鱼同法制。(《食宪鸿秘》)

**蒸鸡** 嫩鸡治净，用盐、酱、椒、茴香等末匀擦腌半日，入锅镟蒸一柱香取出，撕碎、去骨，酌量加调滋味，再蒸一炷香，味甚香美。鹅、鸭、猪、羊同法。(《食宪鸿秘》)

**卷煎** 将蛋摊皮，以碎肉加料卷好，仍用蛋糊口，猪油、白糖、甜酱和烧。切片用。(《食宪鸿秘》)

**烧鸭** 用雏鸭，上叉烧之。(《随园食单》)

**炙鸭** 用雏鸭，铁叉擎炭火上，频扫麻油，酱油烧。家烧猪肉去皮同。(《调鼎集》)

**鸡脯** 鸡脯：煮熟快，酱油、黄酒闷干。(《调鼎集》)

**田鸡腿** 水鸡：水鸡去身，用腿。先用油灼之，加麻油，甜酒，瓜姜起锅，或拆肉炒之，味与鸡相似。(《随园食单》)

**生炒虾** 油炒虾：先入熬油中炒熟，酱、醋、葱调以盐。

**盐炒虾** 用虾投水中，用盐烹熟。宜醋烹熟之，取水淋洁，暴燥，接去壳为虾尾，色常鲜美。宜黄瓜丝，用蒜醋，宜油炒，用韭头。宜为羹，用豆腐。(《宋氏养生部》)

**糟蟹** 一般熟蟹去脐，过冷，入糟。宜醋糟，同鱼。一用生蟹团脐者，每斤先以炒盐四两腌之，次以白酒醋沸稍干，每蟹一层醋一层，入瓮，泥涂其口，勿见火，藏可数月。(《宋氏养生部》)

**煠银鱼** 银鱼干：宜酒，花椒、葱沃之蒸。宜油炒，同韭。宜酒烹，同瓠、鲜竹笋。宜染调面油煎。宜为羹。(《宋氏养生部》)

**鳆鱼** 煮块明法，称洗净，入酒瓶内，满笼糠火煨一

234

番取出。换水浸之，切用。（《云林堂饮食制度集》）

鲦鱼炒薄片甚佳。杨中丞家削片入鸡汤豆腐中，号称鲦鱼豆腐，上加陈糟油浇之。庄太守用大块鲦鱼煨整鸡，亦别有风趣。（《随园食单》）

**蒸鲫鱼** 鲫鱼去肠不去鳞，用布拭去血水，放汤锣内，以花椒、砂仁、酱擂碎，水、酒、葱拌匀其味，和蒸，去鳞供食。（《遵生八笺》）

**风鱼** 每鱼一斤盐四钱，加以花椒、砂仁、葱花、香油、姜丝、桔细丝，腌压十日，挂烟熏处。（《遵生八笺》）

**鲨鱼筋** 煮鱼翅法：鱼翅整个用水泡软，下锅煮至手可撕开就好，不可太烂。取起，冷水泡之，撕去骨头及沙皮，取有条缕整瓣者，不可撕破，铺排扁内，晒干收贮瓷器内。临用酌量碗数，取出用清水泡半日，先煮一二滚，洗净，配煮熟肉丝或鸡丝更妙。香菇同油、蒜下锅，连炒数遍，水少许煮到发香，乃用肉汤，才淹肉就好，另醋再煮数滚，粉水（芡汁：豆粉和水）少许下去，并葱白煮滚下碗。其翅头之肉及嫩皮加醋、肉汤，煮作菜吃之。（《醒园录》）

鱼翅难烂，须煮两日才能摧刚为柔。用有二法：一用好火腿、好鸡汤，加鲜笋、冰糖钱许煨极烂，此一法也；一纯用鸡汤串细萝卜丝、拆碎鳞翅，馋和其中，飘浮碗面，令食者不能辨其为萝卜丝、为鱼翅，此又一法也。用火腿者，汤宜少；用萝卜丝者，汤宜多，总以融洽柔腻为佳。若海参触鼻、鱼翅跳盘，（指海参、鱼翅未发透至软出现的状况）便成笑话。（《随园食单》）

**海参** 海参无味之物，沙多气腥，最难讨好，然天性浓重，断不可以清汤煨也。须检小刺参，先泡去泥沙，用

235

肉汤滚泡三次，然后以鸡、肉两汁红煨极烂，辅佐则用香蕈、木耳，以其色黑相似也。大抵明日请客，则先一日要煨，海参才烂。（《随园食单》）

**鲟鳇鲊** 鲟鱼鲊：切小块，盐腌半日，拌椒末、红谷、麻油，压以鹅卵石。鳇鱼同。（《调鼎集》）

**糟瓜茄** 瓜茄等物每五斤盐十两，和糟拌匀，用铜钱五十文逐层铺上，经十日取钱，不用别换糟，入瓶收，久翠色如新。（《遵生八笺》）

**羊肚菜** 羊肚菜出湖北，食法与葛仙米同。葛仙米即地耳：将米细捡淘净，煮半烂，用鸡汤、火腿汤煨。临上时，要只见米，不见鸡肉、火腿才佳。（《随园食单》）

**炒鸡腿蘑菇** 芜湖大庵和尚洗净鸡腿，蘑菇，去沙，加秋油、酒、炒熟盛盘，宴客甚佳。（《随园食单》）

**鸡子面** 取鸡子同水调混黄白，和面，擀开薄用，折而切如细缕，余同前制。（《宋氏养生部》）

**千层饼** 用生熟水和面，擀开薄，或布鸡鹅膏，或布细切猪脂肪，同花椒盐少许，厚掺干面卷之，直揿数转，接平擀为饼。一用直揿数转，复以生熟水和面，为外皮括于内，擀薄饼。俱热锅熯熟。（《宋氏养生部》）

**酥皮角儿** 用面，以油水少盐和为小剂，擀开，纳前馄饨腥馅、素馅，或熟油盐调干面，而缄其缘，油煎之。（《宋氏养生部》）

**芝麻烧饼** 用酵和面，缄豆沙或糖面，擀饼，润以水，染以熟芝麻。俟酵肥，贴烘炉上自熟。（《宋氏养生部》）

**馓子** 用油水同盐少许，和面，揉匀，切如棋子形，以油润浴，中开一穴通，两手搓作细条，缠络数周，取芦竹两茎贯内，置沸油中，或折之，或纽之，煎燥熟。亦有

236

和赤砂糖煮，似蜜者。（《宋氏养生部》）

**麻叶**　（即芝麻叶）用面同生芝麻水和，擀开薄切小条子，中通一道，屈其头于内而伸之，投热油内煎燥。（《宋氏养生部》）

**玉菱白**　用白糯糢粉一升，干山药坋半升，芋魁劖去皮，捣糜烂，和水滤去汁，溲二物揉实，长若菱白状，暴燥。取香油一斤、蜜一斤，同煎肥，复以蜜染，取炒熟芝麻衣之。（《宋氏养生部》）

**髓饼（即骨髓饼）**　用白糯粉五升，牛骨髓半斤，白砂糖半斤、酥四两，沸汤溲为饼，铁锅中糢熟。（《宋氏养生部》）

**米糒（即米线）**　一粳米湛洁，碓筛绝细粉，汤溲稍坚，置锅中煮熟，杂生粉少许，擀使开。折切细条，暴燥，入肥汁中煮。以胡椒、施椒、酱油、葱调和。一粉中加米浆为糯揉以索绿豆粉，入汤釜中，取起。（《宋氏养生部》）

**蓼花**　取芋魁劖去皮，捣糜烂七分，杂白糯米绝细粉三分，复捣一处，为厚饼数十枚，水煮过熟，置器中，调搅甚匀。先将一木板傅侉在上，擀开，暴半燥，切片段。复暴燥用。又切小颗，同干沙炒肥。或同小石子炒为后四制，（另有四种制法，名曰，檀香球，七香球、芝麻球、薄荷球）以猪脂熬为油，入煎之，尤肥是松也。（《宋氏养生部》）

**抱螺**　素酥、糖酥、有藏白砂糖者，有叠赤砂糖者。（《宋氏养生部》）

**椒盐饼**　白面二斤、香油半斤，盐半两，好椒皮一两，茴香半两，三分为率。以一分纯用油、椒盐、茴香和面为穰，更入芝麻屑尤好。每一饼夹穰一块，捏薄入炉。又法：

用汤与油对半，内用糖与芝麻屑，并油为穰。（《遵生八笺》）

**馄饨** 白面一斤，盐半两和如落索面，更频入水搜和为饼剂，少顷，操百十遍，捌为小块，擀开，绿豆粉为粹，四边要薄。入馅，其皮坚。膇脂不可搭在精肉，用葱白，先以油炒熟，则不荤气。花椒、姜末、杏仁、砂仁、酱调和得所。更宜笋菜，煤过莱菔之类，或虾肉、蟹肉、藤花、诸鱼肉尤妙。下锅煮时，先用汤搅动，一条箸在汤内，沸则频频洒水，令汤常如鱼津样滚，则不破其而坚滑。（《易牙遗意》）

**雪花糕** 蒸糯饭捣烂，用芝麻屑加糖为馅，打成一饼，再切方块。（《随园食单》）

**内府玫瑰火饼** 面一斤，香油四两，白糖四两（热水化开）、和匀，作饼。用制就玫瑰糖加胡桃白仁、榛松瓜子仁、杏仁（煮七次，去皮尖）、薄荷及小茴香末擦匀作馅，两面粘芝麻煨熟。（《食宪鸿秘》）

**脆薄饼** 蒸面，每斤入糖四两，油五两，加水和，擀开半指厚，取圆，粘芝麻，入炉。（《食宪鸿秘》）

糖薄脆法：白糖一斤四两，清油一斤四两，水二碗，白面五斤，加酥油、椒盐水少许，搜和成剂，擀薄如酒钟口大，上用去皮芝麻撒匀，入炉烧熟，食之香脆。（《遵生八笺》）

238

# 清宫御膳述闻

徐启宪

在中国饮食文化中，紫禁城清宫御膳占有极重要的一页。它以满族传统饮食为基底，不断吸收以汉族为主体的中华饮食文化的精华，并使之发展，形成了别具特色的清宫膳饮文化，至今为中外各界所瞩目。

清代皇帝用餐，宫廷中设有专管皇帝的饮食机构，叫"御膳房"。它座落在清代皇帝居住和处理政务的养心殿南侧，由清宫总管内务府衙门直接管理，设专职管理事务大臣若干人，管理事务大臣由皇帝亲自任命。清宫御膳房又设尚膳正、尚膳副、尚膳、主事、委署主事、笔帖式等官职，具体负责管理皇帝的用膳事宜。御膳房中有侍候皇帝用膳的官员、厨师、大小太监等多达二百余人。另外皇后有内外膳房，皇太后等有专设的外膳房，皇子、皇孙娶福晋（妻子）后则有专门的膳房。

清宫帝后用餐为什么叫"用膳"、"传膳"、"进膳"，就

239

是不用"吃饭"二字，则是取吉利、膳用善谐音，有亲和之意，饭同犯谐音、如有异地口音者则把饭念成"反"。再则要显示皇室和平民面姓得有区别，表现皇权的至高无限和生活上的豪华。

在紫禁城皇宫大内，皇帝的进膳又分为两类；一类是常膳、即平日吃的便饭；一类为筵宴，即大型宴会，另外还有皇帝零星赐宴等。清朝初期，有茶房、清茶房和膳房之分，膳房分布在宫内各处，茶房和清茶房是专门承办乳茶和各种清茶的场所。膳房一般以制作菜肴为主，兼做粥品和面食。做饽饽和各种糕点、炉食（烧烤食品），专有饽饽房。饽饽房又分内饽饽房和外饽饽房。内饽饽房专为皇帝和皇家人承办主食；外饽饽房主要承办筵宴和祭供所需的米面食品。内饽饽房和外饽饽房归内务府属下的掌管关防管理的内管领事物处管理。乾隆时期（1736—1795），御茶膳房管理的膳房体系又划分为内膳房和外膳房。内膳房下设荤局、素局、挂炉局（满语称包哈局）、点心局、饭局。荤局负责制作山珍海味类、家畜、家禽、野禽、菜肴，如乳猪、挂炉鸭、挂炉鸡等；点心局负责制作各种糕点、饽饽等；饭局负责制作各种米饭、粥品等。外膳房主要负责制作内廷筵宴和摆供桌张等。

在圆明园、颐和园、热河行宫等处也分设许多御膳房。另外，为御膳房服务的还有买办肉类处、内房和菜库、干肉库等机构，以保证供应御膳房每日所需的原材料。这类膳房（包括茶房）都有餐具库，储藏各种金、银、玉、锡、铜、瓷等器皿，以备随时应用。

清宫御膳，是皇室日常生活的重要组成部分。就其进膳时的礼仪、规模、用度、开销，以及肴馔的品种和质量、技艺等方面，都已达到我国历代封建王朝御膳的最高水平。

## 清 宫 御 厨

顺治入关（1644 年）后，清宫的司厨者多是满族人，以及明宫留下来的厨师。当时的清宫御膳和其它膳食与在沈阳盛京时期的基本相同。明宫留下来的厨师也不敢擅制汉菜，恐有悖于满族统治者的饮食习惯和民族心理意识。这样，很长一段时期，清宫御膳实际上就是满族烹饪。

但是，顺治入关后，清宫中的膳事机构、组织形式以及许多有关膳事都沿袭明制。比如顺治初期，宫中设立了光禄寺，负责为国家举办各种筵宴；膳事机构的各级官员都由太监和侍卫们担任。明宫中留下来的厨师大都是山东人，他们制作山东菜的技艺有很多先进之处，他们在宫内长期服差中，这些技艺自然要影响满族厨师。从此清宫肴馔制作的质量和花色品种不断提高和增加。

当时在光禄寺举办的宴席分满席和汉席。各等满席都以面食为主食，俗称饽饽席，是传统的满族风味；各等汉席多用鹅、鸡、鸭、鱼、猪肉等原料制作。在汉席中也渗入许多满族烹饪的特色，原料大都是东北的关东货；另外，受满族祭祀活动的影响和制约，其肴馔也有祭品的特色。但多数菜肴属于山东菜。

当时的清宫御膳中，反映出较强的民族观念。满清入关后，为了强化满族统治，防止汉化，在各个方面都采取了一些措施，包括清宫中的膳食。御膳以满族风味为主，也不排除汉菜风味的影响。在光禄寺举办的各种筵宴中，满、汉风味掺杂。

乾隆时期清宫御厨的成分和御膳风味有一定的变化。乾隆时期政局稳定，经济发达，饮食市场空前繁荣。南方一些古老的城市，如苏州、杭州、扬州酒楼林立，庖厨技艺精湛。乾隆六次下江南，吃遍了这里的佳肴美馔，并从这里选调了一批身怀绝艺的厨师来到清宫。在清宫御膳房服差的厨师，都是终身和世袭的，老厨师去世，下一代继承。清宫的厨师，以满族厨师为主体，由于厨师的继承制，使山东风味和苏杭风味也被完好地保存下来。这就使清宫御膳既有东北风味，也有中原味和江南风味。

乾嘉时期（1736—1820），清宫中的厨师有 400 名之多，可谓全盛时期。道光时期（1821—1850）因国力衰退，道光皇帝自己的膳食大大从简，将宫中厨师裁去一半，约剩 200 余名。慈禧时期，宫中的厨师又大大增多起来，膳食用度也空前铺张豪华。关于这一时期的情况，请阅《慈禧私厨西膳房》一文。清宫中技艺精湛的上手厨师是少数，多数是配手，还有管生火、洗菜和各种杂事的。另有很多人在茶房服差。

清宫膳房厨师的待遇分不同等级。最优厚的待遇可得七品官的俸禄，相当于知县的薪水。一般厨师每天俸禄为白银三、四、五、六两不等。这在当时也是不低的收入。上等厨师除俸禄外，还常能受到皇帝和皇家人员的赏赐，因此生活比较富裕。他们的家属一般都住在西郊海淀一带。清末民初这些厨师从御膳房出来，流落到北京、天津和东北地区，有人开了饭馆，把清宫风味传到社会上来。

# 皇帝用膳

清代皇帝用膳，没有固定的地方，经常在他居住和活动的地方用膳，各种大小宴会在宫中太和殿、保和殿、乾清宫和西苑（今中南海）紫光阁举行；日常用膳多在养心殿、重华宫、御书房等宫殿，在清宫内务府膳食档案中都有明确详实的记载，如乾隆皇帝用膳就是如此。乾隆十二年"九月三十日，辰初，万岁爷（即乾隆皇帝）弘德殿进早膳"，"十月初一未正，万岁爷重华宫正谊明道东暖阁进晚膳"。"十月初一日，茶膳房侍候，万岁爷霁红盘野意酒膳一桌，十五品……至养心殿侍候"。两天之内，变换三个用膳的地方。

皇帝用膳，按照清代皇室的生活习惯，分早晚两顿正餐。早膳一般在卯正一刻（上午六点以后），有时推迟到辰正（上午八点以后）；午膳在午正一刻（上午十二点以后），或推迟到未正（下午二点以后），二顿正餐以外，还有酒膳及各种小吃，一般在下午四点以后进食，没有固定的时间，其进膳食谱由皇帝随意命进。每到用膳的时间，皇帝命御前侍卫开始传膳，负责皇帝用膳的御膳房大小官员，立即命令有关的大大小小的太监在皇帝用膳的宫殿布陈膳桌，并按皇帝膳单上菜谱作好的饭菜迅速从御膳房抬来，按照傅膳的严格规定布菜。因为封建皇帝总是害怕有人谋害他，就是对他的近臣、侍卫和管理御膳的官员、太监也不放心，所以饭、菜布陈后，皇帝并不马上用膳，而是用一块小小银牌在每道菜上插几次。据说只要饭菜中有毒，银牌就会变色。用银牌验菜皇帝仍不放心，还要让随侍的太监将每道饭菜都先尝上一点，叫做"尝膳"，如果饭菜里有毒，太监尝了会先中毒，就轮不到皇帝受害了。可见，皇帝一旦登上了金銮宝殿，就把一切人都看成自己的敌人，无形中就把自己牢牢地禁锢起来。

此外，凡是遇到直班奏事引见的日子，照例文武臣僚都于皇帝用膳的时间呈递牌子，要求皇帝召见和奏事。王公宗室用的是红头牌子；文职官员副都御史以上，武职官员副都统以上用的是绿头牌子；外官来京者按察使以上、武官总兵以上用的是一般的牌子。奏事处官员将牌子呈进皇帝阅览后，决定是否召见和奏事，因为要求召见和奏事的牌子是在皇帝用膳时呈递的，所以召见臣僚的牌子叫"膳牌"。

清代皇帝的饮食配制有其深刻的哲学思想和认识渊源。在中国古代文献《国语．郑语》中说："夫和实牲物，同则不继，以他平他谓之和，故能丰长而物归之。"也就是说，饮食不能单一或几种单调的原料，必须多样性，而且这种多样性不是简单的混合，而是合理的搭配，这种合理的搭配就是"和"，"和"就是达到科学协调的地步。中国古代哲学的中庸之道反映在皇帝饮食上就是"和为贵"，"和"的内容和境界，就是食要五谷，味要五味。只有吃用五谷杂粮，食甘、苦、酸、辛、咸五味食物，才能营养全面，促进食欲，身体健康，古文献《内经》说的好，"五味入口，以养五气，气和而生，津液相生，神乃自生"。这种食物的多样性且合理搭配，就是达到"和"的境界，清宫皇帝御膳就是这种"和为贵"的典型代表。

清宫皇帝饮食的结构和变化大体可分两个阶段。以乾隆时期为分水岭。首先，是饮食原料的变化：清代前期，

244

清宫饮食的原料大多来自东北地区，其中有板鸭、宁鸭、东鸭、鸭蛋、燕窝、各种鱼、鹿及其制品、獐、狍、熊、野鸡及各种野味、火腿等肉食制品；菜果有小根菜、青笋、百合、山药、水梨等，热量大的肉食较多，而五谷杂粮和蔬菜水果较少。乾隆以后，饮食结构有较大变化，御膳房增加了五谷杂粮的用量，每年除从玉泉山、丰泽园、遵化的汤泉等处进黄、白、紫老米外，还要从全国各地进贡各种好米、小麦、白面、挂面及五谷杂粮；为保证皇帝和宫廷内有充足的干鲜水果，全国各地都将本地出产的特产和水果运往北京宫内，如山东的万年青、长生果、金丝枣、柿霜、莲子等；河南的柿霜、百合、桃脯等；陕、甘进桂花、哈蜜瓜；两广进香橙、荔枝、桔子、豆蔻；浙、闽进桔、柑、冰糖、槟榔、桂圆；两湖、川、贵都有水果进呈，皇帝的发祥之地东北各地，每年都有杏、梨、榛子、红果、葡萄进内，御膳所需蔬菜则由清宫内务府支银到市肆购买。宫中所需各式小菜、酱菜也由全国进贡。从皇帝每餐膳食的配制上，也体现了多营养、多品味、多花样的特点。一餐膳食，有冷、热菜肴，有荤、素菜肴，有甜、咸点心，有汤、羹、奶品，有烧烤大菜，有佐餐小菜，有干膳米饭，有面食饽饽以及各式小吃、水果等，体现了膳食搭配的多样性。这种膳食的多样性，在清宫内务府皇帝每天吃饭的膳食单中充分体现出来，我们以乾隆膳食为例即可说明。

例一：乾隆十二年十月初一日，"万岁爷（即乾隆皇帝）重华宫正谊明道东暖阁进晚膳，用洋漆花膳桌摆，燕窝鸡丝香蕈丝火熏丝白菜丝馅平安果一品，红潮水碗、续八仙一品，燕窝鸭子火熏片肘子白菜鸡翅肚子香蕈。合此二品，张东官做。肥鸡白菜一品，炖吊子一品，苏脍一品，饭房托汤，烂鸭子一品，野鸡丝酸菜丝一品，此四品铜珐琅碗。后送芽韭抄鹿脯丝，四号黄碗，鹿脯丝太庙供献。烧鹿肉锅塌鸡丝晾羊肉攒盘一品，祭祀猪羊肉一品，此二品银盘。糗饵粉餐一品，象眼棋饼小馒头一品，黄盘、拆摺奶皮一品，银碗。祭神糕一品，银盘。酥油豆面一品，银碗。蜂蜜一品，紫龙碟。拉拉一品，二号金碗，内有豆泥。珐琅葵花盒小菜一品，南小菜一品，菠菜一品，桂花萝卜一品，此四品五福捧寿铜胎珐琅碟。匙箸手布安毕进呈。随送粳米膳进一碗，照常珐琅碗，金碗盖。羊肉卧蛋粉汤一品，萝卜汤一品，野鸡汤一品"。

例二：乾隆三十五年七月"二十八日卯初一刻请驾，辰初养心殿进早膳，用填漆花膳桌摆，总管王成进菜八品。

燕窝鸭丝寿意一品，香蕈蜜豆锅烧鸡一品，蜜鸭子一品，香蕈火燻白鸭子一品，红白鸭子苏脍一品，酒炖福尔肉一品，五香羊肉一品，燕窝火燻肥鸡一品，挂炉鸭子攒盘一品，鸭子馅桃一品，油糕一品。蒸肥鸡烧狍肉攒盘一品，竹节卷小馒首一品，银葵花盒小菜一品，银碟小菜四品，随送万福万寿面进一品，（系王成进），粳米干膳进些"。

例三：乾隆三十五年八月"初六日未正，同乐园进晚膳，用填漆花膳桌摆。

鸭羹一品，鹿筋拆鸡一品，燕窝火燻肥鸡一品，肥鸡拆肘子一品，燕窝火燻白鸭子一品，香蕈白鸭子一品，燕窝火燻鸭丝一品，后送煤鸡咕噜一品，摊鸡蛋一品（俱系铺内侍候）。蒸肥鸡挂炉鸭子攒盘一品，象眼小馒首一品，祭神糕一品，鲜蘑菇猪肉馅包子一品、鸡肉馅烫面饺子一品，（此二品铺内侍候），珐琅葵花盒小菜一品，珐琅碟小菜四品。随送粳米干膳进一品。

额食七桌，饽饽二桌，奶子一桌，盘肉二桌，上进毕，尝用。"

例四：乾隆三十五年"八月初七日卯初请驾，辰初，东书房进早膳，用填漆花膳桌摆。

燕窝红白鸭子肥鸡南鲜热锅一品，脍银丝一品，燕窝锅烧鸭子一品（此三品铺内侍候，野意碗）。莲子烂鸭子一品，厢子豆腐一品，羊肉片一品。清蒸鸭子糊猪肉攒盘一品，竹节卷小馒首一品，祭神糕一品，羊肉馅包子一品，素包子一品，（此二品铺内侍候）、珐琅葵花盒小菜一品，珐琅碟小菜四品，随送红白鸭子苏脍汤膳进一品。

额食五桌，饽饽十二品，奶子七品，祭神肉片十二品，共二十品一桌"。

例五：乾隆四十五年"七月廿七日未正，勤政殿进晚膳，用摺叠膳桌摆。

肉丁镶鸭子一品，锅烧肥鸡五香猪肚一品，口蘑大炒肉炖白菜一品，羊西尔占一品，后送鲜口蘑爆炒鸡一品，藕造鸭子肘子肉攒盘一品，烧鹿肉鹿尾攒盘一品，象眼小馒首一品，白面丝糕糜子面糕一品，大馒首一品，家常饼一品，江米镶藕一品，银葵花盒小菜一品，银碟小菜四品，醡肉一碟。随送粳米干膳进一品"。

清代皇帝的饮食，特别注意养生健体，这也是中国古代美食与养身相结合的优良传统。古文献《内经.素问》中曾有明确记载："五谷为养，五果为助，五畜为益，五菜为充"，五谷杂粮，干鲜水果，各种动物肉食和多样蔬菜为人类健康提供了保证。清代皇帝膳食除合理搭配外，还针对季节性的变化来安排自己的食谱，春夏季节多尚清淡食品，秋冬季节多用滋腻食品，清淡养阴，滋腻养阳，符合人体新陈代谢的规律。我们再以乾隆膳食为例，乾隆春夏两季膳食以清淡为主。

例如，乾隆五十四年六月八日，“倚虹堂进早膳，用填漆花膳桌摆，燕窝挂炉鸭子挂炉肉野意热锅一品，山药鸭羹热锅一品，拌老虎菜一品，拌冰粉一品，菜花头酒炖鸭子一品，小虾米炒菠菜一品，煮藕一品，江米瓤藕一品，香蕈蘑菇炖豆腐一品，脍银丝一品，竹节卷小馒首一品，倭瓜羊肉馅包子一品，黄焖鸡炖豇豆角一品，珐琅葵花盒小菜一品，珐琅碟小菜四品，随送粳米干膳进一品，豇豆水膳一品，上传萝卜丝汤送一些。”

乾隆皇帝秋冬季的御膳多用热量多的滋腻食品。如乾隆五十四年十二月十三日初二刻，“养心殿东暖阁进晚膳，用填漆花膳桌摆。燕窝松子鸡热锅一品，肥鸡火熏白菜热锅一品，羊肚丝羊肉丝热锅一品，口蘑蒸肥鸡一品，口蘑盐煎肉一品，蒸肥鸡秃鲁木羊肉攒盘一品，清蒸鸭子鹿尾攒盘一品，糊猪肉攒盘一品，竹节饺子小馒首一品，匙子饽子红糕一品，螺蛳包一品，鸡肉馅烫面饺一品，银葵花盒小菜一品，银碟小菜四品，咸肉一品，随送鸡汤老米膳一品，山药野鸭羹一品，燕窝攒丝脊髓汤进一些”。

从不同季节两膳单分析，除去满族饮食风俗的热锅和烤鸭、烤鸡每顿必备外，所余食品就可一目了然，不同季有着不同食品了。

清代皇帝为了滋养身体，还在御膳中食用有药物作用的食品，从清宫膳档中都有不少记载，其中包括各种酒、露、膏、脯、糖等。如：松龄太平春酒、龟龄酒、椿龄益药酒、健脾滋肾状元酒、雄黄酒、玫瑰、西瓜膏、木瓜膏、风梨膏、桂圆膏、薄荷茶膏、桂花糕、八珍糕、姜糕、百合糕、山楂酱、菊花酱、南枣酱、地黄脯、银杏脯、佛手脯、蔷薇脯、薄荷糖、杏仁糖、核桃糖等，这些寓药於食的食品，从中药作用看，有着健胃、补肾、助消化、消热、化痰、滋补、长寿等作用。

清代皇帝的御膳，是清代饮食文化的最典型的代表，也是中国饮食文化的发展和重要组成部分。清代皇帝的膳食不仅内容丰富和形式多样，而且有着严格的礼制和深刻的文化思想，不仅有满菜，而且有汉菜，有北方菜，又有南方味，反映了清代饮食文化的丰富多彩和多民族的优良风格。我们今日所享用的饮食大多是清代皇帝饮食文化的继续，社会上出现的各种御膳、仿膳、清宫点心、御酒、药膳等等，无不是在挖掘、继承和发展清代饮食文化的表现。研究和发展清代饮食文化，也是发展当代饮食文化的重要任务。

为了研究清代皇帝的御膳，现将部分清代皇帝的食品告诉读者，以便更好地了解清代皇帝的御膳和饮食文化。

热锅炒菜部分主要有：燕窝口蘑蒸白鸭子热锅，燕窝莲子鸭子热锅，燕窝野意热锅，松鸡锅烧肘子热锅，炒鸡丝肉丝炖海带丝热锅，炒鸡肉片炖豆腐热锅，炒鸡肉片炖菠菜豆腐热锅，炒鸡大炒肉酸菜肘子热锅，大炒肉炒白菜热锅，肉丝水笋丝热锅，红白鸭子炖白菜热锅，酸辣羊肠羊肚热锅，山药火燻葱椒鸭子火锅，锅烧鸡烩三鲜丸子热锅，肥鸡糟戒刀肉热锅，酒炖羊肉豆腐丸子热锅，烩银丝热锅，燕窝冬笋白鸭丝，燕窝口蘑白鸭子，燕窝冬笋锅烧鸭丝，燕窝冬笋锅烧鸡，鹿筋冬笋拆鸭子，鹿筋酒炖羊肉，肥鸡拆肘子，冬笋火烧肥鸡，烧狗肉，炒木樨肉，酒炖东坡蹄，万年青酒炖肉，鸭丁炒豆腐，鸭丝炒菠菜，鸡蛋丝鸡丝炒菠菜，什锦拆鸭子肉丝水笋丝，扒烂肘子，炸紫茄盖，小葱摊鸡蛋，羊肚丝，狗肉火烤，醋溜鸭腰等。

攒盘：蒸肥鸡鹿尾攒盘，挂炉鸭子攒盘，挂炉猪攒盘，藕造鸭子肘子肉攒盘，烧鹿肉鹿尾攒盘，蒸肥鸡烧狍肉攒盘，蒸肥鸡爆羊肉条攒盘，挂炉乳猪攒盘，蒸肥鸡挂炉鸭子攒盘，清蒸鸭子糊猪肉攒盘，蒸肥鸡五香塞勒攒盘，蒸肥鸡烧想皮攒盘，蒸肥鸡炸羊羔攒盘，清蒸鸭子鹿尾野猪攒盘，五香肘子丝攒盘，锅他狍肉攒盘，羊肉卷烧野猪肉攒盘，醋烹绿豆菜攒盘，百果鸭子攒盘等。

汤类：鸡丝燕窝汤，燕窝红白鸭丝汤，豆腐片汤，燕窝八仙汤，羊肠羊肚汤，鸭子豆瓣汤，红白鸭子苏烩汤等。

主食：粳米干膳，象眼大小馒首，孙尼额芬白糕（饼），荷叶饼，匙子饽饽红糕，白面丝糕，糜子米面糕，枣儿糕，豇豆水膳，鸭子馅提摺包子，鸭子口蘑馅手包子，鸭子口蘑馅烧麦，鸡肉香蕈馅烧麦，韭菜馅包子，猪肉馅炸三角饺子，猪肉馅烫面饺子，羊肉馅包子，素包子，白面丝糕糜子面糕，家常饼，鸭子馅桃油炸糕，老米面糕，猪肉馅爆饺子，鸡肉馅烫面饺子，鲜蘑菇猪肉馅包子，倭瓜羊肉馅包子，火燻豆腐包子等。


## 清宫御膳的特色


清宫御膳以满族食风为主，包括山东风味和苏杭风味，三者互相影响，互相渗杂。御膳中的某一款菜肴，取料可能是关东货，烹制技法和口味可能是山东和苏杭的特色；同样，山东或苏杭的菜肴，往往又由满族厨师来烹制。满、汉厨师经过长时期的合作、交流，又必须迎合清朝统治者的品味和筵宴意图，在清宫各种典制礼仪的制约下，相互学习、配合，创造了一种新的膳食格局，反映出来的特色，不同于各个地方菜点，也不同清以前的历代宫廷御膳。

满族食风显著。在清宫御膳中，满族食风和满族传统烹饪起主导作用。清宫御膳大体局限于专为皇帝和皇家服务的内务府御膳房和内饽饽房制作出来的肴馔。这两个膳房制做出来的肴馔前期满族食品多，后来满汉菜点兼有。在清宫举办的各种筵宴中，满席和汉席有严格的区分，满席的规格和供应对象高于汉席。清宫中举办的各种筵宴中，最盛大和最著名的要算千叟宴了（主要是康熙帝于1713年为庆祝60寿辰、乾隆帝于1790年为庆祝80寿辰而举办的大型寿宴），宴上供应的主要食品是野味火锅和满洲饽饽，这是满族的代表肴馔。

满族的祭祀，清宫定为国俗。其牺牲、受胙、酒醴、供献等皆有定规，供献食品须遵循祖制。清宫中每年祭品供献的数量非常大，这些祭品供献，循例由皇帝、皇室和宫内官吏、太监、侍卫们分享。这种祭祀食风，对清宫御膳有很大影响，也是清宫御膳的一个组成部分。因为祭品中的肉类、果酒、糕点饽饽、素菜、干菜、蜜食等，常是帝膳食品。

清宫御膳使用的东北膳食原料，在进贡的次数、数量、价值上，远远超过了其它各省，东北气候寒冷，接近北京，运输方便，更重要的是适合清朝统治者的饮食习惯。这习惯是在东北地区形成的。定都北京后，皇帝每年举办的除夕家宴，都是传统的满族风味。另外，东北的山珍野味、土特名产、河鲜海味有很高的营养和滋补价值，可烹制出各种名贵的菜肴。在清代初期，东北膳食原料是清宫御膳原料的主体。满族食风和烹饪特色在清宫御膳中一度占主导地位。

清宫厨师原先满族人占大多数，是烹饪技术力量的主体，清代中叶以后，情况有些变化。

取料珍贵、广泛。清宫御膳取料集当时天下珍贵食品之大成。肴馔档高、珍奇、名贵、质精。

但是，在清朝的260余年中，随着社会和经济的发展，宫内筵宴的开销多少和皇室成员的口味不同，清宫御膳的原料，在不同时期是有变化的。康熙（1662—1722）之前，由于入关不久，还基本保持着东北的饮食习惯，烹饪原料大体上由北京、蒙古和东北地区供应，其它各省的膳食供品很少。乾隆以后，宫膳原料有了明显的变化，西北、新疆和南方的膳食贡品增加很多。南方的膳食供品，为清宫御膳增加了很多新内容，这与乾隆喜食南味有关。道光、咸丰（1821—1861）时期，南味减少了。道光只偶尔吃一顿乾隆时期的御膳，平时以北方口味为主。同治以后，宫中御膳比乾隆时期更丰富多彩，但使用原料仍以黄河以北和东北地区供应的为主。除了福建的燕窝是清宫的必贡之品外，南方一些特产如火腿、菇笋、鲜蔬等，北方地区亦能制作和栽培。光绪喜食海产品，沿海地区向清宫供献的鱼翅、鲍鱼、海参、大虾、海蜇、海带等原料大大增加了。总之，御膳原料在不同时期有不同的特点。

民间稀有的物料在清宫中常年不断。据考有："回疆（新疆）葡萄，种类各殊，有白、红、紫三色，及长如马乳者。又大葡萄中有小者，名公领孙。又一种小者，名琐琐葡萄。康熙间皆移植御苑。又绿葡萄，回语谓之奇石蜜食。

凡葡萄皆有子，此独无子，截条植地而生。……文官果、花嫣红，实大二三寸许，剖之，中有子数枚，再剖之，有仁作旋螺形。味甘淡而有微香……此果亦入祭品也。""康熙二十年前，圣祖于丰泽园稻田中，偶见一穗与众迥异。次年使择膏壤以布此种。其米做微红色。嗣后四十余年，悉炊此米作御膳，外间不可得也。"乾隆辛未秋狝，塞上蒙古台吉必力滚达以狍献，色纯白如雪，目睛如丹砂。是年恭值皇太后六十大寿，高宗遂命瑞狍而系以诗。次年秋狝，复于巴颜河落围中生致一狍，毛色纯洁周陆；所仅见也。"堪达汉，出黑龙江。似鹿而大，生山中而喜水。"清朝统治的二三百年间，天下珍奇果物禽兽、海味河鲜，或御获、或捕牲兵获、或各地贡献，无所不有、无所不致也；天下珍奇美味，御膳房无不烹制。

馔名朴实，少花色而重食用。现今一些城市仿清御膳中，多以龙凤冠名，或菜名华美俏丽，玄妙无稽。这有悖于清宫御膳的原貌。清宫中，龙，喻皇帝；凤，喻皇后，菜肴不能以龙、凤命名，取名。取名浮华玄妙，重观不重食，不是清宫御膳的本来风格。

查阅有关史料和清宫膳档，从康熙到溥仪各代御膳的馔名，无一龙、凤字样，皆朴实无华。从肴馔名称便可知所用物料，烹制方法或盛装器皿。与当时市肆酒楼饭庄里的肴馔名称无大差别，只是制作得更讲究、更精细罢了。

乾隆时期的宫中御膳比较讲究。菜名朴实，讲究火候和味道，这也是清宫御膳的一贯特点。

操作严谨，投料定规。清宫御膳肴馔是一代一代传下来的。这些肴馔虽然是御膳房首席厨师负责制定的，但都经过皇帝口味的检验，吃得多的是皇帝喜欢的菜；吃得少的或不动的是不太喜欢的，下次列食单时就要考虑撤换。皇帝食单中常有的菜是他喜欢吃的，这样的菜，一律要标准化，即做多少次也不准变样、走味。原材料搭配有严格规定，不准随意更换和增减。

讲究原汁原味，不许串味。比如做鸭菜，只能用鸭油、鸭汁或鸭汤来制作，不能用鸡汤或其它油类。同样，做鸡菜，用鸡油、鸡汁和鸡汤。做羊肉、猪肉菜时亦循此法。

制菜的调味品和佐料也有严格规定，制鸭汤只用鸭，制鸡汤只用鸡，制羊汤只用羊。制汤和煮菜都用玉泉山的水，"玉泉山之水最轻、清，向来尚膳，尚茶，日取水于此，内管领司其事"（《养古斋丛录》卷二十四）。在清代，市场上已有舶来品调味料，如胡椒、番茄酱、奶油等，清宫御膳一概不用。

制作肴馔使用的主料、配料、调料，均有固定的数量，菜码的大小，锛锛成品的大小，长短和高矮，都有规定，不能任意增减。

清代历代皇帝的饮食口味不同，他们膳单上的肴馔也不同。康熙膳食使用的原料主要是东北出产的各类兽肉和羊、鸡、猪肉等。乾隆的肴馔丰富多彩。除东北的山珍海味外，主要喜食燕窝、鸭子、苏州菜点、锅子菜和素食，也爱品茶和食水果，但很少见食海河产品，现今保存下来的记载他日常膳食的大量食单中，几乎找不出一款由鱼翅、海参、大虾、鲍鱼和各种鱼类烹制的菜肴。晚清的光绪皇帝喜欢吃海味菜。慈禧喜欢吃鸭子、熏烤菜和带有糖醋味、果味的菜肴，也喜欢吃菌蘑菇耳和新鲜的蔬菜。溥仪喜欢吃素食和西餐，不喜欢酒。

# 慈禧私厨——西膳房

汪莱茵

清朝到了慈禧独揽大权的时期也就进入了晚期，这一时期人们往往称之为光绪、宣统年间，也是最黑暗、最腐败的政治时代。

慈禧以骄奢淫逸著称，是中国历史上的一位祸国殃民的统治者。她一爱穿、二爱吃、三爱排场。

按清朝制度，皇帝的膳食无定额银两，用今天的话说叫作"实报实销"。太后的膳食费，乾隆时期是每日六十两白银。慈禧执掌朝政时期，她不仅是清朝的"圣母皇太后"，而且是大权独揽的最高统治者，是实际上的皇帝。她每天的膳食费是不会满足于六十两白银的。有人估计，可能要两倍于此，也就是说要一百多两白银。

慈禧在宫中的颐和园都有规模很大的膳房。在宫里，有专为她设立的膳房，称为"西膳房"。

西膳房设有总管太监总客五局，各局都有众多的厨役、苏拉（杂工）等。慈禧膳房五局为：

一、荤菜局。专做烹、炒、炸、熘、蒸、炖各种山珍海味，鸡、鸭、鱼、肉等荤菜。

二、素菜局。专用豆腐、面筋等素菜做各种炒菜、炸菜、熘菜等。

三、饭局。专做饭、粥、馒头、花卷、烙饼、面条等各种主食。仅每顿要做的粥就有：绿豆粥、肉粥、小米粥、薏仁米粥、大麦粥、大米粥等，有时还要做荷叶粥、藕粥、莲子粥等。

四、点心局。专做早点、午后点心，还有夜宵所用的各种蒸、煮、炸、烙点心。

五、饽食局。专做酥皮饽饽（满族称点心为饽饽）、酥盒子、奶油琪子、小炸食、萨其玛等点心。

各局下边是青年徒弟小太监，还有临时入宫帮忙的人，称效力。每局下边又分股办事。专管捧膳食盒送饭菜的小太监就有几百人。若慈禧巡幸，离开紫禁城，西膳房也随驾伺候。膳房的太监各有俸给，厨师中有特长的有较多的月银，遇到慈禧太后高兴时，另外有赏赐。

当时在西膳房担任首领的是谢太监。其弟谢二及王玉山、张永祥等，都是有名厨师，都能挖空心思制做各种新颖味美的膳食，不敢稍有怠慢或疏忽，因而受到慈禧的赏识。

谢二，因慈禧想吃油性炸糕被传入宫当效力，后来留用膳房做蒸炸厨师。拿手的是烧麦，做得皮薄如纸，馅的味道鲜美可口。有次慈禧去东陵祭祀，西膳房派人随行，谢二因为有事未能随行。到了东陵，慈禧要吃烧麦。吃完

256

后感到味道很差，吃得不香，问了问，才知谢二未随驾，是刘大做的。慈禧盛怒，责怪刘大不用心伺候，责打四十大板，立即传旨命谢二火速赶来。

王玉山（他于1925年与其他五人合办了设于北海公园道宁斋的仿膳饭庄），在宫内以擅长烹炒而著名。他创做了"四大抓"，抓炒里脊、抓炒鱼片、抓炒腰花、抓炒虾仁。特点是外松脆，里鲜嫩，略带酸味，食而不腻。慈禧赏赐王玉山为"抓炒王"，因此名震京师，他做的菜成为北京名菜。

张永祥做的菜制作精细，色形美观，在口味上讲究清、鲜、酥、嫩。他的拿手菜有酿豆芽、酿扁豆、即选挺直肥大的豆芽菜去两头，用铜丝挖空，然后塞进用鸡肉或猪肉切成碎末的馅，蒸熟；扁豆也是如此，去两头，挖出豆粒，放进肉馅，上笼屉蒸熟，味道清香鲜美。

每年立夏之后，慈禧就要到颐和园或三海（今北海、中南海）、热河行宫（今承德避暑山庄）等地消夏。西膳房的太监、名厨、杂役都要随行。颐和园里慈禧的私膳房叫"寿膳房"。

"寿膳房"地处仁寿北殿的后身，大戏楼东侧，共有八个大院，一百多间房屋。专门为她烹调饮食的首领太监、厨役、茶役等有一百二十八人之多。比乾隆时期的御膳房还多一、二十人。

在慈禧爱吃的菜品中，有一个菜叫"酿豆芽"。这种菜做起来颇费功夫，十个人做一天也够忙累的。在她爱吃的面食里有一个叫"小窝头"。这种小窝头不是因为比平民百姓吃的大窝头小而得名，而是用料精、做工细。它的主要原料是栗子粉，另外加上小米面、豆粉、糜子面和玉米面，用细罗筛净，然后分料加工，一种加桂花白糖，一种加红糖和枣泥，一种加其它果料，和好面后，精心做成如同拇指般大小的窝头，放在一起蒸熟。

慈禧膳房制做的食品花样繁多。能制点心四百多种，菜品四千样，各种上等高级食品，如燕窝、鱼翅、熊掌、鸡鸭鱼肉等，应有尽有。

慈禧用膳每天有固定时间，一般早膳六点，中饭十二点，晚饭下午六点，另外还有晚点。传膳前，各局将做好的菜食，一律装入菜食盒中，放在廊下几案上。盛菜的用具是淡黄色的绘有二龙戏珠的木制膳盒，膳盒底部有一个用锡制成的底座，座内装有热水，外包棉垫，能保温较长时间。在正常情况下，慈禧吃饭的地方是在她居住的乐寿堂，离"寿膳房"一百多米。每次进膳前，乐寿堂正厅内临时用几张桌子拼成一张大餐桌。只有当首领太监发出"传膳"时，所有的膳食才能从"寿膳房"向乐寿堂运送。传膳时，膳房学徒的小太监排成一个长队，他们身穿蓝布袍，两臂带有白套袖，在廊下候旨。

等传膳太监传旨开膳，小太监每人把自己的膳食盒搭在右肩上。管膳太监和西膳房首领谢太监领着这些小太监依次而入，再由内侍太监把菜放在膳桌上。总管李莲英先用银筷子试尝，如银筷子变黑色，说明有毒不能吃。

用膳时慈禧用眼看哪样菜，太监就把那个菜送到眼前吃上一两口。膳桌上的菜只动几样，余下的赏给皇后、贵妃或宫内其他人。有时还把食物赏给宫外的人。京都西城受赏的有三四家：醇王府、恭王府、庆王府，还有总管李莲英家和李莲英的三第李宝泰家。赏给各府的食盒比八仙桌子略小点，也是淡黄底子上描蓝龙红珠的"二龙戏珠"

图案，由两名太监抬着，捆食盒的麻绳染成红绿色，用的扁担两头漆绿色，中间糅红漆。食盒里的碗和碟子是蓝色和豆绿色的。太监把食盒送到各府，领常而回。

查阅光绪十年的有关资料，仅慈禧膳房做菜及其它零用的清宫玉泉酒，一年就有八千八十斤零二两。据传就是在她乘火车去河北易县清西陵祭陵时，还用了四节车厢做膳房，"备正菜一百种"，"糕点、糖果一百种"，"炉灶五十座"，"厨子一百名"。由此可见，慈禧在宫中每餐的奢侈程度是何等的惊人。

每当盛夏清宫都有食荔枝的习惯。荔枝是中国的果中珍品，皮色红艳似火，果肉甘甜多汁、晶莹明润，产于广东、广西、福建、云南、四川、台湾等省，以福建荔枝最为有名。特别是福建福州，兴化、泉州、潭州、福宁、永春等地区的荔枝，品种多、果实大，以六七月份成熟的状元红为最佳。

宫廷中盛夏食用鲜荔枝并非易事。由于自秦汉以来，中国的都城都在北方的中原地区，远离荔枝产地。荔枝汁多，极易变质腐烂，其产地只好把它做成蜜饯或干果。根据中医养生的理论，鲜荔枝生食，能生津止渴、和胃平逆（健胃），凡胃燥气逆、津液不足、口燥、牙痛、喉痛都宜服荔枝。鲜荔枝煎水或与米煮粥食用能补肝肾、健脾胃，因些荔枝又被视为极富养生价值的珍果。这样，历代封建帝王都不惜任何代价，从数千里之外，往皇宫中送运鲜荔枝。据说唐玄宗（712—756 在位）的宠妃杨贵妃嗜荔枝，乃置骑传送，走数千里。故唐代诗人杜牧有"一骑红尘妃子笑，无人知是荔枝来"的诗句。由此可见宫廷生活的奢侈。

据雍正皇帝（1723—1735 在位）时期的贡单上看，每年五月由福建水师战船专程海运荔枝树六十桶进京，历六十余日。荔枝树整棵运送，果实保鲜当然比唐代驿马奔送要好，但花费十分昂贵，因此皇帝对荔枝树上的果实数量十分留意。内务府从收到荔枝树之日起，逐日将摘食鲜荔枝及赏赐情况登记入薄，皇帝本人每天也只尝鲜几枚，其余赏赐大臣，以示恩宠。此举始于乾隆皇帝（1736—1795 在位）时期。那时除了皇帝、后妃、皇子、公主、亲王及重臣外，任何人都吃不到鲜荔枝。一般进贡皇宫的荔枝树可采食廿余天。

用荔枝和各地进贡皇宫大内的时令鲜果做的祛暑冰镇的甜碗子，更是诱人异常，它是用顶好的琼脂、杏仁霜、蜂蜜、冰糖、桂花等熬的浆，放入各种时鲜水果和难得的荔枝，冰镇后从碗中看去晶莹如玉、果色斑驳、清凉爽口，那时如侍奉慈禧左右的人能得到她格外恩赏的甜碗子，是极为荣幸的。

慈禧每逢年节十分讲究用膳时的排场，这里给读者讲一段慈禧大年初一吃晚膳的情景。这顿晚膳排场之大，无与伦比，要由四"金刚"五百"罗汉"伺候。这晚膳地点一般在外东路的宁寿宫，或是在储秀宫南边的体和殿，因为这是慈禧晚年常住的二个宫殿，都必须同时摆三桌同样的菜。这三桌菜分别叫做天、地、人，天一桌在东，地一桌在西，人一桌在中间。这人一桌便是西太后独占了。表示除了天地以外，西太后自己便是独尊的了。

什么叫"四金刚"？便是穿着公服的四个老太监，一般都在先朝有功的，现已不当差了，只在这隆重日子出来当差。他们之中有给道光皇帝当书僮的；有在咸丰大殓时，把咸丰的寿衣，从夏天的纱、单，到各色夹衣，以至冬天的棉、皮衣，先在这个太监身上套好后再往咸丰尸身上套。这四个太监在殿堂的四角站好，宫里管这四个给西太后站堂的太监，叫做"四金刚"。另外，由宫门口外的门坎算起，到寿膳房的门坎止，不多不少整整站着五百个太监，这叫"五百罗汉"。"五百罗汉"一律穿崭新的宁绸袍，粉白底的靴子，新剃的头，透着精神气。殿内、院内灯火通明，仅在院内五百太监的长龙前，每隔五步一盏灯笼，一条火龙从寿膳房，直到进膳的宫殿。这五百太监是经过挑选的，年老的不要，太小的不要。每年从腊月初八开始训练，训练的内容是托盘，训练时以粗碗或砖块代替，用白布托着，要求他们托碗平稳迅速。据说每练一次就得撕用两匹白布。

晚膳开始，听得司礼太监喊一声"膳齐"，就是请慈禧入席了。慈禧由光绪和皇后陪侍着来到座位，她先向东一桌天合手致意，再向西一桌地合手致意，然后自己才端端正正坐在正中膳桌前。接着是"四大金刚"向西太后垂手请安，过后是"五百罗汉"齐声高呼"老佛爷——万寿无疆!"声音一直传到寿膳房，传到大内各个角落。同时万字头的鞭炮在庭院内燃放起来，再加上一种用几股羊肠拧成约一丈多长特制的鞭子，由经过训练的年轻太监不停地抖不停地抽，抽出各种不同的声响。鞭炮声和鞭子声，既热闹又驱邪。

大年初一的这餐晚宴，布陈的菜肴分三大类：一类是应节的吉祥菜，诸如寿比南山、吉祥如意、江山一统等等；二类是贡品菜，都是各地进贡的熊掌、大犴子、飞龙、鹿脯、龙虾、酒蟹等等；第三类是寿膳房按照节日膳谱做的例菜。皇帝、皇后一个在东、一个在西侍膳，他们素来知道慈禧非常迷信，皇帝也极知趣，先布吉祥菜，祝福西太后万寿无疆、吉祥如意。皇帝布一道菜，皇后念一道菜名，其实这菜名是由一个老太监在递菜时候就说出来了，否则皇帝、皇后哪里知道这许多的菜名！

清宫内规矩，皇帝绝不说出"我爱吃什么"，或"我今天想吃什么"，绝不能让旁人猜透他准定爱吃某个菜，皇帝也故意做出明明今天爱吃的菜，而明天却绝对不吃。因此，膳房餐餐按常规备膳而已。另外，皇帝的餐桌旁必须由体面的大太监站立侍膳，皇帝每吃一菜只能舀第二匙，绝不能再动第三筷子，假如要吃这第三匙，这侍膳的老太监就要发话了，喊一声"撤!"这个菜就十天半个月不露面了。这叫执行家法，勿贪食，免遭害。哪一朝哪一代宫里没有暴死的呢？这是历史的经验。这种安全措施，餐餐如此，成了必不可少的例行公事。

皇帝吃饭，旁人从来都是侍膳不劝膳，侍膳的人从来不说："这个菜好吃，请您尝尝。"或"这个菜是新下来的，您尝个鲜。"如果侍膳的太监或后妃（晚清皇帝要向西太后侍膳）一旦说出劝膳的话语，则家法不容，马上被站立一旁执家法的老太监呵斥道："不许多嘴!"尔后还要挨几巴掌（用戴着皮手套的手打嘴巴）。因此，尽管在皇宫大内侍候皇帝、西太后几十年的宫女、太监，也不知道他们爱吃什么；皇帝也好，慈禧也好，也从来不表现出来喜欢哪种菜。他们今天吃贡菜，明天吃例菜，后天又吃时鲜了，绝不能表现或让旁人发现喜欢吃什么。这叫清代宫廷内的规矩。

据说晚清的寿膳房，做饭炒菜的大约不下三百多人，共设有一百多个炉灶。每个炉灶规定有三个人，一个掌勺的，一个是配菜的，一个是打杂的。炉灶都排成号，规矩非常严格。如此说来，每个炉灶烧的菜都是有规定的。只要"传膳"的一声令下，由掌勺的按照上菜的次序，听从指挥安排，做成一个一个菜肴，再按顺序呈递上去，膳房的工作是有条不紊的，而且不允许闲杂人员入内。每天，膳房内的哪一道菜是哪一个人洗的，由哪一个人配菜的，由哪一个人掌勺炒烧的，都记载得一清二楚。一旦怪罪下来，就马上有着落，找着事主。其间每一道工序完毕之后，都由内务府派来的笔贴式检查合格后，才能移交给下一道工序。

俗话说，"帝后一顿饭，百姓数年粮"。慈禧每天膳食费按一百两白银计算，在当时可买大米一万二千斤。按当时一般农民的正常用粮第人每年三百斤计算，可够一人吃四十年的。在慈禧执政后期，全国各地不断发生水、旱灾害。1889 年，东北发生数百年来未有的大水灾，"沿江沿河，田庐漂没，人口淹毙，不计其数"，侥幸活下来的，也因没有粮吃被活活饿死，"哀鸿遍野，惨不忍言"。


## 宫内用火之奥秘


我们在故宫约七十二万平方米的偌大方圆内，见不到烟囱，难道生活在这里的人们从皇帝到太监、宫女们，他们不吃饭吗？不取暖吗？

大家看到紫禁城的建筑都是木结构，最怕火，五百余年间，火始终是宫殿的大敌，稍有不慎，玉石俱焚。皇宫内在使用火的方面，特别小心，同时还要使环境不受烟尘污染。古人认为唯一理想的燃料首推木炭，于是宫内做饭烧水，冬季取暖都离不开木炭，宫内做饭烧水用的炉子是肚大口小，没有烟囱的特制无灰木炉子，（这种炉子，专烧炭，民国初年北京居民也有使用），烧燃炭火。皇宫里有多处膳房，重华宫厨房等，还有多处御茶膳房，兼做各色糕点，此外，在三宫六院凡是有主子住的宫殿，都置有炉子，以便随时加热和煮食物。据晚清侍候过慈禧的宫女荣儿回忆，她在宫中侍候慈禧八年，慈禧的寿膳房一处大约就有不下三百多号人，共设一百多个炉灶，排成号，规矩严格，打杂者对各种草，各种原料，进行严格检查，合格后才交给配菜的，经配菜的切、割、剁、片，并配好各种调料，需经检验合格方能交于掌勺的，而掌勺的则听从传膳命令，按顺序烹制。厨役并不是太监，都住在紫禁城外，听从命令入宫内值班。据清宫有关档案，宫内各处需用木炭的记载常常是几百几千，数量之多足可想见。宫内的木炭都是经过反复挑选的，统统如同筷子一般长短的上等硬木炭，敲击之则叮当作响，坚实耐烧。这种木炭火苗旺，热量大，无火星、无烟尘、无怪味，异常干净，不污染空气。

紫禁城内殿堂寝宫都是金砖（当时由苏州特制的一种澄泥砖，极细密厚实，名金砖）墁地。全部精工磨砖对缝，平整光滑、洁明如镜。凡在后三宫生活区内殿宇金砖底下都建有地道和烧炭的炉膛。宫里称之为暖阁。宫殿建筑物的开间一般都是奇数（单数）。中间为明阁即正间，明阁设有宝座，暖阁在两旁，分别称东暖阁或西暖阁。东西暖阁各设地道，分别烧炭取暖，东西各二间的暖阁暖和了，正间的宝座间也就暖和了，在宝座间还设有大炭盆，烧明炭取暖。每年霜降后，暖客的炉膛里便燃起熊熊炭火，温度均匀、柔和地扩及房内的每个角落。所用木炭，初烧时须先在别处引燃之后，再用铁辘辘车把通红的明炭推进地下的炉膛里，昼夜燃烧不断。根据殿大小所设火盆大小各异，为避免火星爆出，盆外都加盖了做工精细考究、外形优美的高高金属网罩，既实用美观，又安全周到。

# 宫廷火锅趣谈

王光尧

火锅之有始於辽（约公元 10 世纪），经宋、金、元、明至清炽盛，从宫廷到民间、自天子至庶人多有使用。

清宫旧制每年"从（农历）十月十五起每顿饭添锅子（火锅），有什锦锅、涮羊肉，东北的习惯爱吃酸菜、血肠、白肉、白片鸡、切肚混在一起。我们吃这种锅子的时候多。有时也吃山鸡锅子。反正一年里我们有三个整月吃锅子。正月十六日撤锅子换砂锅"（金易《宫女谈往录》第 12 页）。每年冬季三个月用火锅，为的是"吃着热菜"，至於菜、汤的质料内容，则无多的讲究和严格的规矩，可以说是有什么吃什么，只要能做成热汤御寒即可，这不能不算是北方人对付寒冬的一手妙着。正是有这样深厚的基础，慈禧太后才能在久食之中独创出一道"菊花火锅"的名菜。其做法大抵是先从御膳房拿来盛有原鸡汁或肉汤的小温锅和其他一些原料。小太监掀开盖子后，由那拉氏捡几片生鸡或

266

生鱼片投入汤内，由小太监把盖子盖上闷数分钟后，再由小太监打开盖子，那拉氏这时就酌量将金菊花数瓣投入汤中，这种金菊花系经精心摘选，并由稀矾水浸泡而成。汤成后清香、鲜美，别具风味，而今一直为宫廷菜系中的名贵菜肴（何本方等主编《中国宫廷知识词典》第187页）。

至於用火锅涮羊肉之法，耆老相传首倡於元太祖忽必烈。平日以牛羊为主食的蒙古将士们，一日正埋锅造饭，羊肉、调料均已准备就绪，只待入锅烹炒。不料敌人突至，战情紧急，容不得他们再一一按程序烹炒，只好在出发之前拿了羊肉在沸水中烫一下就沾了调料充饥，以免战死沙场也是饿死鬼。不料这原本是无奈之际纯粹填饱肚子的吃法，却赢得忽必烈君臣们的啧啧称奇。尔后经不断改进和完善其做法、用具，涮羊肉之法便迅速地传播和普及。这种说法虽然不足作为史凭，可它却反映了涮羊肉之法起源於寒地游牧民族的史实。

经几百年发展，到火锅成为冬季菜肴中不可缺少的清代时，宫廷对火锅的需求以及对其要求之高就可想而知了。故宫现存清宫旧用火锅，因其铸造、物主均有相当的明确性，故而多外溢着皇家独有的高贵。无论是用料之讲究、做工之精细、造型之完美都为民间同类器所不及。从实物看，其质地有金、银、银镀金、铜、铜镀金、锡、铁数种。造型配件上，除有锅、盖、烟囱、闭火盖组成的四件套外，还有配加锅底座盘更复杂的件套。纹饰方面多见各种镂空、錾刻出的动、植物纹样，和"万寿无疆"、"寿"、"福、禄、寿"、"万"、"龙凤呈祥"之类的吉语。部分火锅的锅、盖、底座盘等件还铸刻有铭文，内容有铸造日期、用料、作坊名等等，多少有些先秦铜器铭文上那种"物勒工名"的遗

267

风"。从铭文中显示有"泰丰楼"等作坊名字看，昔日清宫所用火锅的铸造，似乎并没有为内务府造办处所垄断。火锅的来源似乎为内务府官造、购自民间作坊两种途径。

火锅作为清宫饮食用具中的一种，在故宫百万件旧藏中似也微不足道。可是，自辽而清经数代的发展变化，它不仅在铸造、造型、用料、纹饰各方面均臻完备，且在用途上也正如前引文献所说一样，一改其原始的、仅用於涮羊肉的单一用途，成了人们在冬季吃各种热汤菜的炊具，浓缩了它所深蕴的几百年的文化发展史。

# 宫廷茶事琐谈

王　玲

　　茶自古以来就是中国的主要饮料，饮茶的习俗由来已久。唐代饮茶之风盛行，明清之际品茗则成为达官显贵、文人墨客喜好，借以交流情感，谈诗论经。宫廷中历来十分重视饮茶，饮茶构成宫廷生活的重要组成部分。

　　紫禁城是明清两代皇宫，宫中帝后嫔妃日常用茶，主要为产茶各省贡茶，收贮於宫内茶库，各宫室用茶，俱向茶库领用，茶质之精美自不待言，而宫廷茶事活动不仅繁多，且直接与朝廷的文事、教化、礼仪相结合，具有独特深厚的含意。

　　清宫茶事活动最多的地方，是紫禁城里的文华殿、重华宫与乾清宫。

　　进入故宫午门之后，迎面可见太和门。太和门东协和门外有一座独立的院落，其中主要有三种建筑：最前的主殿称文华殿，中间是主敬殿，最后面是文渊阁。清代，这

269

里是皇帝祭祀先师孔子、与群臣举行经筵和存放《四库全书》的地方，是紫禁城里的"文化区"。茶，正是在这里体现出它典型的文化含意，被用於皇帝的经筵。

其实，早在明代，文华殿的经筵即形成制度，并将赐茶作为重要礼仪与讲经论史相结合。明朝每月三次由皇帝与大臣在文华殿共同讲经论史。至时，讲官进讲，先书，次经，再史。讲罢经史，一个重要内容便是皇帝於文华殿向讲官及群臣"赐茶"。在这时，赐茶并不是仅作为讲书润喉之物出现，而是作为宣扬教化的象徵物来使用。

清代，承继了文华殿经筵制度，而礼仪更加隆重。乾隆朝会举行四十九次大型经筵，每次规模都十分可观。皇帝到来，诸官行礼，首先由满汉官员四人进讲《四书》，然后由皇帝亲自阐发《四书》之意，与会官员全部跪听。再讲《五经》，同样又按例一遍。宣讲完毕，皇帝给予讲官及与会官员的最高礼遇，一是赐坐，二是赐茶。在这样庄严的气氛中饮茶自然既无林泉野趣，也没有茶寮的风雅，但却把饮茶的含意提高到空前的庄重意义上。不仅在宫内，皇帝到孔庙和国子监举行"视学礼"，也要对百官赐茶。这说明，赐茶与皇帝一般赐酒、赐物不同，它是阐发儒理，宣扬伦理、教化的象徵。

紫禁城中另一处举行大的茶事活动场所，便是重华宫。重华宫在西六宫之北一个院落中，清代这里几乎每年都有一次大型"茶宴"。

茶宴起於唐，宋代朝廷开始举行大型茶宴，由皇帝"赐茶"。蔡京（1047—1126）曾作《延福宫曲宴记》说："宣和二年十二月癸巳，召宰执亲王等曲宴於延福宫"，"上命近侍取茶具，亲手注汤击沸，少顷乳浮盏面，如疏星淡月，顾诸臣曰：'此自布茶'。饮毕皆顿首谢。"宋徽宗赵佶确实是个懂茶的人，他在茶宴上亲自注汤、击茶，一则为表现自己的茶学知识，二则为向臣工表示其"同苦共苦"之意。这个风流皇帝虽然不会治国，但此举确是文雅，包含很深的寓意。从此，皇帝赐茶成为一种很高的礼遇。但一般皇帝其实并不真正懂茶，所以样自主持茶宴者也不多。

　　到清朝，又出了个极爱茶的皇帝，这就是乾隆。乾隆嗜茶如命，据说他在晚年准备隐退，有的大臣说："国不可一日无君"；乾隆却笑着说："君不可一日无茶"。且不论这传说的可靠与否，乾隆好茶却是真的。重华宫原是乾隆登极前的住所，后来登极，升之为宫。乾隆既好饮茶，又爱作诗附庸风雅，於于效法古代文士，把文人茶会搬到了宫廷，这便是在重华宫年年举行的清宫茶宴。茶宴在每年正月初二至初十选吉日举行，主要内容一是作诗，二是饮茶。最初人无定数，大抵为内廷当值词臣。以后以时事命题作诗，非长篇不能赅瞻。后定为七十二韵，直接在宫内参加赋诗茶宴者仅十八人，分八排，每人作四句。题目是乾隆亲自指定，会前即预知。但"御定元韵"却要临时发下，憋一憋这些御用词臣。诗成，先后进览，不待汇呈。乾隆随即赐茶并颁赏珍物，得赐者亲捧而出，以为荣耀。重华宫内的十八人取"学士登瀛"之意，宫外还有许多人和诗，但不得入宴。

　　乾隆以后，历代皇帝也有在重华宫举行茶宴的，但远不如乾隆时之盛。这样的茶宴诗会自然都是些歌功颂德阿谀奉承之词。况且，深宫之中，侍卫森严，皇帝老儿又亲自坐镇，真正发挥"茶宴"的作用，像文人於山野之间，将茶与诗，人与自然、内心世界与客观意境交融一体，那是根本不可能的。但通过茶宴，茶与文化界的关系进一步得到肯定。上行下效，对推动茶与艺术的结合还是起了重大作用。

清代最大的茶宴还要数乾清宫举行的千叟宴。

乾清宫在明代是皇帝寝宫，清代稍有改变，皇帝临朝听政，召对臣工，引见庶僚，内廷典礼，接见外国使臣，读书学习，批改奏章，都可以在此进行。康乾两朝（1662—1795），在此举行了规模巨大的"千叟宴"，从而把宫廷茶宴推向茶文化史上最高最大的规模。康熙五十二年（1713年），适逢康熙皇帝六十大寿，各地官员为奉迎皇帝鼓励一些老人进京贺寿。於是，康熙帝决定举行"千叟宴"。不过，这首次千叟宴并未在故宫内，而是在畅春园举行。有一千八百余人参加宴会。千叟宴的一项重要内容便是饮茶。大宴开始，第一步叫"就位进茶"。乐队奏丹陛清乐，膳茶房官员向皇帝父子先进红奶茶各一杯，王公大臣行礼。皇帝饮毕，再分赐王公大臣共饮。饭后，所用茶具皆赐饮者。被赐茶的王公大臣接茶后原地行一叩礼，以谢赏茶之恩，这道仪式过后，方能进酒、进肴。我国自唐以来，向有"茶在酒上"之说，这从千叟宴上得到体现。八年之后，康熙又举行一次千叟宴，这一次是在故宫内的乾清宫内外举行，六十五岁以上老人又多达一千余人。另外两次则是在乾隆时期。乾隆五十年正月在乾清宫举行的千叟宴多达三千人与会，最高龄者为一百零四岁。为参加这次活动，许多人提前多日便来到北京。乾隆六十一年，再次在皇极殿举行千叟宴，与宴者竟达三千多人。另有受到邀赏而未入座的五千人。殿内左右为一品大臣，殿檐下左右为二品和外国使者，丹陛甬路上为三品，丹墀下左右为四品、五品和蒙古台吉席。其余在宁寿门外两旁。此宴共设席八百桌，桌分东西，每路六排，最少每排二十二席，最多每排一百席。这样多的人参与宴会，并不都赐茶，但茶膳房官员向皇帝"进茶"却代表了几千与宴人的意思。赏茶者得茶具，赏酒者得酒具，也只有皇家才有这种能力。这大约是我国历史上，也是世界各国集体茶会的冠军之作了。

清宫把饮茶融汇在政治、文化活动中，主要表现在以下五个方面：

1. 清代将茶仪用於尊孔、视学、经筵，与儒家思想进一步明确挂钩，作为一种明君臣、伦理、思想、教化的手段。

2. 与宫廷诗会、文事结合，表示弘扬文明之意。如乾隆帝重华宫联句，与《四库全书》修纂活动结合，与视察国子监结合，都有这种含意。

3. 用於祝寿、庆典、贺仪。这样，便在传统的"明伦序"、"表敬意"、"利交际"之外又延伸到祝福、喜庆的意思。中国历史上的茶文化思想，向来是文人、道士、佛家重清苦、隐幽，而朝廷、民间重欢快、喜庆，清代宫廷茶宴把后一种推向高潮。

4. 清代千叟宴的"进茶"与"赐茶"均用红奶茶，清代宫廷日常生活中也爱用奶茶。《养吉斋丛录》说："旧俗尚奶茶。每日供御用乳牛，及各主位应用乳牛，皆有定数。

取乳交尚茶房。又清茶房春秋二季造乳饼。"由此可知，清宫饮茶原有清茶与乳茶两类。奶茶本是北方民族习惯，清宫用奶茶本来是从饮食保健角度出发，而在千叟宴中用於进茶的礼仪，使传统的茶文化增加了北方民族色彩。它从一个角度表明中国茶文化与民族融合的进程同步而行，茶作为文化观念已得到各民族的认同，而不仅是汉民族所独有。

5. 清代宫廷茶文化活动，最兴盛时期是在乾隆时期，最好茶的皇帝是乾隆帝。自乾隆八年至乾隆六十年，五十二年间，除因皇太后丧事之外，四十八个年头皆有茶宴。之所以如此，除乾隆本人特别爱茶之外，也是因为这一时期经济上正处於康乾盛世，文化上也正是满文化与汉文化大融合及文事上大兴的时期。这与整个中国茶文化的发展规律也是相符合的。一般说，茶文化的发展兴盛有三个必备条件：一是经济繁荣，二是文事兴盛，三是和平安宁。清代乾隆时期茶事特多，再次证明了这个规律。

### 茶的饮用及保健功能

茶作为一种饮料，在我国大概已有四五千年的悠久历史了。对于茶叶的发现与其药用的价值，历代学者都功推神农。《神农本草》是我国有关茶叶记载的最早书籍，书中说："神农尝百草，日遇七十二毒，得茶而解之。"有关这段记载有两种不同的传说：一种传说，神农为人民治病，亲尝试探各种草木治病功效，在烧水时，偶然有茶的鲜叶枝头飘入锅中，因此发现锅中的水苦中带甜，芳香可口，

274

后来就开始把茶叶作为了一种饮料；另有一种传说，神农尝试草木治病的功效，尝到金绿色滚山珠而中毒，死在树下，这时茶树上面的水流入口中，因而得救，茶叶的解毒功用说是这样发现的。

茶叶，古名茗。从神农发现茶叶开始，就显露了茶能治病的萌芽。经过历代劳动人民不断地、反复地实践、认识，总结提高，到现在已知茶中有几百种化学成分，并对多种疾病有预防和治疗作用，可以说茶确为治病良药之一。从最初把茶作为祭品到用其治病和作为一种饮料来看，我们绝不能低估它的价值。有关茶的药用价值，在古代的中医本草书中多有论述，记载最早的是唐代的《新修本草》，书中说："茗，苦荼。茗味甘、苦、微寒，无毒。主瘘疮、利小便，去痰、热渴，令人少睡，春采之。苦荼，主下气，消宿食。"但这样不否认茶的药用起源于神农时期，后经历代劳动人民不断发现和总结，至唐代茶的药用范围更加扩大，才真正开始了对茶的药用研究。唐朝陆羽是古代对茶深有研究的最早人物，从宋朝起就尊他为"茶神"，在他的名著《茶经》中，提出了："茶之为饮，发乎神农"的论断，并且指出："茶茗久服，令人有力，悦志。"还有很多关于茶的药用记载和便方。

近年来通过中国茶叶专家的研究，发现茶叶中含有多种化学成分，这些成分中一类是正常人体所必需的营养成分，别一类虽非正常生理所需要，但在某些病理情况下对恢复人体健康有益，所以称为药效成分。

1、生物碱类　茶叶中含有的生物碱包括咖啡碱、茶碱、可可碱等。其中主要的是咖啡碱（三甲基黄嘌呤），其含量因茶叶的品种不同，而有较大差异。咖啡碱溶于水，如按每日饮茶 5—6 杯计算，则咖啡碱摄取量约为0.3克，剂量虽然不少，但咖啡碱及其代谢产物并不在人体内积累，而是排出体外。

在茶叶的生物碱类中，主要起药理作用的是咖啡碱，其次是茶碱。二者药理作用相似，相互间起协同作用。其中咖啡碱的主要药理作用：

中枢兴奋作用。咖啡碱能够兴奋中枢神经系统，增强大脑皮层的兴奋过程，增进思维，振奋精神，消失睡意，因而有助于提高工作效率。兴奋脊髓则可增加肌力，有利于消除疲劳。

利尿作用。这个作用被认为是由咖啡碱和茶碱共同协作完成的。一方面通过扩张肾血管促进体内多余水分经肾脏排出，另一方面刺激膀胱利尿。饮茶对心源性水肿、经前期综合症等病症有一定的疗效。

心肌兴奋作用。通过动物试验，可以发现茶叶的水浸液能使蛙和蟾蜍的心脏兴奋，左心室的收缩力加强。

扩张血管作用。医学研究人员用龙井在家兔身上做试验，与对照组比较，结果显示其血清胆固醇的浓度和胆固醇与磷的比值均明显低于对照组。经过解剖学的观察，进一步证实其动脉粥样硬化病变程度也明显轻于对照组。

此外，咖啡碱还可以松弛支气管平滑肌、刺激胃酸分泌，故饮茶可减缓支气管哮喘的发作，并有助消化。

除茶咖啡碱具有上述作用以外，作为茶生物碱类物质之一的茶碱，也有松弛支气管平滑肌、兴奋心脏、兴奋中枢神经系统和利尿作用。据报道，茶碱还有增强雌性激素的作用。

2、茶多酚类　茶多酚又称茶单宁。茶多酚的药理作用主要有以下几个方面：

多酚类对儿茶酚胺的影响。它不但刺激肾上腺合成儿茶胺酚的速度，提高血中浓度，还可能抑制儿茶胺酚的分解。所以茶起着双重作用：茶咖啡碱加强儿茶胺酚的生物合成，多酚类物质又抑制儿茶胺酚的分解。从这个意义上讲，饮茶有益不无道理。因为，儿茶胺酚在人体内的作用非常重要。

增强毛细血管的作用。许多外国学者研究证明：茶多酚能改善毛细血管壁的通透性，增强血管的抵抗能力，甚至在血管遭到破坏的情况下，只要每月内服 100—200 毫克茶多酚，可以使毛细血管的抵抗能力自行恢复。

抗炎作用。有人将茶多酚配合抗坏血酸给小鼠进行皮下注射，结果发现：减轻了甲醛和粘朊酶引起的炎症。而切除了肾上腺的白鼠却没有同样的效果。这可能是茶中某些药效成分刺激肾上腺皮质的结果。茶中能增强毛细血管的抵抗力和抗炎的成分包括黄酮醇和黄烷醇。

影响维生素 C 的代谢。用含有维生素 C 和含有绿茶黄烷醇的食物喂养白鼠、豚鼠，增强了其抗感染能力。而红茶没有这种功效。但是，这种抗感染能力，必须是二者的协同作用。有学者发现茶多酚可以保护维生素 C 的氧化。目前，茶提取液已作为食物防氧化剂，其作用是增加肝、脾、肾脏和肠道、脑部、血液等组织中维生素 C 的积累，降低维生素 C 的分解和尿中排泄率。

抗菌作用。绿茶冲泡液在体外已发现对伤寒沙门氏菌、痢疾杆菌、金黄色葡萄球菌、霍乱孤菌等均有抑菌作用。我国的研究证明，不同品种、不同制作方法取得的茶的提取液，对各种痢疾杆菌均有不同程度的抑菌和杀菌作用。茶叶中的茶多酚，它有凝结蛋白质的收敛作用，能与菌体蛋白质结合而起抗菌作用。

3、脂多糖　是组成茶叶细胞壁的重要成份。将适量的植物脂多糖注入动物或人体，短时间内可以增强机体的非特异性免疫功能。动物试验证明，茶叶脂多糖有防辐射损伤的作用，同时也有改善造血功能、保护血象的功效。

4、蛋白质与氨基酸类　茶叶中含有氨基酸与蛋白质。有人认为，红茶中蛋白质的含量为干重的 15—30％，但是溶于水的不到 2％。如果在茶中加入牛乳，由于牛乳与茶多酚形成酷朊复合物，既可降低茶的收敛性，又不妨碍蛋白质的正常吸收，这大概是中国不少少数民族和一些外国人喜欢饮奶茶的原因。红茶只含少量的游离氨基酸，而绿茶则不同，现已发现绿茶中含有 16—24 种氨基酸，包括胱氨酸、丝氨酸、茶氨酸等，其中茶氨酸为茶叶所特有，约占茶叶氨基酸总量的 50％。人体必需的氨基酸，茶中几乎都有。

5、糖类　茶是低热量的饮料，被水冲泡出的糖类仅占可溶物的 4—5％。但是，饮茶可以帮助高糖的良好摄取。如在茶中加入牛乳、糖，按每日饮茶 6 杯计算，所供给的能量大约为每日进食能量的 7—10％。

6、脂肪类　脂肪类约占原料和成品红茶重量的 2—3％，其中含有磷脂、糖脂、甘油三酸脂以及被糖化和脂化的甾族类和萜品类化合物。红茶所含的脂肪酸是亚油酸和

278

亚麻酸。

7、维生素类　茶叶中含有维生素 A、维生素 B、维生素 C、维生素 E、维生素 K 等多种维生素，大部分是人体不可缺少的。一般讲绿茶中维生素的含量高于红茶。红绿茶含的维生素 B 族种类大致相同，但其组成和含量则随着耕作和加工条件不同而有一定差异。

8、矿物质类　茶叶中含有大量矿物质。鲜叶和红茶中约含 4—9％的矿物质。但世界各地所产茶叶中含的矿物质的数量是有差异的。这些矿物质大多有益于人体健康，前苏联学者认为，虽然茶中铁、铜的含量不高，但由于这两种成分有生血和促进红细胞形成的功能，因此在治疗贫血方面，茶有一定作用。茶叶含钠较低，这对于喜欢饮茶，又同时患有高血压的人来说，不失为有益的饮料。茶树易积累猛、铝、氟等元素和某些稀土元素。

9、芳香化合物类　茶叶含有茉莉花素、紫罗兰酮等芳香物质。这些挥发性物质占茶叶干重的0.6％。饭后用茶水漱口，既去油腻，又可坚齿，防治口臭。

10、含稀土元素"硒"　自从一九七三年硒元素被确认为"人体生命不可缺少的必需十四种微量元素之一"以后，很多专家学者对茶叶中的硒进行了多方面的研究。

他们发现，茶硒在我国不同产地含量也极不均衡，有些地方，茶的茶硒含量很高，其中湖北恩施的茶硒含量平均在1.068ppm，高可达 9ppm。

由于硒本身有很强的抗氧化作用，保护细胞膜的结构和功能，还可预防癌症（可改变致癌剂的代谢活性）及多种疾病，尤其对"缺硒区引起的克山病有肯定效果，对防

279

治大骨节病也属有效。"而茶叶中全部为有机硒，没有4价及6价的硒，因此，作用效果比无机硒要强，并且无副作用。

但有人认为茶中硒浸出率低，只在20%～40%，不足以起到补硒的作用。但是，浸出率是完全可以提高的，如袋泡茶和速溶茶就可把浸出率提高到60%～80%。另外，做茶食品也可提高茶硒利用率，如土家族的酥茶月饼。

目前，中国有72%的地区缺硒，所以必须多渠道的补硒才能满足不同人的需要，而喝茶则是一种主动、不间断的摄硒过程，所以喝茶是一种方便、有效、可靠的补硒途径。

# 中国饮食养生琐谈

国　风

在中国历史上，人们对于长生，似乎有一种持久而又普遍的追求，中国上古神话有黄帝（据说是中原各部族的祖先，姓姬、号轩辕氏，通医药学、文学、音律、算术等）骑龙升天的传说，尔后的帝王从秦始皇到汉武帝，或遣童男童女入东海求不死之药；或宠信方士，敬鬼神之祀，望羽化而登仙与天地共长生。

养生理论是人们为达到去病健身、益寿延年而进行的探索。二千多年前，中国儒家经典《易经》中即有"能协于天地之性，虽得疾病，常可不死"的养生思想。现存的春秋末期的一些思想家、政治家的哲学著作中，如老子的《道德经》、孔子的《论语》、管子的《管子》等书中，都有很多关于养生的论述，可谓是养生学理论的萌芽。

春秋战国（前770—前221）是百家争鸣的时代，政治的多元化为各种学术的发展提供了丰厚自由的土壤。各种学派的代表人物，特别关注政治问题和人生问题。人生自然离不开饮食，故先秦诸子，都或多或少地接触过饮食文化，提出了饮食与养生的关系。

## 道家的养生观

春秋时期，道家提出了养生思想，为中国后来养生学创立了理论根据和具体途径，在这方面首推其始祖——老子。

老子是道家的创始人，关於他的祖籍及生卒年，被中国史学界尊为史圣的司马迁（约前145或前135—前87?）也未能搞清。后人认为老子主要活动于春秋（前722—前476）后期。一说他即老聃，姓李名耳，楚国苦县（今河南鹿邑县东）厉乡曲仁里人，做过周期管理藏书的史官（守藏史之吏）。又说，老子即太史儋，或老莱子。不过后人以为不确。至于老子为何有此称谓，而他本人又姓李，只有传说可解：老子者，其母怀之七十二年乃生。生来白发，故称之为老子，生而能言，指李树曰："以此为我姓"，故姓李。现存《老子》一书，又叫《道德经》，是否老子所著，历代均有争议。《老子》一书五千言，以诗歌文体写成，辞语精辟、思想深刻，一般认为是老子思想追随者的作品，成书于战国中期（约公元前381前后）。

老子认为养生者应返回到人类的初始状态，有如婴儿一样，抛弃复杂的情绪与欲望，他还主张恬淡虚无，少私寡欲的精神，提倡清虚静泰，在体育锻炼方面提倡呼吸吐纳，导引行气，持之以恒，专心致志。老子在饮食方面主张只要满足口腹的最低需求就可以了，不可有过高的美食美味的追求，以粗茶淡饭为宜。以前人们普遍以为道家是最忽略饮食养生的，但从现代的科学眼光来分析，道家实际上是主张清淡的素食、粗粮，这对预防由于蛋白质、脂肪摄取过量而致发心脑血管疾病的今天，是有一定借鉴价值的。

## 儒家的养生观

儒家起源于古代方士、术士。古代方士、术士类似于后世的巫，掌管祭祀，而祭祀中最重要的是酒食，因此，这些掌管祭祀者娴熟各种礼仪并精于烹饪饮食之道。

孔子（前551—前479），春秋末期思想家、教育家，儒家学派的创始人。他十分重视民食，把它作为立国的三个基本条件（即兵、粮、信）之一，主张统治者应该"节用而爱人"，因此，他赞美"菲饮食"而致力于公共事业的大禹。但他认为"食无求饱、居无求安"只有少数人能做到，大多数人则孜孜以求饮食之美味，他自己就是"食不厌精、脍不厌细"的。

孔子论饮食与祭祀有关，如"割不正不食"，祭祀时，按一定规格对牲体进行选择切割，否则不能进食。又如："祭于公，不宿肉。祭肉不出三日，出三日，不食矣。"为国君助祭后分得的肉食要当天吃完，不能留到次日。家中祭祀的肉，过了三天也不能吃。这是从祭祀中总结出来的。

孔子还提出了许多饮食卫生原则和鉴别食物的卫生标准，包括食物放久变味不食、烹饪不熟不食、食物变颜色不食，从市场上买来酒和脯，因不能保证其清洁也不食。"不时，不食，"指不到吃饭时间不食。"肉虽多，不使胜食气。"吃饭应以主食为主，肉食菜肴虽多，也不多吃。这条除反映了华夏民族的饮食文化意识外，也合乎饮食卫生，因为肉食确实不易消化。"惟酒无量，不及乱"，意为酒不限量（当时酒的酒精度很低），但以不醉为度。另外"不多食"、"食不语"也都是符合饮食养生原则的。"不撤姜食"，是因姜味辛，可祛湿解毒，食前吃一点有益于健康和饮食。

孔子还说"不得其酱不食"，当时肉菜多为淡味，须蘸酱而食；不同的肉食须搭配不同的酱，可见孔子非常重视菜肴配伍，不随意苟且。"虽疏食菜羹、瓜祭，必齐如也。"说明孔子对待饮食十分严肃，既使是粗糙的饮食，也像对简陋的祭祀一样，态度庄重。

孟子在著作中以雄辩家的态度宣布了人们的口腹之欲和对美食、美味要求的合理性。"鱼，我所欲也；熊掌，亦我所欲也。"但他反对统治者为满足自己口腹之欲而剥夺民众的口腹之欲，尖锐地揭露了"狗彘食人食而不知检，途有饿莩而不知发"的黑暗现实，主张君王应和人民一起享受生活的乐趣。他的"仁政"就是为达到这一美好境界的手段。孟子还认为从群体上来说，只有在温饱的基础上才能建立人和人之间的和谐关系，百姓才会文明而富于教养。从个体上来说，人应该富于精神力量，从而战胜人的本能要求（在饮食上表现为战胜饥饿），成为一个能肩负人类使命的人。

从后来中国的饮食文化历史来看儒家，也就是孔、孟的后学者，在饮食文化的发展中是积极的，又由于中国儒道两家在精神上相互渗透，所以在饮食养生的理论及实践方面，二者又是相辅相成的。

# 墨家的养生观

墨家的始祖墨翟（约公元前468—前376），又称墨子，是春秋时期的宋国人，曾学儒术，因不满其繁琐的"礼"，另立新说，成为儒家主要的反对派。他主张艰苦实践，服从纪律，使"饥者得食、寒者得衣、劳者得息、乱则得治"。

墨家的思想与实践代表了当时的社会动荡中极不稳定的人群要求最为迫切的就是衣食问题。墨子说："凡五谷者，民之所仰也，君之所以为养也。故民无仰则君无养，民无食则不可事。"又说："食者，国之宝也。"粮食对百姓和国君同样重要。墨子说："今也农夫之所以早出暮入，强乎耕稼树艺，多聚菽粟，而不敢怠倦者，何也？曰：彼以强必富，不强必贫；强必饱，不强必饥，故不敢怠倦。"因有口腹的驱遣，人们才努力工作。可是由于沉重的剥削，使得"民财不足，冻饿死者，不可胜数也。"因此，墨子主张"去无用之费"，节制过度奢侈的饮食。统治者"厚作敛于百姓，以为美食刍豢，蒸炙鱼鳖。大国累百器，小国累十器；美食方丈，目不能遍视，手不能遍操，口不能遍味，冬则冻冰，夏则饰饐。人君为饮食如此，故左右象之，是以富贵者奢侈，孤寡者冻馁，虽欲无乱，不可得也。君实欲天下治而恶其乱，当为食饮，不可不节。"君主提倡奢侈，左右效法，以致造成极大的浪费，因为人的实际消费能力有限，"食前方丈"只是摆谱，又会有什么意义！他从实用的观点出发，强调饮食与身体健康的关系，么对追逐美味，认为只要做到"充虚继气，强肱股耳目聪明则止。"因此，

285

他理想中"圣王"平日的食物是:"黍稷不二,羹胾不重。"也就是一饭一菜。所用的食具为;"饭于土馏,啜于土形,斗以酌。"只是简陋的陶土器皿而已。这些反映墨家朴素的愿望,实际却是无法实现的。

## 释家的养生观

释家也就是佛家,对于佛家来说,一心成佛是其最高宗旨。佛家崇尚"普渡众生"的精神境界,因此佛家主张的是驱除人心里的一切私欲杂念的善行牺牲精神。这样在佛家的经典里就找不到养生的专门理论。可是释家主张的禅定、劳动、素食、绝欲则被人们认为是养生之道。所谓禅是梵文(古印度的一种文字)Dhyāna(禅那)的略称。"禅"后加"定"字,是译家组成的一个词,意思是"安静而止息杂欲"。在思想修行上主张静坐敛心,专注一境,持之以恒,就能达到一种身心愉悦,明净清心的状态,这就进入了禅定的境界。从医学方面说,人的精神与情绪的波动和思虑的无穷,将会很大程度地干扰人体正常的生理功能,诱发病变。而释家坐禅的好处,就是清滤一切杂欲私念的驱扰,使心理与精神自然安定。与禅相伴的是佛门的念佛。佛教徒包括在家修行的居士们多有高寿者,这与他们虔心佛经丢弃一切杂念,把尘世间的荣辱浮沉看得十分淡薄有关。佛门有句谚语:"一日不作,一日不食。"尤其是在深山庙宇里生活的僧侣,他们禅农相依,亦农亦禅,不仅要亲自务农,还要挑水、砍柴、做饭、洗衣、缝补等,劳动是他们生活中的重要内容。释家的劳动,其出发点并不在于养生,而在节俭自足,而释家以俭为尚,离苦得乐的精神境界，又为其益寿延年奠定了基础。对于中国汉族地区的佛教徒来说，素食也是养生的一个重要因素。素食并非全世界佛教徒要遵守的规定，是中国汉化了的大乘佛教的独特产物。在历史上汉族佛教徒食素的规定，约始于梁武帝（503—549）时期，以后伴随着不准杀生的戒律，汉族佛教徒就一直以素食为尚了。从饮食营养看，蔬菜、豆制品、果类、谷物等素食含有丰富的维生素，无机盐、蛋白质、葡萄糖、少量脂肪和糖份。绝欲也是释家养生术的一个重要内容。因为绝欲可以保精。中国古代帝王纵情酒色、耗损肾精，所以短寿者很多。而那位笃信佛教的梁武帝，却因远离房室，享有八十多岁的高寿，这在中国古代帝王中也是少有的。禅定、劳动、素食、绝欲对佛家来说不是为了养生，而是为了修行，因此"佛家的养生观"是佛门外的人所言而已。

战国（公元前475—前221）时期，一部分全面阐述中医理论的书《黄帝内经》出现，正式确立了医食同源的思想。这本书也是中国现存最早的、全面总结秦汉（公元前221—220）时期以前医学成就的中医经典著作。关于它确切的成书时间，学者历来歧见很大，一般认为约产生于战国时期，后经秦汉医家整理、补充、修改。关于其作者黄帝，据古史传说为有熊氏少典之子，名轩辕，因长于姬水，故姓姬。他先后与其他部族作战，最后统一了中原，成为华夏族的祖先，他与臣下雷公（针刺术的始祖）、歧伯（黄帝的太医、药师）共创医道，因此中医学又被后人称为歧黄（歧伯、黄帝）之术。《黄帝内经》即是托黄帝之名与歧伯、雷公等讨论医学的记录，《内经》虽为一书，但体例极不一致，现多数学者认为它并非出自一家之手，也不是黄

287

帝的医道理论。托名黄帝，用今天的话说是以"名人效应"来立著述信誉。

《内经》认为："百病之始生也，皆生于风雨寒暑、阴阳喜怒、饮食居处、大惊卒恐。"为了抗御外界的变化，增强人的抗病能力，《内经》提出："五谷为养、五果为助、五畜为益、五菜为充、气味合而服之，以补精益气。"五谷是粳米、麦、小豆、大豆、黄黍；五果是桃、李、杏、栗、枣；五畜是牛、羊、猪、鸡、犬；五菜是葵、藿（豆叶）、薤、葱、韭。

《黄帝内经》中说："五脏坚固……，故能久长。""五脏皆坚者，无病。"又说："五脏安定、血气和利、精神乃居。"

饮食种类很多、并不都能滋养五脏，中医学传统的认识是：一种是五味入五脏，另一种是以脏补脏，即以动物的脏器来补益人身的脏器。五味入五脏就是；"酸先入肝，苦先入心，甘先入脾，辛先入肺，咸先入肾。久而增之，物化之常；气增而久，夭之由也。"《黄帝内经》中的这段话是说，各种食物进入人体之后，对人体既有特定的亲和作用，也有不利的作用，凡是味酸的先作用于肝，味苦的作用于脾，辛味的作用于肺，咸味作用于肾。经常以五味服养就能增强五脏的功能，如食之过量，亦能起反作用，使脏气偏盛而生疾病。现以五谷养五脏为例来说：五谷中养心的是黍（黍米），养肝的是麦（大麦），养脾的为稷（高粱米），养肺的是谷（指糯米），养肾的为豆（指黑豆或马料豆类）。据说，古时候有位叫李守愚的人，每天早晨用清水服食黑豆二至七粒，说这叫"五脏谷到老不衰。"再有滋养五脏的办法就是以脏补脏，就是人们服食动物的脏器，达到补益脏器的作用。以脏补脏的的服食中，以猪、羊内脏为多，因其内脏结构基本上与人的内脏相似。医家将这种功用的产生，称为"同气相求"的效应。如猪肝、羊肝，多数中药书上都说它们具有补肝养血明目的功效，可治疗目昏、雀目（夜盲）、青目（青光眼）。其法是猪肝一叶，夜明砂（蝙蝠屎）10克，研细末，纳猪肝中，煮熟，约20分钟，去夜明砂、吃猪肝，连汤渴下，连服七天。中医认为夜盲、青光眼都与肝脏虚弱有关。我们以饮食来滋补五脏就调理食物的味道和品种，也就是"五味入五脏"和"以脏补脏"。不过饮食养生并不是机械式的照搬，实际上很多果蔬都有滋补五脏的功能。中国河北、山东、山西一带盛产的大枣补脾养气，栗子、核桃补肾，龙眼（桂圆）肉补心养血，百合润肺益气，桑椹子补肝。这些果实，都性平、味甘或平，一般可以久食养生，可独服也可杂而食之。如大枣与百合同煮，饮其汁，有补益肺、脾之功效。栗子与桑椹子同煮食，能补肝益肾。特别是栗子补老年人的腰膝无力。宋代文学家苏辙（1039—1112）曾有诗赞栗子强身之功效："老去自添腰脚病，山翁服栗旧传方，客来为说晨与晚（客指山翁，说早晚服食栗子的方法），三咽徐收白玉浆（用三枚生栗子去皮入口细嚼如白玉浆，分三次咽下）。"但生栗子不宜多吃，过多会妨碍消化。

在养生的饮食物中还要注重对人体气血的补养。气泛指元气，也可以解为人的精神状态；血指血脉，两字连用，是指人的精神与血液循环系统是紧密关连的。对人体气血的补养也是中国传统养生学中至关重要的环节。中医认为，"人之所有者，血与气耳。"血和经脉流行，营复阴阳，筋骨强壮，关节清利。中医认为：气是一种极精细而富有活力的精神物质，是无形体的一种力量和精神。天地人之间都存在气，气又是生命力的一种体现。故凡言气虚，则是人全身无力的表现。中医以人参来补元气，所以补气并不能理解为呼吸清气，应理解为营养物质（当然包括良好的空气环境）的补养。中医认为，食物中补气血的分两类，一类是真接补益的食品，如动物的肝脏及血液（中国人作成血"豆腐"）。蔬菜中的菠菜与胡萝卜。因为动物（特别是哺乳类动物）的造血脏器是肝，血液中所含化学成份与人血相近，因此对人的气血有补益。现代医学证实，目前已有科学工作者着手研究用猪血，提取血清作原料，制成"代血浆"，用于输给人体。这足以证明动物血液确实具有补血作用。

在饮食养身中填补精髓的食物，都有强壮筋骨的功效。中医所讲的精，主要是指藏于肾的先天之精。它既是构成人体和维持人体生命活动的基本物质，又是生殖繁衍下一代的精气。男子若此精不足，就不能生育；女子此精不足，就不能怀孕。故《黄帝内经》有云："精者，生之本也。"又说："故生之来谓之精。"髓，是充满于骨腔内的柔软组织，又称为骨中凝脂，是肾精充盈部分贮藏于骨腔之内形成的。中医认为，肾生骨髓。骨者，髓之府。因此，精髓是人体最可贵者，中国人认为凡世间最有价值之物，亦用此作喻。填补精髓之食物亦属"血肉有情之品"。凡动物都有血、有肉，特别是有些动物更是有感情的，如狗、马、牛等，若经人训化能解人意，故称"血肉有情"。血肉有情之物甚多，李时珍在《本草纲目》中记载，凡毛、羽、介、鳞共299种。在日常生活中，猪牛的骨髓、牛筋、猪蹄筋、牛蹄筋都含有丰富的蛋白质、少量脂肪并含动物胶质与名贵中医阿胶功效相仿，有强筋骨、补骨髓的作用。螃蟹也是填补精髓的食品，吃法很有讲究，以农历九至十月为佳。李时珍《本草纲目》曾说，煮蟹时要加白芷则黄不散，加葱、五味子同煮则色不变。白芷、五味子中药店均有售，每次约4～5克即可。但一定要用活蟹，煮蒸熟透。醉蟹不能吃，因不熟，虽酒能消毒，因蟹喜食腐烂性食物及有毒杂物，不熟透易中毒。死蟹也不能食用。另外黄花鱼（又称石首鱼）、鳝鱼、甲鱼、海参、扇贝肉等也都有补精益髓的作用。黄花鱼鳔和中药莎苑蒺藜为丸，名曰聚精丸。海参和淡菜也是极好的益精食品，对男子性功能的增强有很好的功效。从现代科学分析来看，这些都是高蛋白、低脂肪的营养补品。海参含粗蛋白质55.51%，粗脂肪1.85%；淡菜含蛋白质59.1%，脂肪7.6%，这两种食物性味平和，多食有益。

　　在饮食养生中，每个人要视脾胃行事。因饮食被口摄入后，有赖于脾胃的功能，正常消化、吸收、摄取其中的营养，滋养全身。脾胃在人的一生中对维持生命活动起着根本的作用，因此保护脾胃正常发挥功能是十分重要的。要达此目的，必须注意内、外两方面的因素，外在因素是指食物，饮食必须适合胃气。清代名医叶天士（叶桂，1667—1746，著有《温热论》，对后世极有影响）把适合胃气概括为"食物自适"四个字，意思是食物的选择必须适合口味，且吃后胃中舒服，叶天士又称之为"胃喜为补"，而反之，则"胃厌"。凡胃喜之食，多为身体急需的营养素，易于消化吸收。在保持脾胃方面要注要饮食的三宜，即食宜软、食宜暖、食宜细嚼缓咽。很有营养的食品，若不顾脾胃的功能如何，一味强调进食补益，这样就会适得其反。鸡、鸭、鱼、肉等虽营养丰富，油烹之后均不易消化，食之过量，反会加重脾胃负担，形成肠胃积滞，不思饮食。

要使脾胃功能正常，还必须经常保持情志的舒畅，尤抑郁怒。因脾主思、思虑太过则伤脾，脾伤则不思饮食。

天下食物繁多，归纳起来，人类赖以生存所需要的营养物质，主要是蛋白质、脂肪、糖、维生素、无机盐和水等六种。由于各种食物营养的含量各有偏重，因此在饮食养生方面，应泛尝博取，不可偏嗜，偏嗜则失去各种营养相互补充的机会，然而在泛尝的荤荤素素中，中国古代的养生家们，有不少人把兴趣集中在素食上。《内经》有云："膏粱之变，足生大疔，受如持虚。"意思是长期进食鱼肉荤腥，膏粱原味的人，足以在他们身上发生出大疔疮，对于这种受病的可能，就好像用空的容器去接受东西。

对于素食的好处，中国民主革命的伟大先躯孙中山（1866—1925）曾说："中国不独食品发明之多、烹调方法之美，尤为各国所不及，而中国人之饮食习尚，暗合于科学卫生，尤为各国一般人所望尘不及也。中国人常所饮食者为清茶，所食者为淡饭，而加以蔬菜豆腐。……夫豆腐者，实植物中之肉料也。此物有肉料之功，而无肉料之毒，……欧美之人所饮者浊酒，所食者腥味，亦相习成风，……单就饮食一道论之，中国之习尚，当超乎各国之上。"（《中国人应保守中国饮食法》）。

西汉建元二年（公元素前139），汉武帝（公元前156—前87）命张骞（？—公元前114）出使西域（今中国新疆及中亚地区），历十二年，加强了中西文化交流并引进了许多果蔬品种及大豆，相传西汉淮南王刘安（也有说刘长）发

292

明了豆腐，此后梁武帝又首创面筋（又称麸），大大地丰富了素食的内容。素菜并非是佛教所提倡，中国的蒙族、藏族和傣族佛教徒信奉大乘佛教，因当地肉多菜少，一般都吃肉。中国部分佛教徒食素，主要是由梁武帝倡导起来的。

梁武帝萧衍（502—549）是中国南北朝（420—589）时期的一位博学多才的君主，少时学儒、道经典，又奉道教，后广结名僧及奉佛的文士，他认为佛教主张的"不结恶果、先种善因"、"戒杀放生"、"素食清净"等思想与儒家的"仁心闻仁"、"孝道"等思想契合，他便舍道立佛，素食由他这位君主一倡导便带有浓厚的政治色彩和宗教色彩，从此一部分佛教徒（大多数在汉族人生活的地区）把戒杀生同素食联系起来。

素菜的发展及形成体系，其间佛教徒有很大功劳。印度佛教徒本无素食规定，因僧人外出靠托钵乞食，对荤素无选择余地。中国佛僧食品也无严格规定，后来虔诚的佛教徒梁武帝大力提倡素食，戒食热血生灵，禁止僧侣食肉，认为食肉是违反佛教戒律，并靠皇权势力对饮酒食肉僧人惩处，这样佛寺禁绝了酒肉。由于僧人常年食素，使素食者增多，这样也就刺激了素肴的发展。

相传梁武帝时在南京"建业寺"有位厨僧，素肴做得相当精致，颇受当时僧人和进香人的赞美，因而名声大震，影响很深。市井的饮食行业为满足佛教徒的需要，经营并发展全素菜肴，又由于"天下名山僧占多"，古寺名刹不仅是善男信女进香朝拜之地，也是文人墨客、达官显贵游览和消闲的去处，佛寺为迎接这些人的到来也创造出不少美味的全素菜肴，如唐朝之后佛教禅宗五祖弘忍大师首创的"炸春卷"（馅用豆腐丝、面筋、野菜，外用油皮或青菜皮）

已是名享中外的一道素菜（现在也有在馅中加肉的）。汉晋以后，佛道寺院宫观遍布名山大川，其间多有斋厨，善烹茹耳菜蔬瓜果及各种豆腐制品。宋元至明清，意有"全素席"和以素托荤的素鸡、素鹅、素鸭、素鱼、素火腿等菜肴。直到现在上海的玉佛寺、杭州的灵隐寺、扬州的大明寺、湖北黄梅县的五祖寺、四川新都宝光寺、厦门的南普陀寺的素肴都是极负盛名的。

佛家菜与道家菜均尚素食，晋代道家著名医药学家、化学家、养生家葛洪（281—341）提倡"五芝之食"，是我国早期菌食和花食的倡导者。把食用菌类和植物花卉用于菜肴，是佛道两家兼有之食道，特别是花食，中国独占世界之先，如萱花（又称黄花菜、金针花）、百合、莲花、梅花、桂花、芙蓉花、玉兰花、菊花都是花食中的佼佼者。现经学者认定，花类中无毒可食者，含有较多氨基酸、果糖、多种维生素及多种微量元素，如铁、钾、镁、锌等等。在宫廷中莲花与精瘦肉爆炒，清香四溢，又能消暑。古人在粥中撒下几朵梅花名梅花粥，清香爽口，芙蓉花和豆腐可做成雪霁羹，国槐花和鸡蛋清炒味美香甜，菊花、桂花都是制做糕点的上品。

中国进入公元十七世纪后，北方游牧民族——女真族入主中原建立清帝国，素食在清代进入盛期。寺院、市肆、宫廷均有专司素菜的馆房，寺院称素菜师傅为香积厨（厨僧），称素菜为斋菜或释菜，宫廷素菜也称斋菜，主要是帝后斋戒时食用。清宫御膳房特设"素局"，专做素菜，其原料主要是面筋、豆腐、豆皮、腐竹、鲜笋、香蕈、荸荠、山药、金针花、木耳及果蔬等等。素局厨师能用上述原料做出数百种风味各异的素食，这样美味并含有丰富营养的上百种素食菜肴，除中国之外尚无二家。

说到素食，还要提一下佛教庙宇里的腊八粥。相传佛祖释迦牟尼在没有成道前，在整整六年的苦修中，每天都吃得很简单，终于在腊月八日悟道成佛。后来人们为了怀念他，就在腊月八日吃粥以示纪念。庙宇煮腊八粥饷客，一般多在大米或糯米中放进花生、红枣、栗子、桂圆、莲子、核桃、赤豆、白果、黄豆等，由于果品辅料，所以香甜暖口，极富营养。古人曾有把腊八粥称为"福德粥"或"福寿粥"的。意思是吃了这粥，能增寿增福，有益健康。

从现代营养学观点看，饮食最好以素为主，荤素结合。因素食不但有补益的功能，还有疏通肠胃的作用。元代著名医药学家朱丹溪（1281—1358）曾说："若谷、菽、菜、果自然冲和之味，有食（饲）人补阳之功。""《内经》言以菜为充者，恐于饥时顿食，或虑过多，因致胃损，故以菜助其充足，取其疏通而易化，此天地生物之仁也。"这段话，前面是讲素食具有疏通胃肠，帮助消化的主要是素食中的纤维素，它可促进肠道的蠕动，利于通便。上述的食物纤维遇水膨胀，形成致密的网络，能在肠腔内吸附无机盐和有机酸，再吸附水分，这些并不复杂的过程，调整着肠道的消化吸收功能，在人体代谢中发挥着微妙的作用，成为防病治病的重要因素。因此，现有科研人员认为多食有纤维素的食物，如粗粮、豆类、玉米、蔬菜中的芹菜、卷心菜、韭菜、大白菜，可以预防大肠炎和肠癌的发生。现在有些人在吃蔬菜时有吐渣的习惯，这是非常错误的，他们不知道这"渣"也就是人体所必需的粗纤维素。还有人以国外调查资料表明，欧美等国家肠癌的发病率比非洲高十多倍，研究得出的结论是与他们的饮食有密切关系的。

欧美人从食物中获得的纤维素仅为非洲人的 1/6。所以合理的菜肴，荤、素要适当配合，且蔬菜的总量要超过荤菜的一倍，或一倍以上，这也是最符合营养要求的，蔬菜的营养好处有五点：含有多种维生素有助消化；防止各种营养缺乏症；防止肥胖；有益于血管的疏通；防癌治癌。另外牛奶、黑芝麻、蜂蜜也是营养价值很高的食品。因此，中国隋唐时期著名医药学家孙思邈（581—682）指出："此物胜肉远矣"，"为人子者，须供之以常食。"从明清宫廷的食单、菜谱上看，皇帝每天的食物中，水果、蔬菜、奶，粗粮细作的食品，如红小豆、豆面、玉米面制作的糕点种类繁多，在本书《明代宫廷菜》和《清宫膳饮述闻》中均有记载。由此可见，宫廷膳饮的配置，从食疗养生方面说，还是十分科学的。

# 中国的菜系

中国幅原广阔，气候、风俗、各地物产的习俗不同，使中国不同地区的人饮食有很大差异。如东南沿海地区人们尚食水产、海味；西北内陆地区人民尚食陆畜、家禽，南北食物差异很大，有些当地风味菜肴，还令异地人望而生畏，如广东人食蛇、穿山甲、白鼠等。加之气候差别，各地区在口味浓淡方面也各不相同，故有"南甜北咸西酸东辣"之说。这样不同地域的人就创造出适合当地人口味的菜肴，也培养了一批擅长烹调本地区风味菜肴的厨师。过去称中国不同地区的厨师为京帮、鲁帮、闽帮、川帮等，借以区别各地区的肴馔及厨师烹饪特长。新中国成立之后，饮食行业从中国各地区形成富有特色的风味肴馔系列出发，称之为菜系。中国有多少主流菜系，至今尚无定论。在习惯上对中国烹调技术影响较大的有九个菜系，它们是：北京菜、山东菜、淮扬菜、江浙菜、福建菜、广东菜、四川菜、湖北菜和湖南菜。

**北京菜**，又称京菜或京味菜。北京曾是辽、金、元、明、清的都城。除明朝外，辽、金、元、清的统治者都是北方游牧民族。北京在这五百余年中，饮食行业为迎合统治阶级的饮食习惯，菜肴以肉食为主，元蒙统治者又特别喜食羊肉，元代宫廷的珍馔中竟有八成以上是羊肉制做的。羊肉菜肴一直留传至今，如烧羊肉、焖羊肉、涮羊肉、爆羊肚、锅贴等都是极富京味特色的。

满清统治者在关外就嗜食猪肉，其烹调技艺以烧、烤、煮为主。北京菜自清以来猪羊并重，正是受了满族食俗的影响，烤乳猪、烧小猪，以及沙锅居用沙锅烹煮猪肉及下水所制成的多种名菜，最初是为适应满族人需要而逐渐为北京人所接受的。北京又是各地士大夫云集之处，追随他们而至的有技艺高超的各地厨师。这些厨师把具有不同风味的菜肴带进北京，使北京的肴馔吸收和综合了各地烹调技术的长处，从而大大丰富了北京肴馔的风味。对北京影响较大的是山东菜、淮扬菜、江浙菜。山东靠近北京，山东人在北京地区谋生的很多，在北京从事饮食业的山东人尤多，山东人的口味和北京人接近，所以们们烹制的菜肴也很快被接受。清代山东人几乎垄断了北京饮食业，有名的大饭庄如同丰堂、福寿堂、惠丰堂、广和居、同和居等，都是山东人开办的。山东菜中的“爆”、“煸”技艺与其善于运用葱香味的烹调特点对北京菜肴的烹制影响很大。如极普通的爆羊肉，正是吸收了山东的烹调技法和调味特点的典型的北京菜。现在北京人日常炒菜都用葱花炝锅，可见山东菜肴风味影响之深。北京作为都城，文化、商业与外界的交流十分频繁，准扬（指扬州、淮安一带）、江浙（指苏南、浙西一带）这两个地方在北京经商、求官的人特别多，这一带士大夫口味也特别高，而且他们还会设计菜肴，因此北京厨师也多以能“包办南席”相标榜。有些北京人及外埠商绅想足不出城就品尝到自己家乡的江南风味，这样又刺激了淮扬风味菜肴在北京的发展。

南菜北上，其风味也发生了变化，如淮扬、江浙重甜味、淡味，而北方重咸味、厚味。它们要想在北京立足，就得入乡随俗，对调味略加变化，创制出南北合璧的菜肴，如名菜潘先生鱼就是晚清翰林潘祖荫（1830—1890）创制的鱼羊合烹，苏州人吴阎生创制的吴鱼片则是具有江浙色彩的北京菜。从清乾隆间逐渐流行的最高规格的满汉全席菜式，冷碟近二百种，点心几十种。这道宴席以满洲烧烤和南菜中的鱼翅、燕窝、海参、鱿鱼、鲍鱼类为主菜，以满族传统糕点饽饽穿插其间，以淮扬、江浙羹汤为佐菜。它集京菜之大成，比较全面地反映了北京肴馔的技艺和风味。近几十年来被外地甚至外国视为北京特味的北京烤鸭，以北京填鸭为原料，吸取了流行于淮扬一带注重色泽味道的烧烤技艺，调味（用面酱）和食用搭配（配以生葱、荷叶饼）则采取了山东风格，这道北京名菜典型地反映了北京菜系的渊源。总的说来，北京菜系如同北京在中国的地位一样，是万流归宗之处，并且有兼收并蓄之胸怀。它不是以一两种肴馔名世，而是能推出几十种甚至上百种有独特风格的肴馔，从小吃到大餐乃至整桌筵席都为其它菜系不能比及。另外京菜不追求怪诞，善于把平凡普通的食物原料加工成鲜美的菜肴。口味也易于为一般人所接受。它是我国最有代表性的菜系。

**山东菜**，又称鲁菜（因山东省简称鲁）。其烹饪历史悠久，早在距今三千余年前的春秋时期，山东是齐、鲁两诸侯国的领地。齐鲁两国当时经济文化都十分发达。由于其地理环境临海依山，还有富饶的平原，故鱼丰粮足且又产海盐，饮食自古就讲究调味。

　　山东菜系的形成大约在元明（1271—1644）时期，山东的烹调技艺和调味风格逐渐流传于华北、京津、东北一带，并且进入宫廷成为御膳的重要组成部分。山东菜系主要由胶东菜和济南菜两大部分组成。胶东以烹饪海鲜著称，无论是名贵海珍如海参、鱼翅、燕窝、干贝，还有一些小海味如蚧、虾、蟹都能烹调出精洁鲜美的名肴，代表性菜肴如绣球海参、烧五丝、线烧干贝肚、芙蓉蛤仁、芙蓉干贝、炸蛎黄等。济南菜精于制汤，善于用爆、炒、炸、烧等烹调方法，多以淡水鱼、猪肉、蔬菜为原料，其代表性菜肴为奶汤鲫鱼、糖醋黄河鲤鱼，奶汤蒲菜、锅烧肘子、油爆双脆等。另外还有孔府菜肴，在鲁味基础上又提高一步，典雅华贵，带有贵族特点。总之，山东菜在烹饪技艺上重视爆、炒、扒、锅煽，烹制出的菜肴脆、嫩、鲜、滑，调味上以咸味为主，酸甜为辅。调和咸味除用盐外，还常用豆豉、酱等。山东人喜食葱，烹调中也常以葱配菜或作为调料，以葱为辅料的名菜有葱烧海参、葱烧蹄筋、葱烧肉等。烤肉、炸脂盖等山东名菜以生葱段佐食。在爆、炒、烧、溜的诸菜式中都用葱花炝锅，取其葱香味。山东人注重面食，像硬面馒头、烤馒头、煎饼、酥饼、悬饼（一种多人吃的大肉馅饼），虽为人们所常食，但确是山东首创或独有。

　　**淮扬菜**，北京人称南味菜（泛指淮扬、苏杭、上海等地的风味菜）。淮扬是中国江苏省北部的扬州、镇江、淮安等沿京杭大运河的地区。扬州自古就是军事要塞和文化名城。早在唐代（618—907）它已成为极其繁华的都会，是除京都外最繁荣的商业城市。富商大贾奢侈的消费必然会刺激饮食行业的繁荣和烹调技艺的发展。明清两代每个大盐商家都有一位手艺高超的厨师擅长某种菜肴或点心，盐商请客，往往互借厨师，每位厨师都献出他最拿手的菜肴，凑成极精美的一桌筵席。这样，厨师也得以互相交流厨艺，在整体上提高了扬州烹饪水平。扬州又处于江淮湖海之间，盛产鱼虾海味，为烹调的发展提供了丰富的原料。元明清以来扬州的繁荣始终不衰，饮食行业也很发达，并有专门出卖烹饪手艺的厨人，人们称之为"外庖"。他们专门为喜庆宴会及游宴服务。厨人的多种服务方式反映了他们之间竞争的激烈，但也促进了扬州烹调技艺的发展。如果说山东菜以急火快炒见长的话，淮扬菜则以炖、焖、焐、蒸、烩见功。这些烹饪法往往需要文火，加工时间较长。其名肴如栗子黄焖鸡、荷叶蒸肉、八宝鸭、扬州狮子头、蝴蝶海参（把海参切成类似蝴蝶的形状，加各种调料烧制）等，都有此特点。因此淮扬菜注重原汤原汁，要求鸡有鸡味、鱼有鱼味、突出主料味道，恰当地配以辅料，使两者相得益彰。在运用小火烹制时，密封加盖，使原料精髓尽出，不失原味，不变原形。这种做法充分体现了淮扬菜文火慢煮之特色。其炖的技艺，尤有特色，能保持原汤的清鲜（这也是"炖"借以区别"焖"、"煨"的显著标志），制出的菜肴质地酥烂，香味浓郁。隔水炖法是炖法中的一种，即把食物原料（最好是体积较大的，如整鸡、整鸭），先经去腥除臭的处理，然后放入密闭容器，并把容器置于沸水锅中长时间加热（一般要数小时）。淮扬系的清炖技艺对于北京菜也颇有影响。淮扬菜口味偏甜，但不过当，而且往往糖盐并用，糖实际起了提鲜的作用，使得菜肴鲜味悠长。淮扬菜十分重视色泽，善于运用糖色、红曲色、清酱色、

301

原料本色以及蛋清料的颜色。如"雪里藏蛟"，此菜以爆炒鳝丝为主，用蒸制而成的雪白的蛋清泡为底色，上覆以乌黄发亮的爆炒鳝丝，真如蛟卧雪中，其它如清炖鸡、叉烧鳜鱼、清蒸鲥鱼、翡翠烧麦，无不色泽晶莹光润，搭配得当，十分悦目。镇江的水晶菜（以鱼畜皮胶凝冻而配制的菜肴）晶莹透明，软韧鲜醇，其口感、色泽、造型均属上乘。淮扬菜还注意色味的配合，色彩浓亮则味也浓，汁也厚；色彩清淡素雅，其味亦清鲜利口，汤清见底。淮扬菜中的全素席也很有特色，北京的素菜系列基本上属于淮扬风味，这是其它菜系的素菜难以做到的。淮扬小吃也很精致，如扬州茶食中的煮干丝、汤饺、烧麦、灌汤肉包、蟹黄汤包、笋肉菜包、黄桥烧饼、千层油糕、没骨鱼面、脆鳝面、浇头面、镇江的水晶包等。

**江浙菜**，北京人也称南味菜，"江"指江苏南部，即苏州、无锡一带，"浙"指浙西，即杭州、湖州一带。江浙的经济是中唐（约公元五世纪）以后逐渐发展起来的，五代（907—960）以后经济文化的中心南移，此地文人云集。如果说淮扬一带烹饪发展主要是为了满足富商大贾消费需求的话，那么江浙一带烹调技艺的发展和烹调特色则反映了士大夫的趣味与追求。江浙菜还十分注重食物原料方面对蔬菜的使用，特别是对笋、蕈、莼菜的擅用，使江浙菜体现了清鲜淳美之味。这些以蔬菜为主的菜肴不仅为人们日常所食，而且成为流行于饭馆酒楼的名肴，如鸡油菜心、锦绣鱼丝、油焖春笋、虾油菠菜、西湖醋鱼，以及久享大名的莼菜羹等，另外许多以鱼肉为主的菜肴，亦常常配以蔬菜。其次是注重产于河湖港汊的鱼虾蟹贝。江浙一带是鱼米之乡，鱼虾现捕现食，十分新鲜。

江浙菜中以鱼虾为原料的名菜很多，如被清乾隆皇帝誉为"天下第一菜"的松鼠鳜鱼，饮誉数百年的西湖醋鱼，被人赞美千余载的松江鲈鱼脍等。再如杭州用龙井茶配伍的龙井虾仁，苏州以洞庭岛碧螺春配伍的碧螺虾仁也都脍炙人口。江浙菜偏甜、偏淡，也有不少糖醋味的菜肴。运用香糟是江浙菜的一个特色，糟本是带酒的渣滓，有除异味、增加香味的作用。据考南宋时杭州食品中就有糟蟹、糟鹅等，后来几乎无菜不可用香糟调味，如糟茄、糟蒸肉。江浙菜在烹调技法上与淮扬菜接近，注重煨、炖、焖、烩、蒸等烹制法，大多数菜肴有鲜美的汤汁。其形、色，取其自然，不刻意追求，与富丽堂皇的淮扬菜形成鲜明的对比。小吃方面，江浙糕粿极负盛名，不仅春节的年糕、金粿、银粿，正月十五的元宵，清明的青白汤粿，立夏的乌饭糕，中元节的石花菜凉糕，重阳的重阳花糕，应时应景，为人家所必备，就是平时作为点心的汤圆、饭粿、凉糕以及松子糕、茯苓糕、黄松糕、水晶糕、梳糕等，也都精致可爱，十分诱人。

**福建菜**，又称闽菜（因福建简称闽）。闽菜在东南诸省中形成较晚，福建地处沿海，盛产海鲜，故闽人喜食海鲜鱼虾，据考福建沿海地区有各种鱼类167种，龟、鳖、蚌、螺等90种。另外还产燕窝、土笋、西施舌（蛤、蚌之类）、墨鱼、鲟鱼等，这些特产为福建菜肴提供了丰富的原料。福建的经济文化是南宋以后逐渐发展起来的，清中叶后出了一些颇著名的显宦名士，经他们的弘扬，福建菜肴逐渐为世人所知。闽菜中最有特色的在于汤菜。所谓汤菜，乃是富于汤汁的菜，并非菜汤，它在福建饮食中的地位仿佛两汉以前的羹。所运用的烹饪技法多为炖、煮、煨、汆、蒸，如闽菜中最著名的佛跳墙（言即使是佛，也要闻香跳墙来吃），就是把海鲜、鸡、鸭、肉放在绍兴酒坛中用文火煨制而成，鸡汤汆海蚌则是在炖鸡汤的基础上加以汆制而成。汤菜的原料及调汤都很讲究，烹调上富于变化，从而出现"一汤多变"乃至"十变"的效果。闽菜还重视刀工，这是由于它所加工的食物原料多为海鲜，如果用刀不精，其味难出，外味也难入。闽菜口味一般偏淡、偏甜、偏酸，如荔枝肉、酸甜竹节肉、葱烧酥鲫、白炒鲜竹蛏都能体现其味道。"淡"能突出鲜味，"甜"能提鲜，"酸"能清除海产品中的腥味，除了食物原料的原因外，与福建地区的湿、热气候也有关系。闽菜还注重使用红糟调味、着色。红糟是用红曲、糯米酿造而成，其制法是将糯米、红米用酒药泡制，封藏一年后便成了具有甜酸香味、红玫瑰色的"红糟"。红糟酒香浓郁，颜色鲜艳，不仅鸡、鸭、鱼、肉可用红糟调味，螺、蛤、蚌、蚶、竹笋、蔬菜也可使用红糟。用红糟调味时所采用的烹饪方法也是多种多样的，有炝糟、煎糟、汆糟汁、腌糟汁等。

闽菜如果细加区别还可分为福州、闽南、闽西三支，除共同之处外，略有区别。福州菜偏重清鲜、淡爽和甜酸；闽南菜偏重甜辣，多用辣椒酱、沙茶酱、芥末酱、桔汁作调料；闽西则偏重咸辣。随着福建人飘洋渡海，闽菜也流行于台湾及海外。

**广东菜**，又称粤菜（因广东简称粤），广东菜系是我国众菜系中比较独特的，其食物原料、烹调技法、调料运用都有迥异于其它地区（特别是中原地区）。广东地处岭南，背山临海，与中原长期隔绝，古为百越民族所居，秦汉间又移居了很大一批中原居民，因此，广东饮食文化中保留了不少古越人和秦汉间的食俗，如吃蛇就是越人的习俗。总之，对广东人来说，无论是天上飞的，还是地下走的、水里游的，无一例外地都可入口。当然，许多奇异食品难以登大雅之堂，有的为了尊重其它地区人们的食性也逐渐被淘汰了，也有些奇异食品却备受重视，最著名的是用"三蛇"和"狸猫"烩制而成的"龙虎斗"（或名龙虎烩），它甚至成为最高规格筵席的主菜，其著名者还有"菊花龙虎凤"（用"王蛇"、"竹丝鸡"、"狸猫"烹成）、"烧凤肝蛇片"（鸡肝蛇片）、"五彩炒蛇丝"等。

明清以来，广东日趋繁荣，与中原联系更加紧密，特别是西洋文化传入后，粤菜的烹饪技艺在继承其它地区技法的基础上又吸收了西餐的菜肴烹制法，并融汇成为有自己独特性的烹饪法，其中最有特色的是"盐焗"、"酒焗"、"锅烤"、"软炒"等。焗本为西菜烹饪法，其原理是使物料受热膨胀变松软，蒸发其水份，将辅料的味道吸收过来。"盐焗"，或称"盐煨"、"盐烙"，是把加工腌制好的食物原料（如整鸡）埋入烧红、烧热的盐粒中至熟，最著名的是东江盐焗鸡。"酒焗"是用酒蒸气加工，如其典型菜例"玫瑰酒焗双鸽"，即用破膛净鸽两只置于瓦钵中，鸽下放筷子两根，使鸽身与钵底有一定距离。两鸽间放玫瑰酒一杯，然后把钵放在铁锅中，锅下用火烧，至鸽熟，杯中尚余清酒半杯，但酒味全无，鸽肉则酒香扑鼻。"锅烤"则是用一种带铸铁盖的铁锅，把要烹制的食物置于锅上，然后在锅底加热，并将烧红的铸铁盖盖上，成上烤下烧之势，典型菜例为"锅烤蛋"。"软炒"也是粤菜独有的烹饪法，所用主料多为液体或半流体，如鲜牛奶、鸡茸，其特点是初用旺火烧锅，下油滑锅。滑锅后下少许油，用中火或小火炒，典型菜例为炒鲜奶、黄浦蛋等。粤菜注重海鲜味。粤菜调料也有独特之处，多用复合味料，如喼汁，用姜葱蒜糖盐香料等制成；卤水是用花生油、姜、葱、绍兴酒、冰糖、八角、桂皮、甘草、草果丁香、沙姜粉、陈皮、罗汉果等制成；五香盐以精盐、白糖、五香粉、八角末调成；还喜用蚝油、鱼露、蛏油、咖喱等调味品，这些调料也是粤菜风味独特的重要原因。粤菜中分为三支：一为广州，为粤菜正宗；一为潮州，因接近福建，其肴馔风格有与闽菜接近之处（如善烹海鲜，菜多汤汁），口味偏重香浓、鲜、甜，喜用鱼露、沙茶酱、梅兰酱、红醋等调味品；一为东江菜，以惠州菜为代表，擅长烹制用家畜、家禽作原料的菜肴，口味偏咸，用酱料比较简单。广东菜系是受外国烹饪文化影响较大的一个菜系。

**四川菜，**又称川菜（因四川简称川），提到川菜，人们会想到麻辣酸甜咸，或鱼香、怪味等，其实这种风味的形成不过是近百年的事，而且最初也只在下层社会流行，因为作为现在川菜风味的重要调料辣椒传入中国不过才二三百年。

三国（220—265）时，四川是蜀国的所在地。据考，那时蜀人尚甜，到了晋（265—420）代，蜀人喜食辛香，不过那时的辛香泛指姜、芥、韭、葱之味。直到二百年前，川菜不仅无麻辣味菜肴，就是用蜀椒等辛辣调料的菜肴也不多，调味十分温和，与今日流行菜肴（如麻婆豆腐、鱼香类炒菜等）大异。直至今日，一些高档川菜如芙蓉鱼翅、一品熊掌、樟茶鸭子、家常海参、鸡茸葵菜、蒜泥白肉、干烧鲤里、开水白菜等仍然保持着传统川菜的风味。四川古称天府之国，物产丰富，除海鲜外，几乎无所不产。家畜家禽、淡水鱼虾十分丰富，因此川菜也以烹制鱼肉见长。四处肴馔作为一种有独特风格的饮食，早在八百多年前的南宋时期，在临安就有专营"川饭"的餐馆。其经营的菜肴为"诸色羹汤"、"诸煎鱼肉"。现在流行的川菜除了味重清鲜、工艺考究的高档筵席菜外，就是从辛、辣、麻、怪、咸、鲜为特色的大众菜肴，它的历史虽不长，但一出现就很快影响、甚至取代了高档菜肴。其实，辣椒是清初（约十七世纪末叶）从南美洲传入中国的，入川后蜀人在烹饪中对辣椒的钟爱无以复加。由于四川空气湿度大，阴雨天气居多，辣椒的引进既迎合了蜀人好香辛的传统，又有除湿的作用。于是经厨师精心调配，使辣椒在川菜中迅速普及，麻辣鲜红的菜肴成了川菜的代表。现在人们所熟知的川菜就是这种大众化的川菜。因此川菜具有一定的平民性质，能为大多数人所食用，并且十分下饭，这也是为平民所喜用的原因之一。这与京菜主要为达官贵人服务，淮扬菜主要被富商大贾垄断，江浙菜主要为文人学士所欣赏是不同的。像回锅肉、鱼香肉丝、豆瓣鲫鱼、宫保鸡丁、水煮肉片这些典型的现代川味菜肴也是一般老百姓在打牙祭时常能吃到的。

川味的特点是：味美、味多、味浓、味厚，有一菜一格、百菜百味之美誉。这与四川本地生产的口味丰富、醇美、富于特色的调味品分不开，如中坝的酱油、保宁的食醋、三汇的特醋、潼川的豆豉、涪陵的榨菜、重庆的辣酱、郫县的豆瓣、宜宾的芽菜、自贡的井盐等。四川泡菜芳香脆嫩，咸酸辣甜，极有特色。如果在其它地方泡制，即使完全照其泡制程序及原料做，也很难达到四川泡菜的味道。这是因为四川泡菜用的是自贡井盐，味纯正，而其它地区多用海盐，不免有回味略苦之感。从这个例子可见，四川风味的形成除了有高明厨师的调制外，调味原料也是个重要因素。川菜很少用单纯味，多用复合味，通过多种调料可调出白油、咸鲜、糖醋、荔枝、酸辣、麻辣、椒麻、蒜泥、香糟、鱼香、姜汁、酱香、怪味等几十种别具特色的复合味。而且同是一味，在具体菜肴中的表现也不同，如同是麻辣味的水煮肉片的麻辣与麻婆豆腐的麻辣就有很大区别。在调味手法上，有集中用味（指两种以上的单一味合用）、收汁浓味（借用急火收汁以增加菜肴味的浓度）以及注重本味、清除异味、增加香味等。在烹调技艺上，川菜擅长小煎、小炒、干煸、干烧。小煎、小炒的特点为食物原料不过油，加工烹制时不换锅，急火短炒、一锅成菜。如炒肝尖、炒腰花，只需一分钟左右，成菜嫩而不生、滚热鲜香，有"肝腰下锅十八铲"之说。"干煸"的原料多为纤维较长的食物，如牛肉、萝卜、苦瓜、四季豆。把它们切成细丝，在锅中加热，翻炒直至见油不见水时再放调料，成菜后有干香酥软的特点。"干烧"与京菜"红烧"类似，但需将原汤汁用小火收干，加豆瓣酱或红辣椒为调料，不勾芡，成菜红润油亮、浓厚酥烂，代表菜例为"干烧鱼"、"干烧冬笋"。川式肴馔中一些精美的小吃和民间风味也占有重要地位，如棒棒鸡、怪味鸡、灯影牛肉，夫妻肺片、小笼蒸牛肉、担担面、赖汤元等，已走向全国乃至海外。

**湖南菜，**又称湘菜（因湖南简称湘），早在西汉（公元前206—公元8）时期，湘菜的烹调技术就达到了一定水平。今天湘菜如从西汉算起，至少已有2100多年的历史。

湖南位于中国东南部，居长江中流，南岭以北，境内河流、湖泊、山脉、丘陵、平原、盆地兼而有之，山珍野味、鱼虾龟蟹无所不有。当地人民利用本地的丰富资源，创造了本地的美味佳肴，湘菜至今已发展有4000多个品种，其中名菜有300多种。湘菜以酸辣、焦麻、鲜香、油重、色浓、主味突出为特点，形成以湘江流域、洞庭湖区、湘西山区等各具地区特色的菜肴。

湘菜注重辣味，因这与湖南地理气候有关。这里空气湿度大，人体散湿不畅，故当地人习惯吃辣椒，用以去湿、祛风。

湘江流域以长沙、湘潭、衡阳为代表。这一带交通方便，人材荟萃，物产富饶，当地的菜肴制作精细，用料丰富，特别注重刀工、火候、色彩和造型。烹调方法煨、炖、腊、蒸、炒、煮、烧、爆等无所不用。口味讲究辛辣、软嫩、鲜香、浓香，如麻辣子鸡、炒细牛百页、鸭掌汤泡肚、干贝无黄蛋、砂锅狗肉等都十分具有这一地区的特色。

洞庭洞区以常德、益阳、岳阳等地为中心，素称鱼米之乡，也是旅游区。宋代文学家、政治家范仲淹的《岳阳楼记》不仅为这里的山川增色，也使这里的菜肴在制作及命名上显得精致雅典而富于文化色彩。其代表菜有潇湘五元龟、原汁武陵水鱼、莲蓬虾茸、洞庭野鸭、玉带鱼卷、芙蓉鱼排等都是这里的名菜。这一地区的菜肴色重，咸辣香软，造型配色十分美观。

湘西地区以吉首、怀化、大庸等地为代表。由于地处山区，野味山珍及香蕈地耳丰富，故菜肴质朴浓醇。这里的山民还擅制作腊肉及各种腌肉，口味咸香酸辣，熏腊清香适口。如：腊味合蒸、重阳寒菌、焦炸鳅鱼、麻辣泥蛙腿等菜肴，都洋溢着浓郁的山乡风味。

总的来说，湘菜注重辣味，同时用腊味品做的各种菜肴——俗称腊菜，也是湘菜的重要特色。

**湖北菜**，又称鄂菜（因湖北简称鄂），湖北是古楚国的故地，早在战国时期楚国肴馔就形成了自己的独特风味，后经两千多年的发展变化，形成了今日的湖北菜系。鄂菜以擅长烹饪河鲜著称，湖北有名的水产品几乎都可自成一席，如全鱼席、全武昌鱼席、全鳜鱼席、财鱼席、鳝鱼席、甲鱼席、娃娃鱼席、鮰鱼肚席、蟹席、虾席、蚶席、菱席、藕席、野鸭席、皮蛋席等，名目众多，变化纷繁，其中的清蒸武昌鱼、红烧鮰鱼、冬瓜鳖裙羹（系用冬瓜配甲鱼制成）、桔瓣鱼氽、仔鸡焖板栗等都是早已闻名遐迩的美味佳肴了。鄂菜重视多料合烹，当地所产的水产品多能独立成席的原因，除了烹调技艺的多种多样外，还由于擅长搭配，许多名菜用两种以上的原料制成，既突出了主料，也重视了配料。如"清炖全甲鱼"除甲鱼外还配有相当主料（甲鱼）重量一半的猪大骨，其它象"滑三丝"（猪里脊丝、鸡丝、猪肚丝）、"龙凤配"（鳝鱼、母鸡），从名目中就可以看出是多种原料制成的。鄂菜在烹饪方法上擅长蒸和煨。"蒸"法前面已经讲过；"煨"，用以烹制富于汤汁菜肴，其制法为：先将原料煸炒调味，然后分装瓦罐，置小火上用较长时间加热而成。菜肴特点为骨酥肉烂、汤汁浓醇，颇能下饭。鄂菜可分为荆南、襄阳、鄂州、汉沔四大流派。荆南擅长烧炖野味；襄阳则以烹制肉禽菜品为主；鄂州菜中多以粮豆蔬果为原料的素菜；汉沔则长于以禽兽海鲜为原料的菜肴，"沔阳三蒸"（粉蒸、酱菹蒸、清蒸）也是极富特色的汉沔代表菜肴。

310

# 仿　膳　菜

　　明代（1368—1644）以前的宫廷菜，流传至今者极少。保留较完整的是清代（1644—1911）宫廷菜，清宫菜能够流传民间，除了清宫饮食档案资料保存完整可提供研究外，就要归功于原清宫御膳房的几位老厨师了。1924年冯玉祥（1882—1948）将军把末代皇帝溥仪（1906—1967）逐出紫禁城后三宫，御膳房解散。1925年北海公园开放，原清宫御膳房的厨师孙绍然、王玉山、温宝田、牛文质、赵永寿等人经赵仁斋（原清宫菜库主管之一）牵头，在北海公园开设了茶庄，取名"仿膳"，专营正宗清宫糕点，在经营茶点小吃的同时，仿膳逐渐推出了一些清宫传统炒菜，不少文人游客慕名而来，不惜破费、以享受一下皇帝的菜点为快。当时由于用料精到、手艺出色、风味独特，很快成为北京著名的饭馆。

　　仿膳饭庄所在的北海琼岛北面的漪澜堂道宁斋，原是慈禧太后（1835—1908）在北海游逛时就餐的地方，这里背山面水，景色怡人。

　　清宫皇帝的膳食称御膳，在宫外办一家承做御膳的饭庄，只是模仿御膳的做法而已。这家饭庄最初的主人为饭庄起名时用了"仿膳"而没有称御膳，倒也显得求实高明。

　　仿膳主食以面食为主，如肉末火烧及用面做成各种形状的面点，如苹果、寿桃、佛手、如意花卷等。人们无论食那种食品，都会得到一句吉祥话：苹果——平平安安；寿桃——益寿延年；花卷——万事如意等。糕点有慈禧爱吃的小窝头、芸豆卷、豌豆黄之类。仿膳中最有气派的是

311

"满汉全席"。仿膳菜肴属北京菜系中的宫廷风味菜，除北京北海公园仿膳饭庄外，经营正宗宫廷菜的还有东单仿膳饭庄和西郊颐和园的听鹂馆饭庄。

宫廷菜来源于民间，它与民间菜的区别在于用料讲究，所用米、面、肉、蔬、瓜果、禽鱼、山珍海味，多为全国各地官员精选的贡品。无论其质量、成色，世上无任何人家可比。如御膳房用的米，在北京海淀区的玉泉山、汤泉等地有专人种植，人称京西稻或海淀稻。由于产量低，味道、口感极好，除皇帝外，官民皆不可亨用。此外，全国进贡的上乘"贡米"也只供宫廷食用。羊肉取之宫中庆丰司；清代御膳房不用牛肉，只取牛奶，也由庆丰司供应。天下奇瓜异果、海味山珍由各地呈贡，做菜用水是从乾隆皇帝御封的"天下第一泉"的玉泉山每日凌晨运来宫中。一般家禽、时令蔬菜，则由宫中菜户当家的到市上选购成色最好的。这样精选的原料，是烹制宫廷菜肴的先决条件。

宫廷菜肴的厨师皆是名厨，不仅做菜的味道要好，在菜的配色及造型上也无可挑剔；每道菜不仅好吃，而且好看，是菜中的艺术上品。许多厨师一生只负责一种或数种菜点的制作，分工越细，制作越精，与其说他们是做菜，不如说是精制菜点的艺术珍品。这样优秀的厨师技艺，是烹制宫廷美食的关键。

宫廷菜配料严格，不能任意搭配辅料。民间厨师在制作菜肴时，可以根据手头原料多寡有无，临时做些调整或用此代彼，只要烹调出的菜色、香、味俱佳，则无人追究。而宫廷中任何菜的辅料都不可更换，厨师要创新，则要冒险。如果一道新菜受到皇帝的赏识，丰厚的赐予十分可观，如皇帝说不好吃则要挨打受罚。

312

宫廷菜讲究原汁原味，在菜肴的外形和味道二者中，更加注重味道，如一道菜的主料是鸡，那么，一定要突出鸡的本味，无论使用什么辅料和调料，都不能影响鸡的原味。烹制鹿肉、水产、海味，都是如此，热菜、冷菜也是如此。宫廷菜讲究色、香、味俱全，中看不中吃不行；中吃不中看也不行。宫廷中的冷菜也不能混放在一盘，如白斩鸡就是一盘白斩鸡，拌海蜇就是一盘拌海蜇，熏鱼、松花、酱肉等各自单放一盘。做成象现代工艺美术品的冷荤冷素拼盘并做成龙凤图案的样子，在宫廷中是绝没有的，龙凤是帝后的象征，是吃不得的。宫廷菜中有专门的看菜，也叫大碗菜四品，是在四碗菜上分别用雪白的官燕摆出的四个字，如燕窝万字八仙鸭子、燕窝寿字口磨肥鸡、燕窝无字五绺鸡丝、燕窝疆字锅烧鸭子，摆在一起就是"万寿无疆"，当然还随不同节令摆出"庆贺中秋"、"蟾宫折桂"、"寿比南山"、"万年如意"、"庆贺新年"等等。这类看菜一般是专供皇帝看的，但味道也要好，万一皇上非要尝一口呢。

宫廷菜命名朴实无华，多以烹调方法加上主料名称命名，或是主料名称加配菜名称命名，使皇上一看就知道此菜的内容，如"鲜蘑爆炒鸡"、"三鲜丸子"、"鹿筋炮肉"、抓炒鱼片"、葱爆羊肉"等等。统观满清二百余年来的御膳档案，没有发现花里胡哨的命名，这也许是皇上一贯要求臣下表里如一的原故吧。宫廷菜在命名上与市井餐馆有所不同而与民间相似。宫廷菜可以说集中了中国菜肴的一切长处，1925年创办仿膳饭庄的几位清宫御厨将宫廷菜的烹制技术传了下来，使我们能够品尝到仿制的宫廷菜——仿膳菜，使神秘的宫廷菜又回到了民间。

# 满 汉 全 席

满汉全席最早约形成于清康熙（1662—1723）年间，但并不始于皇宫，而是形成于上层衙署及官府中。

满汉全席的形成与满族入关前后饮食习俗的改变有很大关系。在满清入关前，其筵宴称"饽饽席"，烹调简单，花色品种不多，以面食为主，讲求数量，富有浓郁的游牧民族的饮食风格。到了清代中叶，由于吸收了各民族，特别是汉族的饮食习尚和烹调技艺，满族的饮食风格发生了很大的变化。如康熙五十三年（1714），正值圣祖皇帝玄烨六十大寿，为恭贺天子福寿无疆，并炫耀大清的太平盛世，康熙皇帝别开生面地在宫廷摆下"千叟宴"。于当年3月25日和27日，两度设满汉全席宴赏园内耆老，先后有年龄65岁以上，至耄耋之年老叟2800余人赴宴，康熙皇帝与老叟们同席进餐，并乘兴挥毫写了"满汉全席"四个大字，从而确立了这一稀世珍馔的地位。

满汉全席的用料都是些珍奇昂贵的山珍海味，名贵蔺蕈，上品蔬果，包括世间一切可食美味。且讲究质量，非上品优质者不选。如熊掌要用秋天的东北黑熊前掌，因为这种熊的前掌侧面短，掌花明显，胶元蛋白丰富，加上秋天适宜它口胃的食物丰富，所以脚掌最健壮，脂膏最丰。烹饪后味道鲜美，营养丰富。再如烤乳猪，要选十二、三斤重的乳猪，宰杀前，还要用稀饭喂养三、四日，以清肠促膘，烧烤后口味鲜香滋润。此外，还必备北京烤鸭、哈尔巴（猪肘）、烤童子鸡等。

清末，满汉全席流入民间，各地都有许多菜馆、酒楼以此为名广为招徕。但其菜肴的品种、数量、质量也随各地风情习俗的不同，饮食爱好各异，而发生变化。如以广州为代表的南方各地，设满汉全席往往喜欢增加一道"龙虎凤大烩"风味名菜，以蛇为"龙"，以猫为"虎"，以鸡为"凤"。每席用"三蛇肉"（眼镜蛇、金环蛇、过树榕蛇）250克，猫肉或果子狸肉150克，鸡肉丝100克，水发鱼肚50克，配以适量香菇丝、木耳丝、猪油、麻油、陈皮、精盐、绍兴酒、白酒、生粉、薄脆、白菊花、柠檬汁丝等原料和调味品，精烹细调而成。在古都西安为中心的西北地区，则爱增加一道小巧玲珑、形象各异的饺子宴。把饺子做成拇指般大小，每只形状与馅心都不雷同，并根据不同馅心给予不同的命名，如肉三鲜、干贝、虾仁、麻酱、蘑菇、鱼香之类，冠以典雅美妙的名字。如黑、白木耳馅心称之为"白银墨玉"，上嵌樱桃者名曰"香花独秀"。华北地区的满汉全席总有一道金光灿灿，诸菜喷香，令人叫绝的火锅或涮羊肉。西北边疆地区的满汉全席，按照饮食习俗，必然要用烹制粗放、异香扑鼻、色味俱佳的炖牛羊肉或烤全羊，来作为压轴菜。四川的满汉全席菜肴中有"鱼香肉丝"、"宫保鸡丁"。山西的满汉全席菜肴中有"平遥牛肉"等。凡此种种，不胜枚举，总之，古代的满汉全席，随着烹饪技艺的提高，珍奇食品的出现，以及各地食俗的爱好，发生了不断的变化，但总的风格仍不失满汉全席的韵味。

满汉全席是一种十分讲究礼仪、程序和格局的豪华筵席。有关筵宴的地点、规格（席数）、等级，对陪客人员的品级职位要求，席间座次的排列设置，供宴席用的烹饪的山珍海味、果品、酒类品种和数量等，都有严格的规定。

赴宴的大小官员都必须一律顶戴朝珠，身穿公服。举办此席，还须奏乐、鸣炮、行礼以恭迎宾客入座。客人入座后，用铜盆的温水及干净的毛巾洗脸，然后奉上一杯芬芳诱人的香茗，边品茶边吃四色精美点心和银丝细面。客人还边吃边饮边对弈，或吟诗作画，亦可促膝叙谈，真是悠闲而庄重！茗叙以后，酒席的台子已经摆好，将四果（橙、柑、柚、苹果）及四京果（倭瓜子、炒杏仁、荔枝干、糖莲子）之类放在四周，还要在周围摆设四看果，作为点缀之用。

每个座位前摆有成套餐具。客人入座后，侍者先把鲜果剖开去皮奉上，然后上冷菜（荤菜），开始饮酒，继之上四热荤，酒过三巡，上大菜鱼翅。之后，上第二道菜双拼、热荤。然后再上第三、四道菜，酒尽兴后，门前喝罄（谓之"门前清"）。第五道上饭菜、粥、汤。整桌吃完，侍者用一只精制的小银托盘，盛有牙签及槟榔、蔻仁等，供客人选用（食）。继而，送来一盆洗脸水净面，谓之"槟水"，筵席方告结束。

满汉全席流入民间后，在咸丰年间（1851—1862）十分活跃，咸丰死后，慈禧曾下令，外埠各地一律不许使用满汉全席这个名称。可是后来光绪皇帝又下了一道旨意，王侯将领可以亨用满汉全席，导致后来天津等地大兴满汉全席之风。辛亥革命后，满汉全席在各大城市曾风靡一时，但随着它的推广和普及，筵宴佳馔及习惯礼仪逐渐简化。菜品种类由原来的200余款减少到100款左右。从现在保留下来的各种满汉全席的菜单来看，有110款、108款、64款等。满汉全席的菜肴风格，已无明显的汉满之分，所以，香港、广州等地还称之为"大汉筵席"。民国以后，由于连年的军阀混战，民不聊生，满汉全席才逐渐趋于衰微。近几年来，随着我国旅游业的发展，满汉全席这一炎黄子孙独创的东方名肴，芳香四溢，盛开在中国的烹饪园地。

## 官　府　菜

中国菜的分类法一般有两种：一种按区域划分，即按各地区饮食习惯不同，划分为若干菜系，例如分成川、粤、鲁、淮四大菜系，或分成京、鲁、川、粤、闽、淮扬、鄂、湘、江、浙九大菜系等（也有把淮扬菜和江浙菜合为一系，这样就是八大菜系）；另一种按菜的起源划分，根据各种菜肴的形成过程划分为宫廷菜、官府菜、庶民菜（或称民间菜）、山林寺庙菜、兄弟民族菜、外来菜等六大类。后一种分类方法，并不始于近代。我国数千年封建社会，等级森严，造成了人们生活方式的差异。在饮食上，明显地表现出等级差别。《国语．楚语下》一书便有"天子食太牢（牛、羊、猪），诸侯食牛，卿食羊，大夫食豚，士食鱼炙，庶人食菜"的记载。这种封建礼教和实际上各阶层人士生活水平的不同，使中国菜分化为宫廷菜、官府菜、庶民菜等类型。

官府菜又称官僚士大夫菜，包括一些出自豪富之家的名菜。官府菜在规格上一般不得超过宫廷菜，而又与庶民菜有极大的差别。官府菜是劳动人民创造的，而为封建官僚贵族富豪们所享用。不少官僚贵族之家厨膳奢糜。唐代黄升"日烹鹿肉三斤，自晨煮至日影下门西，则喜曰'火候足矣！'如是者四十年。"宋朝吕蒙正每天必食鸡舌羹，以至鸡毛堆成了山。蔡京的家厨每天杀鹌鹑上千只……。这些官僚家的家厨们天天烹鹿肉，煮鸡舌，烧鹌鹑，自然会总结出烹制的诀窍，使这些菜肴的味道更美，形成独特的风味。贵族官僚之家生活奢侈，资金雄厚，原料丰富，这是形成官府菜的重要条件之一。

官府菜形成的另一重要条件是名厨师与品味家的结合。一道名菜的形成，离不开厨师，也离不开品味家，官府菜往往同品味家的文化修养和生活水准有很大的关系。品味家的嘴，就像一道关口，由他品评，厨师来改进菜肴，使菜肴日臻完美。品味家的嘴，又仿佛是一个筛子，将质味较差的筛去，留下了色、香、味俱佳的肴馔。这样的品味家，历史上不乏其人，多数出自文人墨客、官僚士大夫阶层。如春秋战国时代的孔子，宋代的苏轼（东坡）、陆游（放翁），元代的倪瓒（云林），明末的李渔（笠翁），清代的袁枚等。他们精于饮馔之道，留下了精辟的议论或专著。如东坡肉、云林鹅、孔府菜、随园菜、谭家菜等，都作为著名的官府菜而流传于后世。

官府菜的特点，大体可以概括为以下几点：

选料讲究，烹制精细。袁世凯当年家厨甚多，厨艺亦高。他喜欢吃填鸭，特别喜欢清蒸，入冬以后，每顿必有清蒸鸭。为了使填鸭更富营养，味美，他命人以鹿茸捣屑，与高粱调和后饲鸭。

清代咸丰年间进士，官至工部尚书的潘祖荫，也是一位深谙饮食之道的官吏。潘家烹制豆腐，要用活鸭子的脑子与豆腐合烹，鲜美异常。

官府菜讲究烹调方法，精制细做，例如著名的东坡肉，苏东坡总结出"净洗铛，少着水，柴头罨烟烟不起。待它自熟莫催它。火候足时它自美"的烹调方法，使东坡肉的美名传遍天下。"宫爆鸡丁"，是清末官吏丁宝桢的家厨创制的（丁宝桢曾任山东巡抚，四川总督，加封"太子太保"衔，一般称为宫保，故而此肴名为宫保鸡丁）。在选料上，必须选择当年长成的小公鸡的胸脯肉，在烹制上，要急火速就，不可欠火，也不可过火，鸡脯丁炒散后，放入调好的芡汁，再加入用盐炒过的花生米，颠翻数下即成。

从目前较为完整流传下来的著名官府菜——北京谭家菜和孔府菜来看，其选料之讲究，烹制之精细，也是极为突出的。

家庭气味，崇尚真味。官府菜，注重进餐时的家庭气氛。在这一点上，既不象宫廷中用膳时有那么多使人拘谨的礼仪，也不象在饭庄餐馆里吃饭时会受到邻桌的干扰，它更接近于普通人家的生活，无拘无束，专心于品味。

在封建社会，那些文人士大夫们总把饮食作为一种文化成果来加以享受；他们崇尚真味，讲究洁美，希求食益；寄文化情趣于品尝美味之中，把品尝美味当作一种艺术鉴赏。谭家菜的主人谭瑑青，鉴赏文物极有眼力，品尝佳肴，同样认真。谭家菜之讲究原汁本味，便是谭瑑青及其父谭宗浚两代人崇尚真味的结果。

潘祖荫，也是一位擅于品味的文人。清末，广和居饭庄名厨荟萃，在北京城里很有名气，潘祖荫常去用餐。他教给厨师一种制鱼的方法，让厨师做给他吃。那方法很简单：将整条洗净的鲤鱼入开水烫一下，用手将鱼折成两段，然后加入调料、配料，上屉蒸熟即可。此菜特点是既不用刀，也不用油，纯粹清蒸，好后，原汁原味，鲜嫩可口，肉香，汤美。厨师尝了觉得好，其他客人也都称赞。潘府上的这道菜，便通过餐馆流传到社会上来，并被命名为"潘鱼"，也叫"潘氏清蒸鱼"。

象这样流传到社会上来的官府菜还有不少，其特点都注重原汁本味。

美食美器，相得益彰。精美的餐具，对于菜肴起着衬托的作用，可为宴席增辉。现在，在孔府还可看到全套的精美餐具，其中银器、瓷器俱全，许多餐具造型奇特古雅，非常美观。还有一些餐具，是专为盛装某一种菜而设计制作的。北京谭家菜中，也有许多特制餐具，比如盛装鱼翅的盘子，盘边略低，而中间凸起，这样，便将名贵的鱼翅突出起来。

菜肴要讲究造形美，这种造形，不应当损害菜肴的真味。为了造型，影响火候，影响品味，这是得不偿失的。袁枚的《随园食单》中提出"美食不如美器"的观点，是有道理的。官府菜，以品味为先，用美器相配，来衬托菜肴之美。

菜以人名，肴以人传。官府菜的许多菜肴以发明或偏爱此肴的文人士大夫的名号（或姓氏，或官称）命名，此肴便也随着这位名人的名字得以迅速传扬。例如东坡肉、宫保鸡丁、潘鱼等等。

在早年北京，有几家文人士大夫极喜雅聚的餐馆，里面有不少此类名人菜。例如三胜馆的吴菜，其中最著名的是"吴鱼片"：将鲜鱼切成长条片，配高等酱油和南姚家井之水制成，鲜嫩美味。吴，即指吴均舍（阎生），侍御。承华园的"胡适之鱼"：将鲤鱼肉切丁，加三鲜细丁做成羹，这是胡适之博士自己发明，让厨师替他做的。名堂最多的还要属广和居，这里除了"潘鱼"，还有"江豆腐"：用嫩豆腐加虾子、豆豉、笋丁制成，极为鲜美，因为是江韵涛（树）太守所授，故名"江豆腐"。"韩肘"，用猪肘子，杂以五味佐料烧成，浓香四溢，为韩心畬（朴存）所授，故名"韩肘"。还有"陶菜"，为陶凫侍郎所授。"胡鱼"为胡古青侍郎所授。"曾鱼"为曾国藩所授等等。上述菜原多是公馆菜，当这些文人士大夫们会聚餐馆时，便各献家珍，将这些菜的做法教给厨师，以助雅兴，使这些菜得以流传。当今北京电视台开辟《厨艺大观》节目，不仅请专业厨师高手献艺示范，还特别邀请各方文化人、艺术家在银屏上示范自己的拿手菜肴，这其中也流露着菜以人名、肴以人传的意味吧！

# 中国的炒菜

国　风

炒菜的发明是中国烹调史中的大事，不仅炒菜的配菜品种多，而且加工时间短，使荤素食物中营养流失少。炒菜可荤可素，也可荤素搭配，如中国北方流行于民间的肉末炒豆腐、姜丝炒肉、葱爆羊肉都是物美价廉、家喻户晓的家常炒菜。炒菜在以吃五谷（粮食）为主的中国百姓家，以菜肉齐备的方式适应着广大中国人的饮食习俗。在宫廷、官府的食谱上，以炒或由炒演变来的菜肴，也为数很多。

炒菜的出现约在汉末（220 年）以后，两汉以前的菜肴除羹外，主要是水煮、油炸、火烤三种，而且大多不放调料，口味单调。

“炒”字在成书于东汉永元十二年（100 年）的《说文》中未见有录，在《广韵》中有“𤅞”字，即古炒字，释意为加工粮食、焙之使干的方法。作为菜肴加工的“炒”，是在锅中放入少量的油（油多则为炸煎），在锅热后看油的热度最佳时把肉或蔬菜倒入锅中，并放入调味料，不断搅翻使肉菜至熟。这里要说明的是炒菜必须用中国的炒锅，即近似半圆形的铁锅，如用西式平底锅决炒不出中国炒菜的味道。另外锅底油热度至为重要，如炒辣椒面而言，高手炒辣椒面能炒得血红，象四川的肉末炒豆腐，红油与白豆腐色彩搭配十分好看，要是油的热度掌握不好，炒出的辣椒面就乌赭暗然，失去炒菜的美观。

炒菜的原料多是体积较小的肉或蔬菜，如末、丁、片、丝、条、球、块等。虽然翻炒的时间不长，但调料之味都能进入菜肴之中。

"炒"包括清炒、熬炒、煸炒、抓炒、大炒、小炒、生炒、熟炒、啜炒、干炒、软炒、老炒、托炒、溜炒、爆炒等细别。其它如烧、烩、焖、炖等都是在炒的基础上再辅以其它烹饪方法，也可看作是"炒"的发展。"炒"字出现很晚，用炒的方法制作菜肴至迟南北朝时已发明，只是当时尚未用"炒"命名。贾思勰（北魏末期杰出农学家）的《齐民要术》（中国现存最早最完整的农业百科全书，成书于公元544年）介绍"鸭煎法"时说："用新成鸭子极肥者，其大如雉，去头烂，治却腥翠五脏，又洗净，细剉如笼肉。细切葱白，下盐豉汁，炒令极熟，下椒姜末，食之。"选用野鸭子大小的肥鸭子，去掉头，用热水烫褪洗净毛羽，去掉尾腺和五脏，剁碎，使成肉馅状。细切葱花，加盐和豆豉汁，将肉翻炒至极熟，再加入花椒粉、姜末，然后食用。从原料的加工（切为细末）和在翻炒中加拌调料来看，都符合今天的炒法，只是没有说到锅中是否放油，但从贾思勰的行文顺序和食物名称"鸭煎"来看，锅中应该有油，否则葱花放在干锅中岂不会烧焦？无油又怎能称为"煎"

呢？因此，这种"鸭煎法"就是近世之炒肉末法；还有一种叫"菹肖法"的，也极似近世之炒菜法，即选用较肥的猪肉（或羊肉、鹿肉）切成细丝，下锅，加入豆豉汁和盐末翻炒，再配以酸菜（菹）和酸菜汁。这个菜和近世的肉丝炒酸菜相类似。唐宋（618—1279）两代的菜谱中也载有炒菜，不过往往把炒的过程称为"熬"。唐代（618—907）初春吃的"五生盘"，系用羊、牛、兔、熊、鹿肉片清炒至熟，然后切成细丝，加入佐料拌食。宋代《事林广记》记载了"东坡脯"的做法："鱼取肉，切作横条，盐醋腌片时，粗纸渗干。先以香料豆粉拌匀，却将鱼用粉为衣，轻手捶开，麻油揸过，熬熟。"所谓"熬"熟，即炒熟。此菜作法是把鱼肉切成条状，用盐、醋腌一会儿，以除腥入味，用纸吸干肉上汁液，然后挂上和以香料的淀粉，再经经把鱼肉展开，涂上油，入油锅翻炒即成，实则就是溜鱼条。北宋（960—1279）开始出现了许多以"炒"命名的菜肴，可见其普及。明清两代的炒菜之名更见于各种有关饮食的著述中。

炒作为一种烹饪法，其加工对象极为广泛，蔬菜中的果类蔬菜（如茄子、黄瓜）、叶类蔬菜（如白菜、菠菜）、块根、块茎类蔬菜（如山芋、马铃薯）、茎类蔬菜（如芹菜、春笋）都可用炒的方法加工。其它如山珍海味、家禽家畜、面筋豆腐、粥饭糕饼也无不可以"炒"。对肉质嫩的可用"抓炒"（这种炒法是先把肉丝、肉片挂上薄糊，经油略炸，即捞出，另在炒锅中放油加热，倒入拌有调料的芡汁，烧开，随即把炸好的肉丝或肉片放入翻炒即成）、爆炒（大火急炒）、溜炒（分焦溜、滑溜。焦溜挂厚糊放入油锅炸焦，再入炒锅；滑溜是挂厚糊入开水锅汆熟捞出，再放炒锅翻炒）；对于肉质较老或体积较大者（如块），可在翻炒加调料后，再用"焖"、"爆"、"烩"等烹饪方法进一步加工，使之熟透。可以生炒、干煸（如干煸豆苗、干煸牛肉）；也可以熟炒（如回锅肉），或加定量汤汁的落汤炒；还可以生熟原料合炒（如宫保肉丁中的花生米已用油炸熟）；至于荤素原料合炒，则是极为普通的家常菜。

炒菜多是在翻炒过种中加调料，也有少量炒菜的原料在烹饪前经过了腌制，其味已基本固定，翻炒的主要目的不过是加热使之变熟。炒菜中的调味有许多是复合味，如糖醋、酸辣、甜辣、麻辣、五味、怪味、鱼香味等。炒菜以多种食物原料配合在一起，在快速的加热过程中使其味混和，从而产生一种新的美味。如家喻户晓的姜丝炒肉、肉丝炒蒜苗、京酱肉丝、鱼香肉丝等等。厨师利用蒜、姜、葱等调味植物的香味，使之在烈火的加热中相互渗透，产生刺激人食欲的新味。中国炒菜烹饪术由于文人的参与，在命名、配色和刀法上日渐讲究，中国宋代著名文学家苏轼（1037—1101）、元代著名画家倪瓒（1301—1374）、明代著名画家、文学家徐渭（1521—1593）、清代著名文学家袁枚（1716—1798）等都是兼擅烹饪的美食家。这样中国炒菜在造型和配色上更加十分艺术化。如"五柳鱼"用葱丝、姜丝、冬笋丝、辣椒丝、冬菇丝和草鱼烧得十分漂亮，栗子炒鸡和冬笋炒鸡丝也同样鲜美味香。炒菜的刀法十分丰富，有切丝、切丁、切块、切片之分，在切肉时讲究顺其纹理，厨谚云"横切牛肉顺切鸡"就是这个道理。另外还有花刀，是艺术性极强的刀法，如中国的"炒腰花"这一普通菜肴，可运用的刀法竟达十余种；炒出的腰花可呈麦穗状、荔枝状、寿字状、核桃状，不仅形象美，还利于速熟、除去腥臊味并溶于调料味。

炒菜，对火候要求十分严格，同样的主料和辅料由于厨师对火候的掌握不同，味道和口感就会两样。煎炸食品由于锅中油多，可调度就大。唯独炒菜，锅底油少，全靠油和锅面的双重热度，加工体积小的菜肉、烹饪时间又要短，这是体现厨艺的关键。据清人袁枚《厨者王小余传》中描写厨师王小余当灶时的情景：他倚在灶边，一条腿支撑着，一条腿抬着，目不转睛地站在灶边，观察火候，别人招呼他，他听不见。只听他一会儿说："要猛火！"即时烧火的把火烧旺，有如赤日。一会儿他又说："要撤火！"那么烧火的速即减柴，火势即弱。他说一声："暂且停烧。"烧火人便弃柴停烧。他指挥自若，有如驾御军马的将军。袁枚在《随园食单．火候须知》中说："熟物之法，最重火候。有须武火者，煎炒是也；火弱则疲矣。有须文火者，煨煮是也；火猛则物枯矣。有先用武火而后用文火者，收物之汤是也。"袁枚所言仅是掌握火候的一般体会。火候掌握恰到准确者，必须有长期的烹饪各种食品的经验，因料用火，其法则就只可意会，难于言传。本书虽附有数十道宫廷菜肴的配方及做法，但在每位读者以此为据烹饪菜肴时，由于火候等因素，出锅的菜肴与正宗仿膳菜在色、香、味及口感方面，也是不会相同的。

# 中国菜肴的命名

国　风

　　中国是个相当重视名称、名誉、名声的国家。在中国成语里有不少是与"名"联系在一起的，如"名门闺秀"、"金榜题名"、"名落孙山"、"名利双收"等等。"名利双收"这句成语，道破了重视"名"的本意。只有出了名，名扬天下者，才能有获利的基础。中国历代不少著名的饭庄、餐馆的主人，以兢兢业业、辛辛苦苦的劳作、经营，使自己的餐馆赢得顾客的赞誉而名扬四方，从而使自己的餐馆在美名的传扬中，招揽四方之客，获利致富。如北京的东来顺、全聚德、鸿宾楼，苏州的松鹤楼，杭州的楼外楼，上海的老正兴，天津的狗不理，福州的聚春园……。当然获得美名的前提是经营中的货真价实、诚信无欺，不然美名是会变骂名的。对于菜肴的命名，秦汉时期，主要根据食物原料和加工方法命名。南北朝时期，菜肴的命名出现了花样，很普通的菜，起个美丽的名字，不仅提高了菜的

327

档次，也使食客感到典雅温存。如现今的橙子拌鱼片名之为"金齑玉脍"，驼掌和油菜心煨烧的菜名之为"沙舟踏翠"，鹌鹑和鹌鹑蛋烧的菜名之为"母子大会"，用鸡块与熊掌烧的菜名为"一掌山河"，用虾仁、玉兰片、香菇烧的菜名之为"风霜雪叶"，用海参、明虾、鸡脯、银耳、荸荠等烧的菜名之为"蝴蝶闹牡丹"，仔鸡和甲鱼烧的一道菜名之为"霸王别姬"等等。好的名字能使人们在筵席间产生联想，创造一种娱悦的就餐气氛。

中国肴馔的命名多富于艺术性，人工制成的肴馔往往以自然现象及大自然中的事物来命名。举凡天地四时，风花雪月，金玉瑰宝，动植万类，凡能引起审美联想的，无不取来命名肴馔。如风消饼（一种薄饼，先烙熟，吃的时候再用油炸）、雪花酥（类似今日北京糕点盐方酥）、雪花饼（类似今日脂油饼）、切雪菜（奶饼蒸青菜）、雪花豆腐（炒豆花）、芙蓉鸡片（用蛋清、鸡脯肉片、淀粉爆炒）、百花棋子（面片汤）、松鼠黄鱼、乌龙吐珠（海参、鹌鹑蛋烧制）等等。这些命名多偏重于肴馔的味、色、香、形，从名字上即反映出肴馔的鲜艳晶莹的色彩和浓郁芒馥的气味。起名用到的色彩多为红黄白绿几种，经心理学测定，这几种颜色可促进人们的食欲；而蓝色、青色则会让人们恶心。另外，光彩照人、玲珑剔透则易引起人们的快感，从而刺激食欲，而暗色正相反。菜肴的命名也遵循了这个原则，人们多取有光泽的物品以代替颜色，使肴馔更富于质感。如上面提到的"金齑玉脍"，不仅"金玉"价值高，使人产生珍贵感，而且"金"、玉""二字，光彩熠熠，能引起人的快感；其它如"翡翠"（翡翠虾仁、翡翠羹）、"琥珀"（琥珀肉、琥珀花生）、"水晶"（水晶肘子、水晶虾饼）、

"珍珠"（珍珠元鱼）、"锦"（锦带羹）等；即使食物中有暗色、黑色，也多用"乌"代替"黑"，如"乌龙钻雪"、"乌饭"，因为"乌"较有光彩。

还有一些肴馔的形成包含着生动的故事，以之命名使得肴馔富于情趣，如"五侯鲭"本是一种鱼杂脍。《西京杂记》云："娄护丰辩，传食五侯间，竞致奇膳，护乃合以为鲭，世称'五侯鲭'，以为奇味焉。""五侯"指西汉成帝时同日所封的母舅玉谭、王商、王立、王根、王逢五人。娄护因为口才好，善言辩，奔走于五侯之家，五侯送给他的都是"鲭"（音征，鱼肉合烹），但各家有各家的独特风味。娄护把它们又合烹在一起，遂产生了新的味，而且味至美，于是，后来就有了"五侯鲭"这道名菜。杭州是南宋（1127—1279）的都城，也是南宋抗金名将岳飞的坟墓所在地，杭州人民为了表示对诬陷岳飞的奸臣秦桧的痛恨，把北方人称之为油条的煎炸早点称为"油炸桧"，北京人在日本侵占北京期间借"油炸桧"的谐音，把油条叫做"油炸鬼"，因抗战期间，中国人称日寇为"鬼子"。在抗战期间中国的后方四川，还把一道现叫"什锦锅巴"的菜，又被叫做"轰炸东京"。中国菜肴还有为怀念创菜厨师而命名的，如川菜中的"夫妻肺片"为成都郭朝华夫妻所创。麻婆豆腐是清同治年间（1862—1874）成都北郊福桥边一小饭馆陈麻婆的拿手菜。苏北地区的"沛公狗肉"据说是汉高祖刘邦（公元前206—公元前195在位）所做的一道菜，因刘邦曾受封于沛，故称沛公。"西湖醋鱼"又名"叔嫂醋鱼"、"叔嫂传真"。传说西湖渔家叔嫂擅做醋鱼，因反抗恶霸向渔民勒索，杀死恶霸而远走他乡，当地百姓借方传做以示怀念，"西湖醋鱼"则成为历久不衰的地方名菜。"东坡肉"据说是宋代著名文学家苏东坡（苏轼）首创，他在杭州做地方官时，曾发动民工疏竣西湖。苏东坡用醇香的绍兴酒代水焖猪肉犒劳民工，结果被人们赞为"东坡第一菜"。"龙凤配"这道菜据说三国（220—265）时期，蜀汉将军赵云护送与吴侯孙权胞妹孙尚香与刘备新婚回到荆州，蜀汉丞相诸葛亮率将士、百姓迎接。文武官员、父老百姓在荆州城南门摆起接风洗尘大宴，头道菜就是"龙凤配"，高厨将鳝鱼托为金龙、母鸡托为彩凤，出盘时组成龙飞凤舞的图案，寓意吉祥和美。这道色泽金黄、外酥内烂、鲜香甜酸的名菜流传至今，成为鄂菜中婚宴美馔之一。"皮条鳝"这道菜也有一个典故，清道光八年（1828），湖北监利县人朱才哲出任台湾宜兰县令，上任不久，就遇"拱界虫"案。台湾水田中鳝鱼繁多，常以田埂为穴，拱垮田界，造成民事纠纷。由于宜兰县民不食鳝鱼，拱界案越来越多。朱才哲查清因由后，命家厨做鳝鱼菜，分给原、被告品尝，食者啧啧称叹，此后县民纷纷捕鳝烹食，不再打官司了。据说此菜是一位叫"狗儿"的厨师所创，当地人称"狗儿"为"皮条"，故称"皮条鳝"。此菜香酥爽脆、酸甜腴美，是鄂菜的名肴。当然，中国菜在命名上的典故有许多，它构成了中国饮食文化的组成部分。命名有雅有俗，也有穿凿附会的，但其总的目的是刺激食欲。肴馔之名有一定的针对性，要视食客的身份而定，如商人聚会的宴席，肴馔之名多取双合利钱、发财好市等，宫廷肴馔则多取宫门献鱼、万寿吉祥之类的名字。

# 宫廷菜点

## 的配料与制作 54 例

# 凤 凰 扒 窝

**主料**：母鸡 1 只，鹌鹑蛋 15 个。

**配料**：水发香菇，水发玉兰片，水发鱼肚各 50 克。

**调料**：料酒 20 克，精盐 2 克，酱油 10 克，清汤 600 克，葱段 50 克，姜 25 克，湿淀粉 15 克，鸡油 15 克。

**做法**：1. 从母鸡背部开膛，去五脏，洗净，由鸡腹内撤出大腿骨，用开水余后，将鸡放入沙锅，加入料酒、精盐、葱姜段，在微火炖两小时左右，倒入大碗内，原汁上屉蒸。

2. 将香菇、玉兰片、鱼肚切成细丝，放入水余一遍倒出，勺内加入高汤，加入盐、料酒，下入 3 种丝，煨 3 分钟，捞出摆在盘中。

3. 锅中放入清水，放入鹌鹑蛋，煮熟后捞出，摆在盘中，半埋在三丝中，把蒸好的母鸡控净汤，脯朝上放在盘中。

4. 将 250 克蒸鸡的原汤注入锅中，加入酱油、料酒各少许，对好口味，用水淀粉勾芡，淋入鸡油，浇于菜上即可。

# 金 鱼 鸭 掌

**主料**：鸭掌 12 个。

**配料**：鸡茸 100 克，水发香菇、冬笋、水发鱼肚各 30 克，黄瓜皮 25 克，樱桃、胡萝卜各少许。

**做法**：1. 锅中注入清水，放入鸭掌，上火煮 15 分钟左右，五成熟时捞出，加入清水过凉，将鸭掌从背部去骨，去掉硬筋，然后掌心朝上，摆放在盘中，在鸭掌跟部撒些面粉。

2. 香菇、冬笋、鱼肚切成丝，入水锅中氽一下捞出，再加入高汤，煨2分钟捞出摆在盘中，将鸡蛋清放入盘，用筷子抽成蛋泡状，将黄瓜切成细丝备用。

3. 鸡茸加入高汤、料酒、精盐、玉米粉、鸡油各少许搅上劲，再放入抽好的鸡蛋清，拌匀成糊（鸡泥）备用。

4. 用手将鸡泥挤成1寸左右的金鱼形，放在鸭掌跟部，樱桃切开安在鱼头两侧做眼睛，胡萝卜切成鱼鳍状放在金鱼背部，黄瓜丝摆在两侧做鳞，即成金鱼鸭掌，共做12个，上屉蒸6—8分钟取出放在盘中。

5. 将200克清汤注入锅中，加盐、料酒、精盐，对好口味，烧开，撇出浮沫，勾芡，淋入鸡油浇在菜上即可。

# 鱼 藏 剑

**主料：**鲜草鱼1尾。

**配料：**黄瓜1条。

**调料：**料酒20克，盐1.5克，白糖100克，醋70克，蕃茄酱10克，葱姜末各少许，湿淀粉100克，鸡蛋清2个，花生油，清汤250克。

**做法：**1. 将鱼去鳞、鳃、内脏，剁下头、尾，剔去骨刺、皮，用刀片成1寸5分长，1寸宽，1分厚的长方形片，共20片，放入碗内加料酒、盐少许腌10分钟。

2. 黄瓜取皮，切成1.5寸长条20根，放入盐、料酒腌5分钟。

3. 将鱼片平摆在墩上放入一根黄瓜条，卷成卷共20卷，加蛋清放入碗中加入湿淀粉拌成蛋清糊。

4. 坐煸锅，加入花生油，烧成七成熟，将鱼头、鱼卷、鱼尾裹满蛋清糊下入炸熟，至金黄色捞出控净油，将鱼头、鱼尾摆在盘两侧，鱼卷摆在中央，成鱼形。

5．锅中加少许底油，放入葱姜末煸一下，加入料酒、盐、糖、醋、蕃茄酱烧开后，调入淀粉，淋入花生油浇在盘中鱼头、鱼卷上即成。

## 太 极 发（菜）财

**主料**：水发燕菜 200 克。

**配料**：水发菜 200 克。

**调料**：料酒，精盐，水淀粉，清汤，蚝油。

**做法**：1．将水发燕菜放入烧开的 300 克清汤中煨一遍，放入大盘的一边。

2．将水发菜放入碗中，加汤、葱、姜、鸡汤上屉蒸约 1 小时，控出汤，放在大盘的另一边，与燕菜构成太极图形，各点红绿樱桃一个。

3．起两锅，分别注入清汤，一汤调味后勾芡，淋鸡油在燕菜上，另一汤加蚝油，勾芡浇于发菜上，即可上席。

## 三 鲜 鸭 包

**主料**：酱鸭肉 250 克。

**配料**：笋尖 50 克，水发冬菇 50 克，鸡蛋 4 个。

**调料**：面包料 50 克，葱、姜、盐、料酒、胡椒粉、香菜、面粉、淀粉、香油少许。

**做法**：1．将鸭肉切成1.5寸的粗丝，将葱、姜切细丝，香菜切段，加入盐、料酒、胡椒粉、香油拌匀成鸭馅。

2．将鸡蛋加盐、淀粉调成蛋液，吊成 10 张直径为3.5寸的圆皮。

3. 将面粉加水调成糊，抹在蛋皮上，包入鸭馅成圆柱形，共 10 个，再沾糊裹上面包渣下入 6—7 成的油锅中炸制金黄色时捞出，控净油摆在盘中即可上席。

## 罗 汉 大 虾

**主料**：对虾 12 个。

**配料**：虾茸 100 克，鸡蛋清 1 个，油菜末 5 克，火腿末 5 克。

**调料**：料酒，盐，白糖，湿玉米粉，面粉，花生油，鸡油，葱，姜。

**做法**：1. 将对虾分为两段，将头部去掉沙包、肠肚，用油煸一下为红色时加入料酒、盐、白糖、清汤、葱姜丝，在微火上煨 3—5 分钟，待汤汁发浓时即可出锅，放在鱼盘中的一侧。

2. 将对虾尾部去皮，留下尾巴，把虾片开，剁断虾筋，加盐、料酒、入味。

3. 用蛋清将虾茸拌匀，加盐、料酒、玉米粉、油拌成虾泥。

4. 在每个虾片上抹上虾泥，点上火腿末、油菜末，下入油锅炸熟，放入鱼盘中的另一侧即可上席。

## 黑 米 膳 粥

**做法**：将黑米洗净，放入锅中，加入清水，上火烧开，撇去沫子，改用微火熬两小时即成。

## 茸 鸡 待 哺

**原料**：酥皮面 160 克，豆沙馅 100 克，鸡蛋黄 150 克，黑芝麻、糖水少许。

　　**做法**：1. 将鸡蛋黄放入容器中，用尺板打散，起油锅置中火上，待油温三成熟时，徐徐倒入鸡蛋液，同时用长筷子顺着一个方向快速搅拌，炸约 5 分钟，即可捞出，挤出炸油，即成鸡蛋茸。

　　2. 将酥皮面卷成卷，用手揪成 12 个面剂，压成面皮，包入豆沙馅，用手捏成葫芦形，将上头捏出鸡嘴，嘴两边粘上一粒黑芝麻，放进烤炉烤熟，在鸡身上刷上糖水，裹上鸡蛋茸，即成小茸鸡。

## 鸳　鸯　酥　盒

　　**原料**：面粉 150 克，熟猪油 50 克，豆沙馅 75 克，桂花糖馅 75 克，花生油 750 克（约耗 40 克）。

　　**做法**：1. 将面粉用细罗筛过，分别制成水油皮面和油酥面，将两种面各分成 15 份，用水油皮面包上油酥面，揉圆后再擀长，卷成筒状，轻轻压扁，再擀长，然后从长的一端卷起至剩下 8 分时，将未卷上的一端擀成薄片，用刀从中间切开，再分向左右拉长，贴在圆卷的两端，再用刀从圆圈中间切两半，然后用手压成两个圆剂，将有层次的一面扣在下面，擀成圆皮，共做 30 个。

　　2. 将豆沙馅和桂花糖馅各分成 15 份，分别包入擀好的圆皮中呈饺状，将一个豆沙和一个桂花糖馅肚对在一起，馅边相搭，用手捏牢，呈带有裂缝的圆盒状，再将圆边捏成花边，即成生酥盒，用温花生油炸至金黄色捞出即可。

## 百　寿　桃

　　**原料**：发面 225 克，白糖 25 克，枣泥馅 100 克，香菜

336

叶少许。

**做法**：1. 将发面对好碱，加入白糖揉匀，醒 10 分钟后揪成 15 个面剂，用手揉成扁圆形，再擀成圆皮。

2. 将枣泥馅分成 15 份，分别包入圆皮中，用手揉成圆锥形，上端做出一个桃尖，再用竹刮板在桃身上竖着印出一条印痕，把两片香菜叶贴在寿桃的下部，醒 10 分钟后上屉蒸 8 分钟，取出后在桃尖上稍抹一点红色即可。

## 冰 花 雪 莲

**原料**：莲子 100 克，白糖 200 克。

**做法**：1. 将莲子去皮、捅去莲心，用温水洗净。

2. 将莲子放入容器中，加入清水（水没过食物表面），放入蒸箱中蒸 20 分钟左右，取出，滗净水，放汤碗中。

3. 锅中注入 500 克清水、加入白糖，上火烧开，倒在盛有莲子的汤碗中即可。

## 烧 饼

**原料**：发面 500 克，白糖 50 克，芝麻 25 克，香油 50 克。

**做法**：1. 将对好碱的发面，加入白糖揉匀，揪成 15 个剂，用手掌将面剂压成圆片，另揪一个小面球蘸上一点香油，放在圆片中心，把小面球包起来，揪去捏拢后收口处的面头，再用手把圆球按成直径 1 寸 5 分的扁圆饼，按此方法做出 15 个。

2. 将扁圆饼正面沾上糖水，再沾上芝麻，芝麻面朝上，放进烤盘里按平，入烤炉烤熟即可。

# 棠花吐蕊

**原料：**酥皮面250克，豆沙馅150克，鸡蛋1个。

**做法：**1．将酥皮面卷成卷，揪成18个面剂，用擀面棍擀成面皮，包入豆沙馅，上面捏成五角形，用剪刀分别将每个角从上到下挨着剪两刀，形成两条，用筷子在酥皮中心沾上鸡蛋，然后将每个角落边的第一条卷向酥皮中心，用鸡蛋粘牢，在酥皮中心再放一点红色面点。

2．将酥皮生胚放入油锅中，用微火慢慢炸熟即成。

# 金钱香菇

**主料：**香菇75克。

**配料：**鱼茸50克，马蹄3个，熟火腿75克，鲜豌豆12粒，水发发菜少许，鸡蛋清1个。

**调料：**料酒15克，精盐1.5克，清汤200克，湿玉米粉20克，面粉少许，鸡油10克。

**做法：**1．将香菇放入盆中，注入温水，浸泡1小时左右，然后换水洗净泥沙，用剪刀剪去香菇根，从中挑选出12个直径约1寸的香菇圆片。锅中注入清水，上火烧开，放入挑出的香菇，余一遍捞出，挤干水分，面朝下放入盘中，上面撒些玉米粉。

2．将鱼茸放入碗中，加入料酒、精盐、玉米粉、鸡油各少许，搅拌上劲。将鸡蛋清放入盘中，用筷子抽起，呈雪白泡沫状，然后倒入鱼茸中，搅拌成糊。将马蹄剁成细末，放入鱼茸糊中拌匀。

3．用剪刀将剩余的香菇剪成长1寸、宽1分的长条，共剪24根；将火腿切成长5分、宽2分、厚1分的薄片，

338

共切 48 片，将剩余的火腿剁成末。

4．用手将鱼茸糊挤成直径约 8 分的丸子，放在香菇上，将火腿片、香菇条对称地摆在鱼茸丸子上，做成古钱形，中间放一粒鲜豌豆。在香菇条的外侧撒一些火腿末，在火腿片的外侧点缀些发菜，即成金钱香菇，然后将做好的金钱香菇上屉蒸熟，取出，平码在圆盘中。

5．锅中注入清汤，加入剩余的料酒、精盐，上火烧开，撇去浮沫，倒入湿淀粉勾成茨汁，淋上鸡油，浇在金钱香菇上即成。

## 绣 球 干 贝

**主料**：干贝（水发）200 克，鱼泥 150 克

**配料**：香菇（水）25 克，蛋清 2 个，油菜心 8 棵，火腿末、油菜末各少许，清汤 200 克。

**调料**：味精适量、料酒 10 克、熟猪油 25 克、鸡油 15 克、玉米粉（湿）20 克、盐少许。

**做法**：1．将干贝上屉蒸好，搓成丝放在盘内。

2．将蛋清抽起，同鱼泥、盐少许、料酒 5 克、味清、熟猪油搅成湖，然后挤成直径 5 分的圆球，放在干贝丝上，使球粘满干贝。

3．将香菇剪成 28 条，在干贝球上打 1 个十字放好，中央点些糊，撒些油菜末和火腿末上屉蒸熟。

4．油菜心用水烧熟后码在盘内，根向盘中间，把干贝球摆在上面。

5．把清汤 200 克烧开，加入料酒、味精、盐少许，玉米粉 15 克，勾稀汁蒙于菜上，淋上鸡油即可。

**特点**：此菜形似绣球，味鲜色美。

## 抓 炒 鱼 片

**主料**：鱼肉（最好是桂鱼）200 克。

**调料**：花生油 500 克（实耗用 40 克），白糖 25 克，味精适量，料酒 10 克，酱油 10 克，熟猪油 25 克，醋 10 克，葱末少许，姜末少许，玉米粉（湿）100 克

**做法**：1. 将鱼去净皮骨，用刀片成长 1 寸五分、宽 1 寸、厚 3 分的长方形片，用湿玉米粉（约 85 克），把鱼片拌匀浆好。2. 将花生油 500 克倒入锅中，放在旺火上，待油熟到冒烟时，将鱼片一片一片放入油锅内（这样可以避免粘在一起。）如火太旺油太热，可把油锅端到微火上缓炸一下，约炸 2 分钟左右。当外边呈焦黄色时，鱼片成熟即可取出。

3. 把酱油、醋、白糖、味精、葱末、姜末等调料和湿玉米粉一起在碗中调匀。把锅放在旺火上，倒入熟猪油 25 克，油热后将调好的汁倒入锅内，炒到汁成糊状时，将炸好的鱼片倒入翻炒即成。

**特点**：此菜鱼片呈金黄色，香、甜、酸、咸、味美适口。

## 熘 鸡 脯

**主料**：鸡脯肉 100 克。

**配料**：蛋清 5 个，鲜豌豆 100 克，清汤 1000 克。

**调料**：味精适量，料酒 10 克，玉米粉（湿）35 克，盐少许，鸡油 10 克，熟猪油 500 克（实耗 75 克）。

**做法**：1. 把鸡脯肉砸成鸡泥用 5 个蛋清加入少许玉米粉，将鸡泥搅成稀糊（搅糊时蛋清匀着倒，不要打）并加

入少许料酒、味精、盐。

2．将油锅放在旺火上，倒入熟猪油待油温热时，迅速将鸡糊透过漏勺渗入油锅内，炸成白色的形似豌豆大小的圆球，如果有块大的可用手勺敲碎，然后将鸡球捞出控净油。

3．另坐一锅放入清汤 1000 克，加入料酒 10 克，味精、盐少许，用玉米粉 30 克勾成稀汁，将豌豆倒入锅内，再将鸡球倒入，淋上鸡油 10 克，倒入油碗即可。

**特点**：此菜的制做方法，系由过去宫廷中创始的。其色泽洁白，掺有少许绿色豌豆，白绿相间，色调美观，味清香，柔软而不腻。

## 炒 肉 末

**主料**：肥瘦猪肉 500 克。

**调料**：味精适量，料酒 5 克，白糖 10 克，酱油 10 克，葱、姜、盐各少许。

**做法**：1．将猪肉去皮、筋，剁成碎末。

2．将锅放在火上烧热，不加油，放入肉末直接煸炒。待肉末变成白色时，用漏勺将汤滗净，加入酱油 10 克、白糖 10 克，盐少许继续煸炒，味吃进肉末后，再加入料酒、味精、香油、葱末、姜末再炒，炒干为止。

**特点**：此菜肉嫩鲜香，不腥不腻，用马蹄烧饼夹食，风味更佳。

## 炸 佛 手

**主料**：瘦猪肉末 200 克。

**配料**：鸡蛋 2 个。

**调料**：玉米粉（干）50 克，面粉 10 克，味精适量，料酒 5 克，香油 5 克，花生油 100 克，葱、姜、盐各少许。

**做法**：1．将猪肉末加入味精、料酒、香油、盐和葱姜末，用少许玉米粉拌匀。

2．把鸡蛋磕入碗内，加入少许水、玉米粉、盐搅匀。将炒勺用油擦一下，烧热后，将鸡蛋糊倒入一半，转动炒勺，使鸡蛋吊成一张薄皮，然后将勺底朝上，在火上一烤蛋皮即离勺，此时用手勺接着，即成一张蛋皮，如此做 2 张。

3．将蛋皮中间切开，变成 4 个半张，将肉馅均为 4 份，用 10 克面粉搅成面糊，抹在蛋皮边上，将肉馅用蛋皮卷成长条（宽约 1 寸左右），然后每隔 2 分宽切一刀（上面留 1 分不要切断）。如此连切四刀，第 5 刀时切断，即成佛手形肉卷。

4．坐上油锅，待油七成热时，将佛手下入锅内用温油炸，约炸 10 分钟，捞成即成。

**特点**：此菜色金黄，开似佛手，外焦里嫩。

### 金蟾望月

**主料**：原汁桶鲍鱼 12 个。

**配料**：鱼茸 50 克，水发香菇 30 克，水发玉兰片 25 克，熟火腿 25 克，水发鱼肚 40 克，鲜豌豆 24 粒，发菜 5 克。

**调料**：料酒 15 克，精盐 1.5 克，鸡蛋清 1 个，清汤 400 克，湿玉米粉 25 克，鸡油 10 克，熟猪油 10 克。

**做法**：1．将鲍鱼的毛边从其缺口处各撕开一半（切不可撕断），用刀在上下壳接合处片开三分之二。

2．锅中注入清水，上火烧开，将香菇、玉兰片、鱼肚分别氽一遍，捞出，用清水冲凉，然后同火腿一起切成长1寸的丝，即成"四丝"。

3．把鸡蛋清倒入盘中，用筷子抽起，呈雪白泡沫状。将鱼茸放入碗中，加入料酒、精盐、清汤、熟猪油、玉米粉各少许，搅拌上劲，再放入蛋清，拌匀成糊。

4．用小刀将鱼茸糊抹入鲍鱼开口处内（周围要抹齐），用豌豆按在鱼茸糊的两侧做眼睛，中间点缀些发菜，放入盘中，将撕开的毛边放在前面做爪，即成哈蟆（金蟾），按此方法做12个，上屉蒸熟取出。

5．将150克清汤注入汤锅中，放入四丝、料酒、精盐、在微火上煨两分钟捞出，控净水，撒在盘中，把蒸好的蛤蟆鲍鱼嘴朝外码在丝上呈圆形。

6．锅中注入250克清汤，加入料酒、精盐，上火烧开，撇去浮沫。用水将玉米粉调稀，倒入锅中，勾成芡汁，淋上鸡油，浇在菜上即可。

## 乌 龙 吐 珠

**主料**：水发海参250克，鸽蛋6个。

**调料**：料酒20克，精盐1.5克，酱油15克，清汤150克，葱50克，湿玉米粉15克，花生油150克（约耗20克），鸡油40克。

**做法**：1．用水将海参洗净泥沙，竖着切成两半。葱切寸段。锅中注入清水，上火烧开，放入海参，氽一遍捞出。

2．锅中注入清水，放入鸽蛋，上火煮熟捞出，剥去外皮，用水洗净。火上坐一煸锅，注入花生油，烧至七成熟，下入鸽蛋，炸成金黄色，倒漏勺中，控净油。

3．煸锅注入鸡油，坐火上，放入葱段，炸成金黄色时捞出葱段，即成葱油。将一半葱油倒入小碗内，煸锅中留下一半葱油，起锅上火，下入海参煸炒一下，再加入料酒、精盐、酱油、清汤和鸽蛋，在微火上㸆3分钟左右，待汁浓时，用水将玉米粉调稀，倒入锅中勾成芡汁，淋入小碗中的葱油，即可出锅。

## 龙 凤 丝

**主料**：净鱼肉250克，鸡胸肉250克。

**配料**：冬笋50克。

**调料**：盐，味精，料酒，湿淀粉，清汤，葱姜末，鸡蛋清1个。

**做法**：1. 将鱼肉、鸡胸肉切成1.5寸长的丝，加入盐、料酒、蛋清、湿淀粉上浆备用，冬笋切成丝。

2. 勺上火，烧热加入油，待油温3—4成热时，下入鱼丝、鸡丝、笋丝滑熟倒出。

3. 勺内加底油，下入葱姜末、高汤、盐、味精、料酒，勾芡，下入三丝翻炒，加入明油即可装盘。

## 干 贝 冬 瓜 球

**主料**：冬瓜500克。

**配料**：水发干贝50克。

**调料**：盐，料酒，葱姜末，高汤，水淀粉，鸡油。

**做法**：1. 将冬瓜用瓜勺挖成球状。

2. 勺上火加入高汤、下入盐、料酒、加入冬瓜球、干贝烧透控出。

3. 勺内加葱姜、高汤、盐、料酒烧开，勾芡，下入冬瓜球、干贝，淋入鸡油即可。

## 福字扣肉

**主料**：带皮五花肉 500 克。

**配料**：鸡茸、生菜叶。

**调料**：盐，料酒，酱油，葱姜，味精，湿淀粉，糖。

**做法**：1. 将五花肉下入热油略炸一下，勺内加酱油、盐、味精、料酒、葱姜，下入肉，酱熟，皮朝上装入盘中，用鸡茸在皮上挤上福字，上屉再蒸 2—3 分钟，起出。

2. 勺上火加底油、葱姜、生菜，炒熟围在扣肉周围。

3. 勺内加入高汤、酱油、盐、味精、料酒烧开，勾芡，淋入鸡油，浇在扣肉上即可上席。

## 沙舟踏翠

**主料**：水发净驼掌 1 只。

**配料**：油菜心 500 克，冬菇、冬笋少许。

**调料**：盐，味精，料酒，酱油，胡椒粉，湿淀粉，葱油。

**做法**：1. 将驼掌正面打上一字花刀，加入冬菇、冬笋片，放入碗中加入高汤、盐、料酒、胡椒粉、酱油上屉蒸一小时左右。

2. 勺中加入高汤、盐、料酒、油下入油菜心，熟后，捞出码放在盘中，将蒸好的驼掌扣在菜心上。

3. 两勺上火加入盐、料酒勾成白汁浇在菜心上，另一勺调成红汁浇在驼掌上，即可上席。

## 桃仁鸭方

**主料**：酱鸭半只。

配料：虾茸，马蹄，核桃仁，油菜末，火腿末。

调料：盐，料酒，湿淀粉，花生油，面粉。

做法：1. 酱鸭皮朝下，摆在盘中，表面上撒上少许面。

2. 虾茸加盐、料酒、淀粉、油打成虾泥，抹在鸭子上，摆上桃仁、油菜末、火腿末。

3. 锅内下入油，烧至 7 成热时下入鸭方，炸熟到金黄色时，捞出控净油，上熟墩切成方块装盘即可上席。

## 肘 子 菜 心

主料：净肘子一只。

配料：油菜心。

调料：盐，酱油，料酒，糖，湿淀粉，油，葱姜。

做法：1. 肘子下油略炸捞出，勺上火加入葱、姜、酱油、料酒、糖、水，炖熟装盘。

2. 勺内加入高汤、盐、味精、料酒烧开，下入菜心至熟捞出，码在肘子周围。

3. 勺上火加入高汤、盐、味精、料酒勾成白汁浇入菜心上，再勾成红汁浇于肘子上即可上席。

## 一 品 豆 腐

主料：豆腐 250 克。

配料：肉末，虾茸，水发干贝，水发冬菇，马蹄，冬笋，黄瓜皮，水发发菜，胡萝卜，油菜心。

调料：盐、味精、料酒、鸡蛋清 4 个、鸡油、玉米粉、香油、清汤。

做法：1. 将豆腐用水淖一下，控净水，加入盐、味精、料酒、淀粉、鸡油、鸡蛋，放入搅拌机中打碎成糊状。

2．将肉末、虾茸、水发干贝、冬菇、马蹄、冬笋剁碎加入盐、味精、料酒、香油拌均匀备用。

3．取两个豆腐托上抹上一层鸡油，倒上豆腐糊，抹平上屉蒸熟，取一片放入一个9寸盘中，上面放上什锦馅，另一片再放在馅上面，周围和上面抹上一层薄薄的豆腐糊。

4．冬菇剪成丝，黄瓜皮切成竹叶、竹杆，胡萝卜切成菱形片，备用。

5．在豆腐坯子上，用冬菇丝摆树形，黄瓜皮摆成竹子，胡萝卜码成小花，发菜点缀即成一幅美丽的图案。

6．将做好的豆腐上屉蒸10多分钟，取下，放在盘上，再将淖好的油菜心摆在周围。

7．勺上火加高汤、盐、料酒、勾芡，淋鸡油，浇于豆腐上即可上席。

## 豌　豆　黄

**原料：** 白豌豆500克，白糖375克，冻粉10克，食碱2克。

**做法：** 1．用小磨将豌豆破碎去皮，用凉水洗三遍。铜锅坐水，开锅后将豌豆下入锅内，加入碱，然后将豌豆煮烂成稀粥状，并带原汤过罗。

2．将过了罗的豌豆放入锅内，加入白糖和溶化的冻粉水，上火炒30分钟左右。

3．将炒好的豌豆泥倒入1尺寸长，5寸宽，7分高的白铁模子内，然后放在通风处晾三四个小时，晾透即成豌豆黄，改刀装盘即成。

# 芸 豆 卷

**原料：**白芸豆 500 克，豆沙 250 克，碱少许。

**做法：**1. 用小磨将芸豆破碎去皮，放在盆里，用开水泡一夜，把未磨掉的豆皮泡起来，再用温水把豆皮泡掉。将芸豆碎瓣放在开水锅里煮，加少许碱，煮熟后用漏勺捞出，用布包好，上屉蒸 20 分钟，取出过罗，将瓣擦成泥，泥通过罗而形成小细丝。

2. 将芸丝晾凉后，倒在湿布上，隔着布揉和成泥。取 1 尺 5 寸见方的湿白布，平铺在案板上，将芸豆泥搓成 1 寸粗的条，放湿布中间，用刀面抹成 1 分厚、5 寸长、2 寸宽的长方形薄片，然后抹上一层豆沙，顺着湿白布从长的边缘两面卷起，各卷一半后，合并为一个圆柱形，用双手隔着布轻轻捏一捏、压一压。最后将布拉起，使卷慢慢地滚在案板上，先切去两端不齐的边，再切成六七分长的段，芸豆卷即成。

# 金 银 鹿 肉

**主料：**鹿肉 500 克。

**调料：**鸡蛋 2 个，绍兴酒 5 克，玉米粉 5 克，精盐，葱，姜各少许，鸡油 5 克，花生油 500 克（实耗约 50 克左右）。

**做法：**1. 先洗净鹿肉，放锅中加水煮至五成熟时捞出，再将肉切成 7 公分厚的大片，放于碗中，加入绍兴酒、精盐、葱段、姜块、鸡油、上屉蒸烂为止，然后滤去汤，分为两份。

2. 把两个鸡蛋的蛋清、蛋黄分别放在两个碗中，各用

348

玉米粉5克、面粉2.5克及精盐少许搅拌成糊。坐锅，倒入花生油，油热后，将一份鹿肉蘸满蛋黄糊下入油中，炸至金黄色捞出。另一份鹿肉蘸满蛋清糊下入油中。炸熟后捞出。将两色鹿肉分别切成条，码入盘中，配以鸡蛋松上席。

## 灯 笼 豆 腐

**主料**：豆腐2块。

**配料**：肉末50克，水发香菇25克，水发玉兰片（最好是鲜笋）25克，荸荠2个，豆苗2棵。

**调料**：清汤250克，绍兴酒5克，白糖5克，鸡油10克，香油10克，酱油少许，葱、姜少许，花生油100克。

**做法**：1. 将豆腐切成5厘米长、2.5厘米厚的块，用油炸黄。把香菇、玉兰片、荸荠各一半切成末，和肉末一起用香油煸炒，加入少许绍兴酒、盐、酱油。

2. 将豆腐的一头破一个圆口，掏尽里边的豆腐，装入炒熟的肉末，盖好，抹上一点鸡蛋糊，用温油炸一下。

3. 香菇、玉兰片另一半切成菱形片，用开水氽一下。用清汤250克，加绍兴酒、酱油、盐、白糖和配料下入豆腐烧二三分钟，勾芡、淋上鸡油。

## 如 意 冬 笋

**主料**：冬笋1个（长约20厘米）。

**配料**：鸡肉泥150克，荸荠3个，火腿末25克，油菜末25克，鸡蛋清两个，清汤200克。

**调料**：绍兴酒10克，盐少许，玉米粉（湿）15克，鸡油10克，熟猪油10克。

**做法**：1. 将冬笋去皮剥平，上火煮10分钟，晾凉后用刀切成长约 14 厘米，宽 7 厘米的薄片。

2. 把荸荠剁碎，与抽起的蛋清、鸡肉泥拌成糊，加入绍兴酒、盐、鸡油少许。

3. 将冬笋片平铺在白布上，两头抹上 7 厘米宽的鸡泥糊。在糊上撒上火腿末和油菜末，然后卷起两头，用白布包着蒸熟，晾凉后切成 7 厘米宽的鱼鳞形片，码在碗内，走菜时，上屉蒸热扣在盘内。

4. 用清汤 200 克、绍兴酒 10 克、玉米粉 15 克、盐少许，勾成稀汁，淋鸡油，蒙于菜上。

## 荷 包 里 脊

**原料**：猪里脊 50 克，鸡蛋 3 个，水发香菇 2.5 克，水发玉兰片 25 克，火腿末 5 克，油菜叶少许，绍兴酒 5 克，湿玉米粉 25 克，精盐 1.5 克，猪肥肉 25 克，花生油 100 克，面粉 25 克。

**做法**：1. 将猪里脊肉、香菇、玉兰片剁成末，加入绍兴酒、精盐搅成馅。

2. 把鸡蛋打入碗内，加点盐和湿玉米粉，搅匀。

3. 将小炒锅上火，烤热，再用一块肥猪肉将锅内擦匀，使锅内壁沾上一层油，然后舀一小勺鸡蛋液倒入炒锅内，旋转炒锅，使之摊成杯口大小（直径 8 公分左右）的蛋皮。

4. 把调制好的馅做成直径 3 分（1 公分）左右的小球，放在蛋皮中央，将蛋皮折过一半，用筷子在上边轻轻按一下，要用筷子竖着将蛋皮夹拢，使馅包在蛋皮当中，馅肚上抹一点面糊，撒上一点火腿末和油菜末。最后，把这样的小"荷包"放入温油中炸熟，码在盘中。

# 怀 胎 桂 鱼

**原料：**桂鱼 1 尾（1000 克），清汤 250 克，水发香菇 50 克，水发玉兰片 50 克，水发海参 50 克，火腿 50 克，荸荠 50 克，蛋清 50 克，油菜心两棵，绍兴酒 15 克，玉米粉（湿）15 克，鸡油 10 克，熟猪油 25 克，葱 50 克，姜 50 克，盐少许。

**做法：**1. 从鱼鳃处取出五脏，刮去鳞，用开水氽一遍，从头到尾用刀轻轻刮去鱼青（切一可刮破鱼皮），在鱼身两侧斜剞花刀。

2. 将香菇 3 个、玉兰片 4 片留下，其余同荸荠一起切成丝。

3. 海参切丁，与鱼肉泥、鸡蛋清、绍兴酒、盐、熟猪油 25 克拌成糊，从鱼鳃处放进鱼肚内。然后把少许绍兴酒、盐抹在鱼身上，将留下的香菇、玉兰片顺序摆在鱼身上，加上葱、姜段，上屉蒸至肉刺分离。滗去鱼汤、葱段不要。

4. 把火腿氽一下，码在鱼身上，用清汤 250 克，加入玉米粉 15 克，绍兴酒 10 克，盐少许，勾稀汁，浇在鱼上面，再淋上鸡油。鱼做好后将油菜心码在鱼两旁，一棵向前，一棵向后。

# 扒 四 宝

**原料：**原汁鲍鱼 1 桶（罐头），龙须菜 225 克，盖菜脑 6 棵，火腿 100 克，鸡泥 100 克，鸡蛋清 2 个，豌豆 24 粒，清汤 500 克，发菜少许，绍兴酒 15 克，熟猪油 25 克，鸡油 10 克，玉米粉（湿）15 克，盐少许。

**做法：**1. 将鸡泥、蛋清打成糊，同 12 个鲍鱼做成蛤蟆形。

2．龙须菜去皮，切成两半，加入绍兴酒、盐少许，上屉蒸 10 分钟。

3．削好盖菜脑，根上划十字花刀，用清汤 250 克，加少许调料烧熟。

4．走菜时，将龙须菜放入盘中间，四周放蛤蟆鲍鱼、四角放盖菜脑火腿片。用清汤 250 克，加入剩余调料，勾稀汁，蒙于菜上，淋鸡油 10 克。

**特点**：此菜美观大方，鲜嫩可口。

## 荷 花 鱼 丝

**原料**：生鱼肉 250 克，鲜荷花 1 朵，冬笋 150 克，鸡蛋清 50 克，绍兴酒 15 克，湿淀粉、姜丝、精盐少许，芝麻油 5 克，熟猪油 100 克。

**做法**：1．将剔尽骨刺的鱼肉洗净，切成细丝，将冬笋切成细丝。

2．将鲜荷花瓣洗净，围放在荷花碗中。

3．将鱼丝用蛋清、绍兴酒、淀粉浆调匀，然后连同冬笋丝入温油（熟猪油）中滑透，滗去油，再加姜丝、绍兴酒、精盐回锅烹炒，淋上芝麻油，趁势倒入摆好荷花瓣的盘中。

## 金 斋 玉 脍

**原料**：青鱼肉 200 克，鲜桔子 150 克，冬笋 50 克，料酒 5 克，盐 1．5 克，面粉 50 克，鸡汤 50 克，蛋清 2 个，葱姜各 25 克，白糖 10 克。

**选料**：选青鱼中段去皮精肉，无籽的鲜桔子。

352

**做法**：1. 将鱼肉片切成6.5厘米长，2.5厘米宽的大片，用盐、料酒稍腌一会儿。

2. 再用湿淀粉芡蛋清浆好鱼肉片待用。鲜桔子剥成瓣，葱、冬笋切片。

3. 热锅温油，将鱼片滑出，沥干油。锅中留底油，炸葱姜后，捞出葱姜不要，再放入冬笋片、桔瓣翻拌，随即下入盐、料酒、白糖、鸡汤，再用湿淀粉勾芡并倒入滑好的鱼片搅匀，最后淋少许香油，出锅装盘，盘边围桔瓣、樱桃点缀即可。

**特点**：鱼片鲜嫩，桔瓣清香，色泽典雅。

特别注意：火功，加热时间不宜过长。

典故：据说隋炀帝驾临江都时，令地方官献当地美馔佳肴，吴地官员进献了"鲈鱼脍"，隋炀帝尝后，大加赞扬说："金齑玉脍东南佳味也。"宋代著名诗人陆游曾烹制过此菜，并留有"自摘金橙捣脍齑"的诗句。

# 箸　头　春

**原料**：活鹌鹑5只（以出生3个月的最佳），香菇，冬笋，葱姜和调味品。

**做法**：1. 宰杀鹌鹑除毛放血，去脏洗净除骨，将鹌鹑肉切成筷子头大小的丁，冬笋、香菇也切成小丁。

2. 先用鸡蛋清、料酒、湿淀粉和精盐将鹑肉丁上好浆，放入猪油锅内滑散、熟透捞出，放在砂锅内，加入高级奶汤、葱、姜、精盐、料酒、胡椒煨烧30分钟左右，然后加入用沸水汆过的冬笋、香菇丁，调好味放入小碗，上桌食用。

# 素　脆　鳝

**原料**：水发冬菇250克，生姜50克，干淀粉50克，白糖125克，醋50克，酱油25克，花生油500克（实耗75克），湿淀粉少许。

**做法**：1. 将冬菇用剪刀剪成鳝鱼丝状，拍上干淀粉。生姜去皮，用刀切成丝待用。炒锅上火，放入花生油，烧至9成熟，投入拍过淀粉的冬菇丝，炸至锅内无气泡时捞出。

2. 将炒锅上火，放入清水75克、白糖、酱油烧沸，淋上湿淀粉，放入醋，即成卤汁，浇在脆鳝上面，再放上姜丝即成。

# 金　边　白　菜

**原料**：大白菜500克，干红辣椒7.5克，精盐6克，酱油20克，醋25克，白糖10克，姜末5克，菜籽油75克，芝麻油5克，湿淀粉15克。

**做法**：1. 大白菜去2层老叶、老帮，取嫩的洗净沥干水份。面朝上放砧板上，用刀拍一下（使之发松、易进味），切成2.6厘米长，1厘米宽的条。

2. 干辣椒一劈两半去籽，切成2.6厘米长的段。

3. 旺火上锅，放菜籽油75克，烧至7成熟，将辣椒段放入，炸出辣味，色变褐时，下姜末、白菜。用旺火急煸炒几下，入醋，翻颠几下，加酱油、盐、白糖、煸至刀茬处呈金黄色时，用湿淀粉勾薄芡、淋芝麻油、颠翻起锅装盘。

这一菜据说是庚子之乱（1900年八国联军进北京）时，

慈禧外逃西安，每餐几十道菜肴里，必有"金边白菜"。

## 它 似 蜜

**原料**：羊里脊肉 150 克，甜面酱 5 克，酱油 10 克，白糖 40 克，醋 2.5 克，湿淀粉 25 克，绍兴酒 2.5 克，姜汁 1.5 克，芝麻油 60 克，花生油 500 克（实耗 50 克）。

**做法**：1. 羊里脊洗净用斜刀切成 3.3 厘米长、1.6 厘米宽、0.16 厘米厚的薄片，加入甜面酱、湿淀粉 15 克，抓匀浆好。

2. 把姜汁、酱油、醋、绍兴酒、白糖、湿淀粉 10 克，一起调成芡汁。

3. 花生油倒入锅内，用旺火烧至 7 成热，下入浆好的羊里脊片，迅速拨散，勿使粘连，里脊片变成白色时，连油一起捞出。

4. 将空油锅坐在旺火上，放入 10 克芝麻油烧热，倒入滑好的羊里脊片，烹入调好的芡汁，迅速翻炒，使羊里脊片沾满芡汁，再淋上 10 克芝麻油即成。

## 葱 烧 海 参

**原料**：水发嫩小海参 1000 克，大葱 105 克，青蒜 15 克，姜末 5 克，姜汁 27 克，湿淀粉 10 克，鸡汤 200 克，白糖 27 克，酱油 12 克，绍兴酒 15 克，精盐 2 克，味精 2 克，煳葱油（用猪肉 500 克，放炒勺内，烧至 8 成热，下入葱段 100 克，姜片 75 克，蒜片 50 克，炸成金黄色，再下入香菜段 100 克，炸焦后，将以上原料捞出，余油即为煳葱油）50 克，熟猪油 150 克（约耗 75 克）。

**做法**：1. 洗净水发海参，整个放入凉水锅中烧开，约煮5分钟捞出，沥净水份。

2．大葱100克切成5厘米长的段，取5克切成末。青蒜切成3.3厘米长的段。炒勺内倒入猪油，用旺火烧至8成熟，下入葱段、炸成金黄色，捞在碗中，加入鸡汤50克、绍兴酒5克、姜汁2克、酱油2克、白糖2克和味精1克，用旺火蒸1—2分钟取出，滗出汤汁，留下葱段备用。

3．将汤勺倒入猪油25克，用旺火烧至8成熟，下入白糖5克，炒成金黄色，再下入葱末、姜末、海参煸炒几下，随即下入绍兴酒10克、鸡汤150克、酱油10克、姜汁25克、精盐、煳葱油20克和味精1克。待汤烧开后，挪到微火上爆数分钟，把汤汁爆去三分之二再改用旺火。

4．边颠翻炒勺，边淋入调稀的湿淀粉勾芡，使芡都挂在海参上，随后倒在盘中。

5．将炒勺放在旺火上，倒入煳葱油30克，烧热后下入青蒜段和切好的葱段，略煸一下，撒在海参上即成。

## 炸　响　铃

**原料：** 用杭州特产的泗乡豆腐皮（或用其它地方的油皮、豆油皮，采用豆浆结膜，捞出晾制而成，薄如蝉翼，透明黄亮）15张，猪里脊肉50克，鸡蛋清1/4个，葱白段1克，甜面酱50克，绍兴酒1克，精盐1克，味精1.5克。

**做法：** 1．将里脊肉去筋洗净，剁成细末（不使粘连），放入碗内，加入葱、盐、酒、味精和蛋黄拌成肉馅，分成5份。

2．豆腐皮润潮后切去边筋，将弧形的一端切平，成长方形。

3．取豆腐皮3张，每层揭开摊平重叠，再取肉馅1份，

356

放在豆腐皮的一端，用刀口（或竹片）将肉馅拓成3.5厘米左右的宽的条，放上切下的弧形豆腐皮（边筋不能用），然后揭起有肉馅的一端，向上卷成筒状（卷时不宜太松或太紧）。在豆腐皮的卷合处蘸上清水使之粘牢，做成 5 卷，再切成3.5厘米长的段，直立放置。

4. 炒锅置中火上，下熟菜油，烧至 5 成熟时，将豆腐皮卷陆续放入油锅，用炒勺不断翻动，以防相互粘连，炸至黄亮松脆时，用漏勺捞出，沥干油，装入盘内即成。用甜面酱、葱白段蘸食。

## 锅 烧 鸭 子

**原料：** 填鸭 1 只（2500 克），卤汤 2000 克，花生油 1000 克（实耗 55 克）。

**做法：** 从鸭子背部开膛去五脏，洗净，用开水煮烂捞出，放入卤锅煮 5 分钟捞出，擦去水分。用热油炸鸭子，至枣红色时捞出，控去油，上墩改刀。将翅及大腿摆在盘子两旁，鸭骨垫底，鸭脯码在上面。

**特点：** 此菜颜色油红光润、肉烂皮脆、味道鲜香。

## 核 桃 鸭 子

**原料：** 填鸭 1 只（2500 克），鸡泥 100 克，核桃仁 200 克，油菜末少许，荸荠 150 克，葱、姜、盐各少许，鸡蛋清 100 克，绍兴酒 10 克，玉米粉（湿）50 克，花生油 150 克。

**做法：** 1. 从鸭背开膛去五脏，洗净，用开水氽一遍，加入葱、姜、绍兴酒、盐少许，上屉蒸烂。凉后去骨、分成两半，去皮。

2. 另用鸡泥、蛋清、玉米粉、绍兴酒、盐调成糊，再

357

把核桃仁，荸荠剁碎，加入糊中，抹在鸭子内膛肉上。

3. 把鸭子用温油炸酥，捞出、控去油，用刀切成长条块，码在盘中，四周撒些油菜末。

## 炒 胡 萝 卜 酱

**原料**：瘦猪肉 200 克，胡萝卜 100 克，豆腐干 1 块，海米 25 克，黄酱 10 克，酱油 5 克，绍兴酒 5 克，葱末、姜末各少许，湿淀粉 5 克，高汤少许，熟猪油 50 克，芝麻油 500 克（实耗 50 克）。

**做法**：1. 把瘦猪肉和胡萝卜都切成 0.7 公分的小丁。先将胡萝卜放在油锅（锅内放芝麻油）中炸一下，使颜色变为鲜红。

2. 将豆腐干切成与胡萝卜同样大小的方丁。海米用开水泡一下，把咸味泡出来。将炒锅放在火上烧热，倒入 50 克熟猪油，将肉丁放入、煸炒一下，待肉丁内水份炒出时，锅内响声大，把锅放到微火上，响声变小时（肉的水分已尽），再端到旺火上。

3. 炒至肉的颜色由深变浅时放入葱末，姜末及黄酱，炒 2—3 分钟，待煸出酱香味，加入豆腐干、海米、胡萝卜和绍兴酒、酱油。

4. 待锅内汁干时，加入少许高汤，淀粉勾芡，汤汁变稠后，滴入 25 克芝麻油，翻炒几下。

是清宫风味菜中有名的四大酱之一。所谓四大酱是：炒胡萝卜酱、炒黄瓜酱、炒碗豆酱、炒榛子酱。

**典故**：四大酱历史悠久，据说清初，满族人进兵中原，战争频繁，士兵们往往来不及搭锅做饭，于是想出办法：把肉放在火上烧熟，切成丁，放在碗中，再把可以找到的

358

青菜切碎放入，用黄酱拌匀而食。清朝建立之后，一些满族人依然喜食这道菜。清宫御膳房的厨师将此菜加以改进，将拌改为炒，味道更美，尔后一直是清宫的家常菜，流传至今成为老北京人喜食的一道风味菜。

**饭捲子**：也是宫廷中别有特色的食物，其做法是把米饭和白面混合，用热水和面，然后蒸熟。种类很多，有陈米饭捲子、籼米饭捲子、粳米饭捲子，分甜咸两种。咸的加花椒盐、五香椒盐粉；甜的有枣泥、豆沙泥、白糖加桃仁，或加松子仁、核桃仁等。

**油性炸糕**：用油和面，内包白糖、芝麻、山楂，放点奶油，形状如烧饼大小。包好后放进油锅内炸酥。吃起来外酥、内软、香甜。

**烧麦**：用精白面加水和好，擀成饺子皮略大点等用。将猪肉切末，加上口蘑，做成馅，包在皮里，裂着口不封死，上笼屉蒸20分钟即成。皮薄馅香而不腻人。

**黄色蛋糕**：将鸡蛋打碎，搅拌起沫后，加上白面、白糖、桂花、果料等，放在模子里蒸熟。入口后，感到柔软香甜。

**炸三角**：芝麻酱加水和面备用，将肉切成碎片，加上虾米、口蘑、火腿等佐料，用团粉搅成卤馅，将面擀成比饺子皮略大点的面片，切成两半，切口处捏死，装进卤馅，将口捏死成三角形，再炸呈黄色即熟，外酥里软。炸三角一般和粥配食。

粥的种类也很多，有荷叶粥、藕粥、绿豆粥、肉粥、果料粥、小米粥、薏仁米粥、大麦米粥、老米粥等。这些粥有的是季节应时吃的。慈禧身体不爽时，则吃老米稀饭，用微黄色的陈仓老米煮成。煮出来的粥呈散粒，没有粘性。

**菜包鸽松**：把麻豆腐（豆腐渣）用羊油、黄酱炒熟，然后把各种炒菜都炒成碎末，拌在麻豆腐饭里，再将白菜心里的菜叶去帮洗干净，然后把拌好的料放在菜叶里包好，边菜叶一起吃。

**"和尚跳墙"**：把酥造肉和剥皮蒸过的熟鸭蛋4枚放在一起上屉蒸熟。由於鸭蛋光滑，一半露在肉外有些像秃头，慈禧便赏给这个菜一个别名，叫"和尚跳墙"。这也是西膳房常备的肴馔。

**图书在版编目(CIP)数据**

宫廷餐饮与养生: 英、汉对照/徐启宪等著; 章挺权译.
北京: 中国文学出版社, 1998.1
ISBN 7-5071-0376-5

I. 宫... II.①徐... ②章... III.①宫廷-饮食-中国-古代-英、
汉②③宫廷-食物养生-中国-古代-英、汉 IV.R2-12

中国版本图书馆 CIP 数据核字（96）第 24927 号

## 宫廷餐饮与养生

翻　　译: 章挺权
中文责编: 上官丰

**熊猫丛书**
*
中国文学出版社出版
（中国北京百万庄路 24 号）
中国国际图书贸易总公司发行
（中国北京车公庄西路 35 号）
北京邮政信箱第 399 号　邮政编码 100044
1998 年　第 1 版（英）
ISBN 7-5071-0376-5/I.334
04800
10—EC—3239P